Crystal Journey

Travel Guide for the New Shaman

Crystal Journey

Travel Guide for the New Shaman

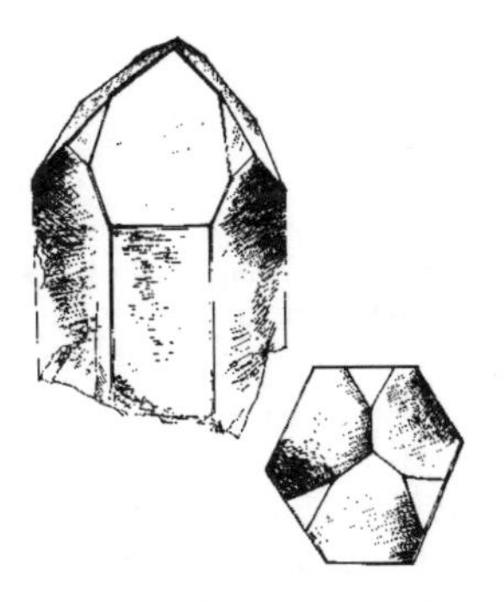

JaneAnn Dow

Journey Books
P.O. Box 23346
Santa Fe, New Mexico U S A
87502

CRYSTAL JOURNEY

— *Travel Guide for the New Shaman*

JOURNEY BOOKS
P.O. Box 23346
Santa Fe, New Mexico 87502
USA

First Quality Paperback Edition 1994

10 9 8 7 6 5 4 3 2 1

LIBRARY OF CONGRESS CATALOG CARD NUMBER: 94-77245

ISBN 0-9642385-0-0

Published in association with CONSCIOUS BOOKS
Reno, Nevada. 1-800-322-9943

Design and prepress by WHITE SAGE STUDIOS
Drawer G, Virginia City, Nevada 89440

Cover produced at ENVISION DESIGN, Reno, Nevada.

PRINTED AND BOUND IN THE UNITED STATES OF AMERICA

Contents

Crystal Index

Acknowledgments

TO THANK EVERYONE who has contributed to my work over the past twenty-five years would be impossible, but there are some people who stand out in my mind and remain in my heart.

If a genie were to pop out of my diet coke can to grant me one wish for this planet, it would be that every marriage could be blessed with a husband like Scott. For over thirty-five years, this man has walked with me through the most extraordinary experiences and supported me in every way possible as I was trying to find myself. What a guy!

My children, S.J. and Kate, continue to be an important part of my life and work. They were with me at the beginning of my own shaman journey and saw me move through some interesting and sometimes mysterious times. They have always been there for me and my love for them just keeps on growing. My family now includes a wonderful daughter-in-law, Cathy, and two adorable, brilliant, beautiful and talented granddaughters, Cherron and Jessica. Grandmothering is what I do best.

There is family to thank, my parents Gladys and Fred, who politely smiled as I presented my New Age ideas and muttered: "That's nice, dear." My brother Don has loved me since the day I was born when he proudly charged all the neighbors 10 cents admission to see his baby sister. My sister-in-law Georgia had a tremendous impact on my life when she introduced me to alternative healing many years ago. Nieces MaryAnne and Marci-nephews: John, Steve, Charlie and Chris, each a treasure. I cherish all of my family.

In between my first small crystal class of four women - Barb, Peg, Jeanine, and Denise - and my present advanced class there have been many hundreds of students and clients who have all shared insights into themselves through my crystals and counseling, expanded my ideas and contributed to my work. I could not have put this book together without them. Thanks to everyone who trusted me to do my thing.

For the company of my friends, wise and wonderful, who have walked alongside me, I am ever grateful — Mel, my pal of many years; Katrina, who started this crystal sojourn with me; Ryokan College, which channeled my mid-life crisis into a doctoral degree; Servando and our Sweat Lodge family, who pray for me a lot; and Dee, my witness and my friend, who always sees my light.

Others in my heart: Yolanda and her girls, Joy, Carla, Maggie, Judith, Vivian and Chuck, Sandy, Gail, Bernard, Melinda, Pamela, Cheri, Binky, Carol, Idelle and the Golden Girls of Piedmont.

Love to Doc and Freckles, who trotted into my life with their "horse medicine" of power at exactly the right time to teach me about trust and courage, reminding me that 'you are never too old to learn'.

AND SPECIAL THANKS to Catherine Bean Weser for the line drawings herein; to Taos Gem and Mineral Shop for their expertise and friendship; to Eric Swanson of Santa Fe for the picture of the Shaman Dow quartz crystal on the cover; to Gary Fleck for sharing the wisdom that inspired me on this crystal journey.

Just about the time
I began to explore crystals
my husband Scott
presented me with a puppy
MerLin
who became
my best friend

•

Just about the time the last words were written
for this book
MerLin
died

•

For thirteen years this small light
stood by my side
sat in my lap
shared my life
and
warmed my soul

•

MerLin
will always be in
my heart

•

Preface

THE CRYSTAL in the book cover photograph is the Shaman Dow, a Dow phantom quartz that has come to epitomize for myself and others the journey one takes in a crystal healing session. The phantoms in most quartz crystals are a dark blue or green color, or sometimes black. They are exact replicas of the quartz termination and indicate where the crystal stopped growing at various intervals in its formation. To find a white phantom is rare. To find a white phantom Dow crystal is even more rare. Thanks to my crystal friend Alysia Hansen in California, who sent one to me, it has now become the symbol for my work. The light from within, the light that surrounds—movement into that light is the crystal shaman journey.

The Dow crystal is named after me and is sometimes called the Tao crystal by those who do not know its history. Years ago when I was assisting Katrina Raphaell in gathering material for *Crystal Enlightenment*, we would sit for hours tuning into the stones. Always present was a large quartz point of mine which was perched in a natural wood stand. It had the quality of balance and light we were seeking in our work and we became quite fond of this special piece which inspired our channeling and provided a certain clarity of focus to our meditations. When Katrina began her second book, *Crystal Healing*, she called one day to ask what I wanted to call this crystal, since I had begun to take an interest in it mathematically and energetically. She wanted to mention it in her book as something unique. "The Dow crystal," I responded, "because Dow is my name and so close to Tao." We both laughed.

I had begun to explore the facets, or faces, of this stone. Three perfect triangles were balanced by seven terminating facets. I was not sure what this meant at the time. I knew that the American Indians called crystals such as this one "grandfather crystals" and considered them powerful healing tools. Balance seemed to be the key. The terminating facets form a mandala-like design, 7-3-7-3-7-3, that equates to balance. Numerologically the Dow combination is a three, the triangle personified—body, mind and spirit in balance create an aura of perfection in our lives, which expresses as a sense of well-being and a deep inner knowing that everything really is all right.

This inner knowing, which is now very much a part of my life, did not happen overnight. For over twenty-five years I have traveled the cutting edge of metaphysics, beginning my own journey in what seems to me now like the dark ages of enlightenment because New Age information was so scarce. Following a near death experience, I searched for books, for teachers, for anything that would help me to understand what had happened to me and why, and to clarify the purpose and direction of my own life.

My friend Mel and I went to a small, local college to sign up for a sewing course but it was full. We ended up in astrology! That class opened our eyes to dimensions of understanding that were new and exciting and seemed to have answers. Although neither of us spent any more time in astrology, we ventured into every other metaphysical seminar and workshop that became available. We pored over the few books we could find at The Bodhi Tree in Los Angeles—Alice Bailey, mostly—sipping herb tea and thinking we were pretty far out. Along came the Seth books by Jane Roberts and we were off and running. Those were the days when no one called "metaphysics" by its real name. We were two crazy ladies searching for answers and most certainly not communicating our thoughts to our Junior League companions. What fun we had exploring philosophy and physics, psychics and phonies! Those were the days when I had two business cards (one black and white, the other purple), two wardrobes (one tailored suits, the other long, hippie dresses), two sets of friends (some conservative, some flower children) and, in effect, two lives.

After years of personal study, I went back to college for a graduate degree in Holistic Studies. I decided to combine my interests in children and metaphysics and began counseling critically ill children and their families.

The holistic umbrella gave me a great deal of latitude. As people became familiar with the concepts, they developed enthusiasm for some of the tools. Using color breathing to facilitate control of mind and body was surprisingly effective with the children. They responded well and soon I discovered I could use quartz crystals to assist in creating visualizations. I put colored gels under the crystals and placed them on light boxes. And the magic began.

The children found stories hidden in the quartz and responded to the energy from the stones, which came to play an important role in their counseling. They were selecting their own crystals, they were breathing color, and they were excited about being able to take part in the healing process. Being in charge, if only of their own breathing, made them feel better. They shared their feelings and reactions to the stones and I learned from them. I was their counselor and they were my teachers. Together we explored new vistas in the understanding of illness, death, and wellness of spirit.

I met someone special, a teenage cancer patient named Billy. We were best friends for the last five years of his life. He taught me and many others about living. As a part of my doctoral project, we established a foundation for the counseling of critically ill children. He and I lectured at medical schools and in psychology classes. We appeared together on TV interviews. What a road show we were—this bald young man with a smile that opened your heart and a silver-haired college student wearing Birkenstock sandals and carrying a purseful of crystals. Together we hung out with Katrina and some zany crystal people in Los

Angeles. Among them was Gary Fleck, who opened up the world of gemstones and minerals for us. He told colorful mining stories, filled our lives with the light of inspiration and encouraged us to continue our own crystal journey.

Most people think crystal work is just physical healing. This book is about using the stones for counseling as well as healing. Certainly many of them have a vibrational energy, a frequency that can be used to enhance the movement and flow of energy through an individual light system. But do the crystals, all by themselves, actually heal? No. If crystals had that much healing capacity on their own, this planet would be in much better shape! There is healing potential in the mineral kingdom, but *intent* is required to activate, focus and utilize that energy, just as with medicinal plants. What the crystals can do is create movement where energy is blocked and this, in itself, can make healing possible. What they can do, acting as indicators, is give us access to the light system where seed thoughts can create a tension or disharmony that may eventually manifest into illness. What they can do is provide us with the picture of a geometric pattern in the soul blueprint which may be responsible for the issues and problems, physical or otherwise, that challenge us as we try to live our lives.

I am often referred to as a crystal healer, a title I am not always comfortable with. It implies that I am responsible for the changes that take place in the light systems of my clients and, ultimately, in their lives. I do not create these changes. I merely facilitate the process. But there is no other way to describe this work—yet. In this book, I am presenting the story of my own journey, my own beliefs, and most of what I have come to know after many years and hundreds of clients and students. Hopefully this material will open a door to your exploration and understanding of just one of the many healing possibilities and potentials this planet holds.

— *JaneAnn Dow*
RED CLOUD RANCH
CERRILLOS, NEW MEXICO

FACET I

Introduction to Patterning

Shamanic Perspective

TRADITIONALLY, among early tribal communities, the shaman was the healer of the tribe, the medicine man or woman who reached into the dreamtime body of the patient, or touched his soul, to retrieve the mystery of an illness or emotional disturbance. Today shamanic healing describes the processes of healing through visualization, soul retrieval, past life regression and a myriad of other alternative healing modalities. It is my understanding that what makes a shaman, irrespective of time period or cultural setting, is the ability to journey to the "other side" of reality in order to experience not only the death cycles but the soul level of our consciousness. What we call a near death experience is actually a rite of passage to the "other side" that gives the soul traveler a broader perspective on what we perceive as reality. This altered awareness remains a part of the physical consciousness and can be utilized as an adjunct to the healing process. When a shaman merges with the consciousness of a client, they journey together through the shadow worlds of mind and body and out into the far greater reaches of the soul.

Medicine people have always had knowledge of the healing powers inherent in Nature. They are specialists in the curative properties of herbs, minerals, crystals, color and sound, as well as authorities on the movement of stars and planets and the interpretation of dreams. The mystic healer was a part of every early culture and has emerged in our time as the New Age practitioner of bodywork techniques, herbology, astrology, iridology, spiritual psychology, crystal healing, and color and sound therapies.

We are no longer tribal communities. We have become a highly specialized society, requiring a variety of healing modalities to meet diverse needs and preferences, and we have many different kinds of healing practitioners, each with a specialty that is more or less individual and has its own advocates. These New Age medicine people have contributed to the practice of conventional medicine in the rediscovery of creative and useful methodologies. It is no longer enough for us to eliminate pain by putting a band-aid on the problem. Taking aspirin for a headache does not reach into the reasons for the headache or teach us how to prevent one in the future. Surgically removing a problem organ or cancerous growth does not prevent the breaking down of other organs or put an end to the process that created the tumor. More and more, we are delving into the meaning behind our personal and global lives and learning to take responsibility for them.

Crystal healing is presented in this book as an adjunct to your own personal healing and as one way of gaining perspective on the journey which is your experience of life and the world around you. A crystal shaman uses the crystals and minerals as a guide to the life process. Taking the crystal journey out to the limits of your own light system can help you to rediscover who you are and why you are here. Most of us are distracted by the dramas of day to day living and, unless we are forced to confront ourselves in a personal crisis, we can get by without looking too closely at the greater scenario in which our lives take place. We are powerful beings. We create the reality we live in. And we create it with such intensity that our entire lives can be colored by patterns of thought and behavior we are not aware of consciously. The stones can assist in bringing a hidden agenda to consciousness. Each shining quartz crystal, each beautiful mineral specimen, has a role to play or a memory to reflect in the much more lengthy drama of soul history, revealing the thread of purpose that runs through all our lives and is the key to reading the tapestry in this one.

The focus of the crystal healing session, or crystal journey, is to bring to consciousness unresolved issues that inhibit the flow of energy through the light system and can manifest in the physical body as illness. Most people perceive the light body on a subconscious level. When you meet up with a friend who seems "out of sorts" and you sense a lack of vitality, what you are perceiving is an absence of light. The aura is withdrawn, compacted and probably moving very slowly. On the other hand, when you think about someone you know who is in high spirits and irrepressibly full of life, the happiness around this person is almost a tangible thing. The aura will be vibrant, fully expanded and very active. You sense light and color without even seeing it.

The light body is, then, the movement and flow of energy. It consists of three distinct and separate energy bodies—emotional, mental and spiritual—each of which has characteristic colors and, most importantly, geometric patterning. Patterning is a fundamental part of the crystal healing session. The stones are selected by the client and placed, whether deliberately or at random, in a pattern. Patterning is important in the individual layouts. In other aspects of this work, which will be covered in more depth later on, grid patterns are constructed to facilitate group teaching and planetary as well as personal healing. The patterning of the crystals is always a reflection of the patterning in the light body, whether the subject is an individual, a group or a planet.

FIGURE 1: *The geometric patterning of the energy body*

The entire light body system is anchored in the physical body, which is our vehicle of physical expression. The physical body is the actor on the stage, playing out scenes from the life script. Sensory information, ideas and emotional reactions that derive from experience are all stored in memory at the cellular level. All input is accepted impartially, including disturbances in thought or feeling, so there is a continuous physical acknowledgment of conflicting messages and ideas, conflicting emotional reactions to people and situations, and the simple challenge of survival. The stress generated by these experiences saturates the physical body and eventually registers as disease or imbalance.

Life becomes physically painful. Sometimes anger and fear grow out of the isolation which is so characteristic of illness. When this happens, the physical breakdown has set up an emotional response. Now the entire physical and light body system is stimulated and reacting to a stress whose origin is long forgotten. Or is it? The physical body is a reflection of the light body patterning. If the physical body retains every thought and action in cellular memory, we can assume that our history is recorded in our light patterning as well. And that history is what makes up our total being.

It is the emotional body which shows itself as the "aura," although this light really encompasses all of the bodies. It reflects the energy of our emotional responses to the world around us, to thoughts received from the mental body, and to our spiritual perceptions and patterning. The patterning here is not static, but changes with every fleeting thought or feeling. The emotional body streams, spirals and swirls around the physical body in every vibrant color of the rainbow—pinks, oranges, greens, blues, violets and yellows. There are as many colors as there are feelings.

The next threshold brings us to the mental body which holds our belief system, all the knowledge derived from experience in this lifetime and others, and our innate wisdom. The mental body can be intuitively perceived as a three-dimensional arrangement of squares and rectangles that actually resembles a computer chip in its structure. The colors that predominate are pale hues of blue, violet and gold—peace of mind, intuition and wisdom. It is the mental body that actually molds our behavior. We act out what we believe about ourselves and our world. Many of these beliefs are predicated on what we were taught as children and remain as a part of the patterning even after they become obsolete. Obsolete patterning, even when we are not conscious of it, can create a conflict in the belief system that the emotional body perceives as distress and the physical body receives as tension.

The last of the energy bodies, the spiritual body, is where the healing journey really begins. The spiritual body houses the soul blueprint, the master plan of our lives. I first became familiar with its geometrics during my early work in death and dying, when I was facilitating soul transitions through the birth and death processes. I noticed a triangular shape, like the head of an arrow, which indicated the direction of the soul energy as it passed to and from the earth plane. The light in the spiritual body is predominantly gold and white. When I am with a client, I do not see the whole blueprint at once. Often the geometrics are far out in the aura. What I am able to see, however, has a triangular patterning and gentle, wavelike movement. Some of the triangles have long tails like comets in slow motion. Here we find the writer of the original script, the creator of the scenario in which we are now living, and the thoughtforms that shape the mind and emotions and, ultimately, the physical body.

Once we have access to the master plan in our light body patterning, it becomes clear that we are in control of our own lives. The world may be a stage, as Shakespeare says, but we are not merely players. We are directors, scriptwriters, stage managers, and set and wardrobe designers as well. We are not at the mercy of a predestined future that is beyond our reach and understanding. These outer limits of our energy and consciousness are a part of the process that creates what we perceive as reality. And we have the ability to access these life patterns and to change them, as long as we remain true to the purpose of the original script.

There is a spiritual responsibility that comes with crystal

healing—to the stones that come to us as gifts from the Earth, to the energy they hold and the role they play in the healing process, to the energy field which is the sacred space of each individual client, and to the planet itself as the source of all life. Our responsibility is to be the quartz crystal. We need to be very clear as we interact with the subtle energies of the mineral kingdom. We need to be very focused as we move into another's personal space. We need to be very aware that, in healing ourselves, we contribute in a small way to the healing of the planetary consciousness. We are emissaries, then, in a very real sense. We have the responsibility, and privilege, to bring ourselves and others into alignment and harmony with the planet that gave us life, and into an acknowledgment of the Dow crystal within us—our own perfection.

Facet II

Crystal Journey Begins

Path of Dow

I NEVER INTENDED to be a healer. I have always been more interested in counseling—taking apart the puzzles of life and putting the pieces back together in a different order. In the early 70's, I began receiving information as a channel. I did not know what to do with this new ability so I asked my sources if I should use it to heal. The answer I received was "Yes, but not like you think. You will be a soul level healer." "Thank you," I said. "But what in heaven's name is that?" The ever popular, ever frustrating, "you will find out" was the only response. It only took me twenty years to find out and fortunately it is very hard to accelerate the ego on that kind of timing. I patiently took up the exploration of different alternative healing modalities. I experimented with color and finally settled into the work I do now with crystals and minerals. Time does not permit the myriad of anecdotes I have amassed over the years. For those you will have to venture to Santa Fe, New Mexico, find me in the mountains and share a pot of tea.

My intention here is to share some of my views on alternative healing and to present my insights on how to work effectively with crystals. I have done my share of clean up work on clients who have been tampered with energetically by people who claim to be psychics or healers. While crystals can never in themselves cause injury or harm to an individual aura, their energies can be creatively misused through ignorance. Interpretations of the stones, or patterns in the light system, can be confusing or misleading if they are not fully understood and a client's thinking and behavior can be permanently affected by this kind of misunderstanding.

One such client came to me several years after consulting with a crystal healer in another state. She had discovered a dark thoughtform in his light body that must have frightened her. Instead of pursuing the issue at hand, she dismissed the client saying that she could no longer help him. You can imagine his state of mind after years of wondering what this darkness meant and thinking he was some kind of sinister soul. After a few sessions, we rediscovered that darkness and found it to be the pattern of an event which had taken place very early in his life cycles. The "evil" attributed to it came out of his own misinterpretation of what had happened and the way of thinking prevalent in the consciousness of that time. The thoughtform which coded this experience into his light body patterning grew larger and more intimidating as the scenario was replayed in subsequent lifetimes. After we had examined and re-interpreted his memory of the event, this thoughtform was found to be relatively harmless and useless to his present life expression.

Another case in point was a man I met in California at the very beginning of my crystal sojourn. He had asked the healing circle at a local spiritual center for energy to expand his spiritual consciousness. Saying that they would remove the blocks that were inhibiting the flow of his kundalini, these people did a laying-on of hands, took his money and sent him home with their blessing. By the time he called me, he was in a constant state of sexual stimulation and quite frightened by this energy in himself that seemed to be out of control. What the healing circle had done was to pour light into the spine via the crown chakra or soul center and then send him away without sealing the aura. A powerful energy had flooded his light system and was continuously charging it. Because they had left him open, he was also vulnerable to any stray etheric energy that was floating around in his vicinity. After I explained what had happened and showed him how to regain control of his light body, he called to tell me that he had put a sign over his desk at work: I follow the Path of Dow.

I have become concerned by the tendency of many psychic healers and bodyworkers today to "pick up" on experiences of sexual abuse in childhood and to present these "impressions" as fact to their clients, even when there is no conscious memory of the event. A close friend of mine was muscle-tested by a massage therapist who told her that her father had molested her as a young child. He insisted that this experience had happened between the ages of six and nine and that, because she was so traumatized by it, she had blocked it completely from her conscious awareness. She came to me distraught, disheartened and very frightened. We psychically explored her relationship with her father and found nothing that could explain what this practitioner had discovered. She did remember, however, that when she was between the ages of six and nine there had been a family crisis which nearly resulted in divorce. She had felt responsible, as many children do, for the difficulties her parents were having in their relationship. The guilt and fear she experienced then, sustained over a three year period, was still present in her light body.

My friend confronted her family and was assured, after much discussion and family therapy, that the accusation was unfounded. Fortunately her family reacted with understanding and was willing to work with her on the issue. This is not always the case with such confrontation. A number of clients have come to me with this kind of misdiagnosis and I have seen families destroyed, personal relationships strained and lives distorted because of it. I am not saying that these "impressions" are *never* valid, but only in rare cases is there no current life memory of the event. The healer should exercise extreme caution in conveying information of this nature to the client.

These stories can teach us some valuable lessons. Bear in mind—should you decide to visit a psychic or a healer—that you will be listening to someone else's viewpoint of who you are, why you are here, and how you are expressing yourself. If these ideas feel right to you, you may want to explore them further. If they do not feel right, if they do not resonate with your own inner knowing, you should reject them without hesitation. The information might be colored by the bias of the channel. It could be right for somebody else, but inappropriate for you. It could be partially right—in which case, you may want to keep whatever seems valuable and discard the rest. It could be altogether wrong. You need to trust your own sense of what to accept and believe about yourself, because you know yourself better than anyone else ever will.

There is a special bond that is formed between the crystal healer or facilitator as I prefer to call myself, who is able to act as a bridge between the conscious mind and the light body patterning, and the client, who trusts enough to put his physical and energy bodies into the hands of a virtual stranger so that the healing process can begin to unfold. The facilitator, however, is *only* the bridge. The client must consciously connect with the thoughtform and decide whether or not to resolve it. This process can sometimes be very painful, so the willingness to trust, to be vulnerable, is paramount to the success of this kind of intervention. When my clients are lying in front of me, covered with stones and ready to review their lives with soul-searching honesty, they are vulnerable energetically to everything that is happening around them and aware, on a superconscious level, of everything I am saying. It is as if they have a built-in recorder that encapsulates the entire session and plays it back into their conscious awareness whenever these memories resurface. With this in mind, I choose my words carefully. I have had clients return to me years later and repeat verbatim everything I said to them in sessions that are no longer a part of my own conscious awareness.

People often ask me how the crystals work. If it is a social, offhand kind of inquiry, I simply reply, "I have no idea. They just do." And, in truth, aside from being able to say with certainty that crystals have vibration and frequency, I am often at a loss to explain in technical detail how all of this really happens. I have a large glass cabinet filled with hundreds of stones. With a sweep of my hand, I tell people who seem genuinely interested, that each stone has a vibration that matches some small frequency within our physical and light systems. Crystals need intent to focus their healing potential, and for this purpose, the intent of the client is more important than my own. It may be the color of a stone or its shape that attracts a client's attention. It is the intent which is set forth at the beginning of a session, however, that seems to decide whether the attention will be drawn to it in the first place. People are often at a loss to explain why, when they first confront the beautiful colors and sparkling facets of so many of my crystals, they are suddenly moved to pick up a stone that is not even pretty. The motivations that govern the selection process are, for the most part, unconscious.

Until recently little thought was given to the expanse of light that surrounds each of us, let alone how to access it. Crystal healing as we know it today began in the early 80's as an adjunct to massage therapy. It was one way of introducing energy into the body. Stones were assigned to the energy centers according to color-based chakra associations in the Hindu system. Healing was restricted to the physical body. We moved slowly into the emotional realm when it became clear that we were not reaching the source of the imbalance or disease. The years I spent counseling critically ill children provided many insights into the ways crystals could be used in working with energy. I transferred these ideas to my own work later on and discovered that when my clients selected their own stones, they felt more a part of the healing process. Moreover, I gained a greater knowledge of who they were and what their issues were.

Eventually the stones fell into categories that identified with the various bodies of energy around us and the reading of these stones became an important part of the therapy. Within a few minutes of beginning a session your client has already told you, even though he does not realize it, what his real problem is and, more specifically, where it can be found in the light system. You will know by the stones he selects whether the issue at hand is coming from the reactive emotional body, from the beliefs or innate wisdom of the mental body, or from the spiritual blueprint. The universal law of "like attracts like" applies to any level of consciousness. The crystals set up patterns of light and energy that assist the client in visualizing the light body to determine the fate of a seed thought. Accessing this light body patterning is essential to resolving outdated issues and beliefs—thoughtforms from the past that hold us back from our personal journeys through life.

When I was first getting started in all of this, I used to have experiences that I called CV's, for clairvoyant visions. They were like little vignettes or filmstrips. I would be sitting quietly and pictures would come into my mind, stories that I recognized as other lives that were somehow related to my present. It was like watching a movie. I could see myself clearly and understand that this was something I had experienced then and could learn from now because each story had some bearing on what was happening in my life at the time—relationship issues or something to do with my work. Looking back on them from many years down the road, I realize that these CV's were actually thoughtforms that had been coded into my light body patterning and that I was reaching out for them because I had a need for the memories they held. These experiences triggered my interest in thoughtforms being scenarios. And these vignettes or filmstrips are what people experience when they go into the spiritual body to find the seed events that have triggered whatever is happening in their present.

In the spiritual body, the body of the soul, are the patterns that dictate our lives. We live in response to these patterns, though very often we have no conscious awareness of them. The thoughtforms that exist here hold very ancient memories. Sometimes these memories are of past or future lifetimes. Sometimes they hold the consciousness of events that occurred in other, nonphysical dimensions. Severe traumas in the present life can code themselves into the patterning of the spiritual body. The thoughtform, to me, is like an encapsulated drama. It is an event that has been recorded and somehow coded into the light body patterning so that when it is accessed, it is experienced as a moving picture or sensory happening that is all done in symbolism, like a dream. The pattern is the code or symbol of what the thoughtform is trying to say. The whole point of a crystal healing session is to access this sacred place in the light system where we can evaluate and restructure these thoughtforms.

Soul level healing has come to portray the true essence of crystal work as it is presented in this book. It took many years to get beyond the physical and emotional body issues and venture out into the mental and spiritual light. We tend to see ourselves as physical vehicles wrapped up in emotional upheaval. Working through the stress and unwinding from the tension of mundane living can take all our waking hours. Sometimes it is all we can do to get through the day, let alone ponder lofty thoughts or think of ourselves as the light bodies of spirit in physical form.

A period of meditation with fluorite taught me how to access the mental body in my own light system. I found the seed thoughts of patterns that were manifesting in my life at the time and I realized that if you can change your thought or image of an issue, you can change the issue itself. The problem with positive thinking, however, is that we rarely know what the issue really is. It is one thing to sit around and think beautiful thoughts but quite another to seek out the thoughtforms in the mental body that are manifesting as what I like to call challenges. Positive thinking, in the way most people practice it today, is a form of denial that can actually do more harm than good, because the source of the initial problem is still registered in the light system that constantly feeds into our consciousness.

The crystal shaman journey uses crystals and minerals to access the soul perspective of a client's situation. Behind every illness or any other kind of imbalance there is a seed, a thoughtform, a source. Often these thoughtforms are filled with dramas in present or past time that need further evaluation or understanding in order to alleviate the tension that has caused the problem. I perceive this tension visually as a kind of rocking motion, not unlike a tug-of-war, between the physical manifestation and the pattern in the light system. This conflict is especially evident in clients who have strong religious belief systems. As years pass, belief systems expand or change with exposure to new ideas. On a conscious level, the client begins to develop new ways of thinking. On a light body level, the original belief holds firm. When the new behaviors do not match the old beliefs or contradict the creeds set forth in the life script, the conflict builds and eventually expresses as frustration, mood swings or emotional traumas.

In crystal work, a bridge is formed between the problem and the source that leads to what is called soul level healing—changing or eliminating patterns of thought which have created distortions in the soul blueprint. Soul level healing is a transformational process. By using crystals to access the initial trauma, we can alter the perspective of the thoughtform and the problem is then transformed from a shadow or glitch in the system into a point of light. When I watch the light body of a client at the moment of transformation, all of the patterning shifts as if to indicate that the entire light body has been altered by the resolution of this one thoughtform. The more shadows that we can transform in ourselves, the more we can let go of our density and become light. Each shadow that becomes infused with light is a new awakening for spirit.

Crystal healing has possibilities that are limited only by the boundaries of your imagination and parameters that are constantly shifting. Your visualizations and interpretations will vary with each session and every client will present you with a different scenario for change. The major key to success in this work is flexibility. If you rely only on what is presented in the "Six Steps to Healing" chapter of this book, you are denying your intimate relationship with your own crystals and your own rhythm with clients. If you memorize everything I have said about the stones and you take my meanings too literally, then you miss the excitement of your own creative thought and intuitive abilities. If you disagree with my understanding of a crystal, then I encourage you to develop your own. My impetus for writing this book was not to convince you that my way is the only way, but to set up a framework of knowledge and method from which you may draw your own conclusions and create your own work. If I had all the answers I would be up for sainthood—most definitely not my calling.

Many people will snicker when you say you use crystals in counseling or healing. Members of my own family do not discuss my work with anyone. Years ago my mother asked my good friend Mel if I was a witch. Mel said, "Well, I suppose if she were, she would be a white witch." My mother pondered this for a while and then exclaimed, "I didn't know they came in colors." How I loved that remark! It is a typical reaction to the idea of crystal healing. There is an aura of magic about it which can be frightening, I suppose, to people who are afraid of magic. For myself and others, however, it has been a powerful adjunct to the healing process. Whether you use this book to enhance the healing practice you already have or to begin your own crystal journey, it is my hope that such wit and wisdom as I am able to offer will help you on your way.

FACET III

Six Steps to Healing

Road to Recovery

SOMEWHERE out in our spiritual patterning is the signed contract which is our agreement to be here, to live this life and assimilate the experience that goes with it. Most of us did not read the fine print at the bottom that says, "By the way, this may hurt a lot." The importance of crystal work is in its ability to alleviate suffering, to help us re-experience life and death traumas as lessons which were never meant, at any time, to overwhelm us. Not all issues come from other lives. Present life situations can also create large and imposing thoughtforms. The childhood image of a shaking finger that says you are worthless can be as powerful as a death trauma in another time and place. A parent or adult partner who wounds with criticism, who abuses you verbally or physically, can create a seed thought that eventually becomes a thoughtform with the ability to interrupt the natural flow of energy through the light system.

Once you hang up your shingle as a crystal healer, you are announcing to the world your intent to help others in a unique and sometimes controversial way. Realize that not everyone is going to be interested in what this particular type of healing has to offer. It is always wise to question clients when they call you for an appointment. Try to find out what it is they are looking for. If they want a psychic reading—that is, if they are interested in advice that is more precognitive in nature—refer them to a channel who is better able to assist with this kind of information. You cannot imagine the kinds of inquiries I received when crystal healing first became available to the public. Will crystals take my cancer away? Will crystals make me spiritual? Can crystals tell me why my boyfriend refuses to marry me?

No, crystals will not take your cancer away, but they may be able to help you discover the reasons for its manifestation in your life and what it is you are supposed to learn from it. And perhaps, once you have worked with these lessons, it will go away on its own. No, crystals cannot make you more spiritual than you already are, though if you are interested in growing spiritually, they can probably provide you with information that will point you in the right direction. As for the boyfriend, unless there is a deeply ingrained thoughtform in both light systems that is able to lock two people into a single life pattern, there is not much that crystals can do about marriage.

You must know that, being a Capricorn, I am much more comfortable when I am working within a structure. I love to set up rules and schedules and rarely deviate from my rituals unless, of course, I am in the process of creating a new one—which I also love to do.

The six definitive steps which structure the crystal healing process are offered here as guidelines to help establish a routine that will enable you to flow naturally and easily from one part of the session to another. If you become addled and confused because you cannot remember what comes when, you will inhibit your flow of light and information and be less effective as a facilitator. Remember, however, that these are only guidelines. This is, indeed, a creative endeavor and there is plenty of room for embellishment. And remember that you are only a guide. It is the client who will ultimately determine the structure of each session.

Before initiating the healing process, it is important that you be very clear and certain of your intent. I cannot stress enough the importance of being absolutely clear. The intent of your client will provide the key to his own process, but it is the intent of the facilitator that links the client to the stones and focuses their healing potential. When someone comes to you for healing, you are being invited into a sacred space. You will be opening up a corridor of light which extends from the physical consciousness to the spiritual body or soul of your client. When you enter this space for the purpose of affecting a healing, you must leave your own issues behind. If you try to project your feelings and beliefs onto the focus of the session, you might miss valuable clues that could lead you to the source of your client's problem. In a "worst case" scenario, your client could integrate your fears and judgments into his own belief system and spend years condemning himself on the basis of your assumptions.

Finally, try to relax and view each session as an adventure rather than a challenge. If you enjoy working with crystals and are stimulated by the energy, you will convey that enthusiasm, along with a sense of your own confidence, to your client. Even when the two of you are working on an issue that seems to inspire anger or fear, perhaps especially then, it is important to hold onto your curiosity, your excitement, your humor. What you are after is a totally different perspective. It is important not to get caught up in the drama, or emotional experience, that is attached to the seed thought. The more years I spend in this work, the more I realize that we are truly mental beings and that our thoughts, past and present, mold our lives.

The Introduction

STEP 1

THE CRYSTAL HEALING SESSION always begins with an introduction to you, the facilitator, and to the stones. Clients coming for the first time are often bewildered by the crystals and anxious about the session because they do not know what to expect. Begin by putting your client at ease. Introduce yourself and talk freely about how you became interested in crystals. A personable approach is the most effective way to relax your client and create an ambience that is conducive to healing.

Because this type of counseling is different from any other, a proper introduction to the crystals and minerals is important. Some interact with and modify our energies while others indicate what portion of the light body needs attention. If you have a vast array of stones, select a few and explain that each stone has its own vibration and role to play in the light system. This is such a colorful medium for healing and it often seems very mysterious to the client. Perhaps you have a story or two about how this process has worked for others, how quickly deep issues can be reached or how certain stones are able to penetrate areas of consciousness that are not usually accessible to us. The introduction sets the tone for the session and creates a spiritual connection between the facilitator and the client.

When you have finished your explanation of how the stones work, go directly to the purpose of the session. If the client has come to you with a problem, now is the time to bring it up. It is important to know why a client feels the need for a session. He may be vague about what has prompted him to seek help—"I just can't seem to make my way in life"—or the issue may be more specific—"I am having difficulty with this relationship" or "how do I resolve this problem." These questions or comments help you to interpret the stones. A far more difficult challenge is the client who wants what I call the "cosmic experience," who just wants to experience the crystals with no real issue in mind. Many of these individuals are what I call "healer junkies," people who spend a major part of their lives as clients on the "healer circuit." They often have real problems but are just not ready for the answers. When calling for an appointment, they will assure you that they have no issues while displaying an inordinate amount of curiosity about you and your work. I generally try to refer them to someone else. If people call and ask me specifically about the stones, however, and I suspect a hidden agenda that needs to be addressed, I will see them—even if they say they have no issues.

On my last trip to Hawaii, I met with one such client who had heard about me through her hairdresser. She came in stylishly dressed and coiffed, with a brisk, businesslike air. I greeted her and she announced that she had come for the crystal experience. "Oh, great," I said to myself—under my breath and without much enthusiasm. She looked at me expectantly and we began the session. The emotional body stones predominated in her selection—rose quartz, aventurine, citrine. As the scenario unfolded, it became clear that she was going through a late-in-life divorce and had been holding in a lot of fear and anger. Suddenly her manner changed from curiosity to concern and she became very emotional. She was quite overwhelmed when she left, shaking her perfectly coiffed hair and looking utterly bewildered.

The majority of my clients in the early years had no exposure at all to the concept of holistic healing. People now seem to be much more aware, but you need to be prepared to work with individuals who know nothing about crystals, who may not understand light and energy in the context of the aura and energy bodies, and who are not spiritual in their orientation to the world. For these clients, long and detailed introductions are necessary. You must make sure they understand your language and explain every nuance of what you intend to do in the session, otherwise they will miss the point and get very little out of it. You may have clients who enter into the healing process with a "show me" attitude. Now there is a difficult session, folks. I had a client once who came in, sat down, crossed his legs and arms and refused to remove his dark glasses. He said to me quite bluntly, "Just what is it that you do and what makes you think you can help me?" The way I figure it is, if a client has come this far in order to see me—many of my clients come from out of town and I am not all that easy to find—then there must be something I can do or should do. So inject a little humor into the situation and try not to tense up. And get on to the next step.

The Selection of the Stones

Step 2

IN THE CRYSTAL HEALING SESSIONS that I guide or supervise, it is the client who selects the stones that will eventually be used in the layout. This approach differs from the method of many other crystal healers—the majority of them, in fact—who prefer to control the selection process by choosing the stones for their clients. My own belief is that this encourages the client to go completely passive during the session and makes it easy for him to deny the validity of the information—"that's not me" or "you didn't get it right." In my work with critically ill children, I learned that the perspective achieved by being directly responsible for the treatment of a problem or situation can give a tremendous boost to the healing process. If I preface the selection by explaining to my clients that the stones mirror or reflect back who we are, it gets their attention. It gives them responsibility. They select the stones; they create the scenario. I do not create it for them. Even if they do not recognize the scenario as their own, they have to acknowledge that they created it. And if they wish to change it, there is more of a sense that this is within the realm of possibility. If they created it, they can 'uncreate' it. So there is less tendency to be passive during the session and more of an attitude of hope and expectancy.

Explain to your client the importance of being part of the healing process. When the client, rather than the facilitator, selects the stones, he is taking responsibility for his part of the session. As he is standing in front of your collection of crystals and minerals, ask him to take several deep breaths and focus for a few moments on the question or issue at hand. This sets the intent and establishes a connection, a kind of agreement, between the client and the stones.

Ask your client to select from your collection any of the stones that he feels drawn to, that attract his attention for whatever reason, and to place them on the floor. You can suggest placing the stones in a pattern or design, or you can say nothing about it and wait for a design to emerge by itself. Or you can give him a choice. Most clients have no experience in working with the stones and will not know what to expect. If you specifically ask them to place the stones in some kind of pattern, they will worry about choosing the wrong stones or making a mistake with the design, so give them a choice. Most clients will just put them randomly on the floor. Sometimes they will sit down afterwards and put them in some kind of order, but I find that very rare unless they have a background in art or color therapy or they are artists. If your client is an artist, the colors and shapes of the stones will take on an even deeper significance because of the intent which dictates their placement.

As I have said before, the motivations governing the selection process are, for the most part, unconscious. And I would like to emphasize here that it is simply not possible to make a mistake in the selection. The universal law of "like attracts like" will apply as your client chooses stones that are compatible with the energy in his light system or have the capacity to trigger the information he needs to clear a shadow or distortion in the patterning. Encourage your client to be spontaneous and tell him not to try to figure out which stone means what. Believe me, even seasoned crystal people can still be spontaneous and amazed at what can come out of the selection process, even though they know what all the stones mean. Once during a class I was teaching, I decided to create a fictitious character and draw stones at random so that my students would have someone to work with who was totally unfamiliar. Every scenario I selected described something that was going on in my own life, even though I deliberately tried to avoid the stones that I ordinarily would have chosen.

As the facilitator, your role in this part of the process is to be still and receptive, to continue to focus on the issue at hand and touch into the stones as they are placed. Be patient. Stay neutral. Watch carefully as the stones are put down on the floor. Which were the first two or three selected? Have they been placed in any kind of pattern or design—a circle, an arrow, a straight line? As important as these initial observations will be to your interpretation of the scenario, which is the next step, you need to wait until the selection process is complete before you begin to analyze the stones. The last stone selected can color the entire reading. Are there any pivotal stones? A pivotal stone can be the first or last stone selected, or a stone like dioptase or aquamarine that pulls the issue up into the soul blueprint. Any stone which seems to dominate the scenario, for whatever reason, is considered a pivotal stone.

Often when I am getting my studio ready in anticipation of a client, I will receive the impression of a stone that best indicates the underlying issue, even when the client is unknown to me and I do not know what the problem is. I was waiting for a client to arrive one day when I suddenly slipped into a meditative state and saw one of my lingams. At the time, this stone was not even in the case. It was sitting on one of my bookshelves. The client arrived and toward the end of her stone selection, she walked over to the shelves and picked up the lingam. She recently had been diagnosed with cancer and the underlying issue was a lack of parental nurturing. For me, the lingam has always had something to do with the planet's gift of nurturing—the birthing of a new relationship to the Earth as a consciousness. This woman had longed for parental nurturing and needed to know that this was simply not within the realm of possibility. If you are not able to get nurturing from your parents, you get it elsewhere—from other people, other activities, from the Earth itself. She needed to seek nurturing from the Earth itself, to see it as a nurturing place to be.

When the selection process is complete, sit quietly for a moment. The first few stones that were selected will define the issue and give you an idea of what you are dealing with. Is this a physical problem, an emotional conflict, or a mental or spiritual disharmony? If there is a predominance of emotional stones such as rose quartz, aventurine or sodalite, then the problem exists in the light body as a present or past emotional trauma. I will say here that the majority of clients—even when their stones depict emotional issues—are really dealing with thoughtforms that reside in the mental or spiritual energy bodies. An emotional trauma will always impact the belief system eventually because information derived from the experience is stored as patterns of thought. We have a feeling sense of who we are which gives rise to the mental constructs of "Who am I" and "I am this kind of person because," which become part of the belief system and are eventually integrated into the spiritual body as what we perceive to be truth.

If your client has selected a majority of mental stones such as azurite, lapis or, most especially, fluorite, know that you are dealing with someone who thinks before he feels and whose way of relating to his world is predominantly mental. Do not expect mental beings to respond to emotional rhetoric—the "open your heart" kinds of comments, for instance—because they simply will not hear you. On the other hand, it is pointless to speak in overly mental terms to what I call the flower child type of client, who has committed to living and speaking solely from the heart and whose function it is to be "the loving light" on the planet. These individuals perceive the world and the people in it from the perspective of feeling and they need to hear the emotions talking. It is very important that you, as the facilitator, use language that will be heard and understood by your clients. You cannot expect to do this work in just one way. You need to be flexible as well as alert all the time, impeccably intuitive and perfectly clear. Your clients must be able to tell you, through the stones they have selected, exactly what they need to know and how you should proceed. And you have to be able to hear what they are saying.

The Scenario

Step 3

WHAT I CALL the scenario part of the session uses the stones your client has selected to give you and your client some valuable insight into how he feels about himself and interacts with the world and where he stands in relation to his issue. Your interpretation of the scenario will bring your client's issue into sharper focus. Begin with some very general observations. Note whether your client has selected just a few stones or a great number of them. People who are not primarily visual in their orientation or who are very direct in their approach to people and situations will tend to select fewer stones. My husband, for example, regardless of the intensity of the situation, rarely selects more than two stones—or four on special occasions. He is an accountant who is very basic and attached to the facts and does not enjoy embellishing them. Sometimes a client who is nervous about being "read" will not select enough stones to give you a clear picture of himself. In either case, you will need to analyze the stones your client has chosen and ask him to select a few more around one that seems pivotal to the issue.

Clients who select a great number of stones may unintentionally be trying to distract themselves, and you, from focusing on the issue at hand. They experience a lot of distraction in their own lives and find it difficult to focus on any one thing. Fear is not the issue here. I once had a pair of clients in a joint session, mother and daughter, who perfectly illustrated these two conflicting approaches to life. The mother selected a great many stones and put them down at random. The daughter selected a few stones and placed them in a straight line. My question to them was, "How do you communicate? Are you able to understand one another?" They seemed surprised at the question but the answer was no, of course. I went on to explain that the mother had a lot going on, was involved in many projects, and expressed herself through innuendo, suggestion and point of view. The daughter dealt with life in a direct and simplistic manner. She became frustrated when she would ask a question and was unable to get an answer that made sense to her. I suggested that the daughter be clear about what she wanted from her mother and that she recognize her mother's need to embellish.

To be able to read specifics into the scenario, you really need to know your stones. Not only do you have to know what they mean, but you must be familiar enough with the way they interact with one another to weave a story around them. It is not enough to say that black tourmaline neutralizes negativity. You need to note where it is placed with regard to the other stones. Was it one of the first stones picked? This will give it special emphasis. Is it part of a group or off by itself? Is it a central focus? On the periphery? Is it an integral part of the pattern if there is one, like at the head of an arrow or the intersection of a cross? You need to be able to see what is negative about the situation and how it can be neutralized, taking into account not only the black tourmaline but the stones around it which help to define the interaction. The next chapter in this book, Facet IV, "Shaman Tool Box," will provide you with detailed information about what the stones mean and in Facet VI, "Grids and Wheels," you will learn to create mini-grid combinations that will give you an idea of how they interact with one another energetically.

Begin with the first few stones selected. Tell your client what they mean and how they apply to the issue at hand.

Then turn his attention to the overall appearance of the stones in the scenario. Comment on the way the stones are arranged on the floor. Have they been placed in a pattern or design? What is the central focus of the pattern? Which stones appear to be working together? Sulfur and malachite together, for example, would indicate some kind of nutritional imbalance or digestive disturbance and the need for energy to be physically moved through the solar plexus area. Is there a stone that does not seem to fit with the others or that you are unsure about? Ask your client to select a few stones around it to clarify its place in the scheme of things. Are there small groups of stones that seem to clarify or give dimension to the message that is being conveyed by the larger picture?

Discuss the design, if there is one, that your client has created with the stones. Straight lines and arrows are wonderful. Clients with this type of configuration like to confront their issues directly. They want straight answers, not innuendo. Circles usually indicate that your client is coming to a conclusion about the issue which has been presented or is completing the pattern that this issue has caused him to focus on. A cross indicates tremendous vulnerability. These clients often feel that they are going through some form of crucifixion, or resurrection, or they are telling you that they feel very open, very vulnerable. They are feeling a need to bring their extremities in somehow and make some sort of spiritual shelter for themselves.

A medicine wheel configuration will have one or more stones in each of the four directions and be open in the middle—sort of like a cross without a center. Clients who create medicine wheels with their stones may have some kind of background in the Native American religions, or the source of the configuration could be totally unconscious. In either case, you have to pay attention to the symbolism. The North is the source of your wisdom. Fluorite, especially blue or violet fluorite, would indicate that your wisdom is an innate part of your consciousness, something you were born with, and that you should trust in what you know. The stones in the South will tell you how best to utilize your own healing abilities. Aventurine would indicate that your focus should be on how the emotions can be positively oriented to alleviate stress in day-to-day living. Topaz would suggest a more empathic approach to healing. East is the direction for the birthing of new ideas and new approaches to life. Sodalite, for example, would be telling you that it is time to begin expressing your own personal truth, to have faith in who you are and respect for what you feel. Whatever you have in the West symbolizes the death of old ideas and the transfiguration of the inner self. Black tourmaline in the West would indicate that you need to put your fears to rest and stop dwelling on the past. The negativity that you perceive around you is an illusion. In this particular configuration, black tourmaline could also indicate a fear of death. Trust your intuition to tell you which reading is the right one.

Sometimes clients will lay out the stones in an outline or contour that resembles their physical selves. The whole body will be there. You'll see a straight line with stones coming out from the center. The head, hands and feet will be apparent, sort of like a stick figure. Children often make stick figures with their stones and this can be very helpful in a session as the crystal language is sometimes difficult for them. Charlie was ten years old when he first came to me. He has his own stones because his mother is a student of mine and he had done a layout that he wanted me to interpret for him. It was a stick figure. You could see his head and his legs and arms. And coming out from the heart were two pink tourmalines. I said to him, "Do you know what this means?" He looked at me, smiled and said, "Yeah. It means I'm a real lovin' guy." And, in fact, he is. We have worked since then on his extraordinary sensitivity. He picks up feelings and impressions from the people around him and, at this time in his life, wants to be able to open his heart and give. The environment does not always reciprocate, however, and life has not been easy for him.

One client came to me with deep-seated fear issues. She announced this outright at the beginning of the session which was, in itself, unusual. Very few clients do that. They are usually much more vague. I asked her what she wanted to work on and she said, "I have to get hold of my fear." She was an artist, but she was not a productive one. She was afraid that all the decisions she had ever made were wrong. She was afraid that she would never be able to do anything meaningful with her art. She was afraid of life, really. Because she was an artist, I asked her if she would like to create some kind of pattern with the stones. She laid them out in the shape of her body, from her head to her toes. She had chosen all dark stones—obsidian, black tourmaline, smoky quartz.

I always see a lot of light and movement in the dark stones, but because she was an artist and color had more than ordinary significance for her, and because she had chosen *all* dark stones, I felt that she was trying to express her fear. Most people think of fear as being very dark. And as it turned out, there was a lot of movement. The predominance of obsidian suggested that there was something hidden within her that needed to come out. So we talked about what her fears were and how they colored her thinking and were manifesting in her life. I asked her to go back to the crystal cabinet and draw stones for the person she wanted to be, whereupon she headed for the shelves holding the brightly colored crystalline pieces and clearly mapped out her own changes.

What surfaced when she started replacing the stones was her own creativity. She had such an abundance of creative stones—red jasper, carnelian, a lot of calcite—that it was obvious she *did* have a choice. She did have ability. I told her that she could stay locked into the shadow which had been created by her fear or she could explore new ways of being creative. Later, she took up pottery and loved it. She was fearful of making decisions, so to allow that creativity to come out was very risky for her.

Interestingly enough, I have never had a client create a square or rectangular shape with the stones though I did have one who laid them out in two parallel lines. I suggested that perhaps he was expressing parallel parts of himself. He concurred with this interpretation and did not seem at all surprised by it. In this particular instance, my client was an actor who projected an outward persona that was debonair and sophisticated and had another, inner side to his personality that was more introspective and shy. The presence of optical calcite in a configuration like this one would suggest that a parallel part of the self, or parallel life, is impacting the present from a past or future lifetime. Sometimes the thoughtform is so powerful that the pattern repeats itself like a physical reflex whenever circumstances combine to create the appropriate environment for it. Or perhaps the soul has decided to continue a pattern that was left unfinished in another life.

The scenario is the part of the session which will draw most heavily on your intuition. The issue has to be clearly defined. Sometimes your client will not be able to define it for you or he will say that he does not have one. You must be able to sense which part of the light body holds the seed thought or pattern from which the issue developed. This will enable you to map out a strategy for leading the client out into the light system during the breathing part of the session. If your client is not able to recognize the thoughtform, it will not matter whether or not you know what it is. In order to release the pattern, he must see it for himself. So the strategy of your approach should minimize your client's resistance and keep him focused. Always follow your client's lead. Give him information and see where he goes with it. Be very gentle and, most importantly, nonjudgmental in telling your client's story.

In isolating the seed thought of an issue, it is important to watch for the spiritual body stones or any member of the beryl family. These stones pull the whole problem up into the master plan of the soul and clarify what your client came into this life to work out or deal with. If, for example, he selects aquamarine, you know immediately you are dealing with someone from the angelic kingdom which originally seeded the template for consciousness on this planet. People who are drawn to aquamarine have had difficulty expressing themselves as part of a density which is so different in essence from their own energy. Many of them have spent lifetimes here wrapped in their wings, afraid to unfold, afraid to be the loving being in an environment where survival is dependent not on mutually beneficial cooperation and loving interaction but on conflict and struggle. So if you have a client who selects aquamarine, your strategy would be to lead him into a recognition and acceptance of these aspects of himself, rather than to encourage the change or release of a seed thought or pattern. This particular pattern *is* the blueprint. And the experience of life in this dimension is characteristically harsh for these individuals. Sometimes just understanding the conditions of a life expression, whatever they are, can alleviate suffering and open up tremendous reserves of strength. When these forerunners of angelic consciousness are functioning at their optimum, they are able to open their wings and feel empowered in their loving, not vulnerable. Even here.

Each one of the spiritual body stones is a key to the master plan and can dictate the entire session. The presence of dioptase in a scenario always indicates a soul wound, a past trauma severe enough to fracture the soul blueprint. If it appears with green apophyllite, it can indicate the ability of your client to heal those fractures in himself or an urgent need for such healing. Without the dioptase, green apophyllite might be suggesting that your client has the ability to reach other people at those levels, to be the soul level healer. Clear apophyllite, on the other hand, emphasizes perception rather than healing of the blueprint. Perhaps, as in the case of aquamarine, your client simply needs to recognize a particular pattern as an aspect of himself and to integrate that recognition into his conscious awareness. The other stones will help to clarify this issue and guide you in explaining the scenario to your client.

Once in a great while you will have a spiritual scenario that does not seem to match its physical counterpart. I had a client who did not tell me, at first, that he was HIV positive. The stones he selected were all spiritually dynamic and powerful and the scenario reflected a brilliant light—no shadows in the system, no glitches. His light was absolutely brilliant. This was a highly evolved spiritual being. He was very quiet when I told him this. His reaction was sort of delayed. Then he told me that he had a serious immune deficiency disorder and wondered why it had not revealed itself in the scenario. The stones gave no indication of any physical deterioration and seemed to be saying that, on a spiritual level, this was immaterial. His soul was using the disease to grow spiritually. I guess you could say it was a spiritually motivated disease, but it did not derive from any kind of wound or imbalance. It was built into the patterning.

In the scenario part of the session, all the stones are functioning as indicators. In other words, the stones are describing a situation or telling a story rather than actively modifying the flow of energy through the light system. I have, for example, a few stones that I use as indicators for Atlantean or Lemurian past lives. When these are selected I know that, whatever the issue happens to be in this life, its roots more than likely derive from a life experience in one of these civilizations. You can have scarabs among your crystals to indicate Egyptian lives, small carvings that seem Mayan or Incan in character, I Ching coins, whatever. It is your own agreement with these pieces that will determine the story they tell.

There are some stones that function only as indicators. These stones, as a general rule, are not capable in themselves of moving energy or activating patterns in the light body. They may trigger a memory or a particular association or simply give you valuable information about how your client functions in the world. The three members of the tiger's eye family, for example, all indicate the need for a particular type of focus on the physical environment. They do not generate or enhance that focus energetically or physically. They simply indicate that your client needs to give it some attention. The indicators are especially valuable in the scenario part of the session, but because they are symbolic of the experience which created the thoughtform around the issue at hand, they can be incorporated into the layout as well.

The Layout

STEP 4

IN CREATING AN INDIVIDUAL LAYOUT, the stones that make up the scenario are placed on and around the physical body of the client. This will intensify the movement and flow of energy through the geometric patterning of the different energy bodies. Let me say here that this part of the process is not always necessary. If your client works well with the patterning and seems to get a clear picture of the issue from the scenario, he may not need to experience the various stages of the light body to locate a particular thoughtform. He might be able to connect with it just by looking at the pattern of the stones as they have been placed on the floor. Sometimes this awareness is all that is needed to trigger the release of a thoughtform. Most clients, however, will need the layout.

Now that your client is more comfortable with you and has some idea of what to expect from the rest of the session, lying down on the floor or massage table will not seem so awkward. If the stones are to be used in conjunction with body work, you can place them in a pattern or grid underneath the table. In a straight crystal session, however, I find the massage table too limiting. It is very difficult to place crystals around a client who is lying on a table and raising your client off the floor will give him the sensation of floating rather than being grounded. This can be important in a session, especially with individuals who are sensitive to the stones and can easily lose touch with their physical surroundings. As a facilitator, I prefer my clients on the floor. They can shift position without having to worry about rolling off a table and I have more flexibility in moving the stones around. And I like sitting on the floor with my clients. It helps me to feel grounded as well.

Whether your client is on a massage table or on the floor, you need to be aware that some people feel extremely vulnerable when they are lying in the anatomical position—that is, flat on the back, arms at the side, palms up. If you sense that your client is feeling insecure, put a stone in each hand. It closes the hands so that he does not feel as open and exposed. It also gives him something physical to hold onto and something else to think about. If your client is fearful about the session or feeling vulnerable about lying on the floor, the aura will be contracted and you will not be able to get an accurate measurement of the energy centers. This is why it is so important to do the introduction properly and make sure that your client is relaxed before beginning this part of the session.

Before you begin placing stones for the layout, explain to your client that you need to measure the aura and energy centers. I have redefined the chakras as energy centers because I wanted a term that gave my clients and students a better understanding of the vital points of energy flow which link the light system to the physical body. Some of my clients even now do not know what a chakra is and I have found that the concept of "energy center" is easier for me to explain and for them to understand. If you are not sure where to locate the energy centers on the physical body, refer to the following diagram.

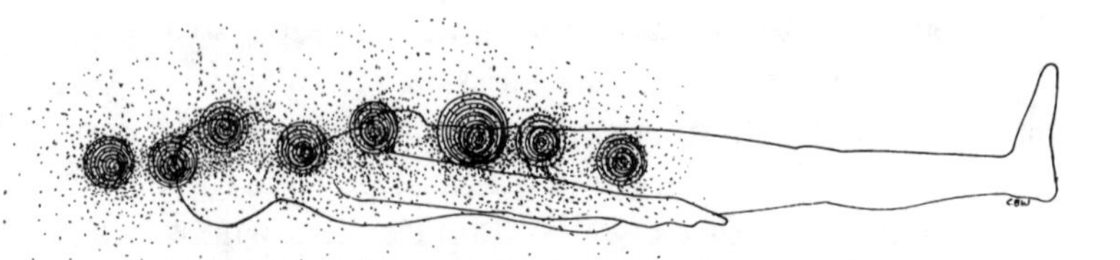

FIGURE 2: *Major energy centers of the physical body*

Holding one hand approximately four feet from the body, internally ask to be shown the extent of the aura at this time. Gently bring your hand toward the body and when you feel a slight resistance, you have touched the outer boundary of the auric field. Holding your hand over each of the energy centers, measure them in the same way. The measurements for the energy centers will be inside the aura reading and will give you some idea of which centers are depleted, or considerably lower than the aura reading, and which centers are operating as close as they can to their optimum potential.

If your client is balanced, all the readings should be pretty much the same. What you will probably find, however, is that some centers will be depleted while others extend all the way out to the end of the aura. In this case, there is a lack of balance that needs to be addressed. It is important that you explain these measurements to your client in a way that can be easily understood. If your client is depleted in the lower triad, for example—root, second center and solar plexus—and the upper triad extends out to the end of the aura, it will be obvious that those centers which have the most to do with being physical are low in energy and the more spiritual and etheric centers are overinflated. So you would explain to your client that, as important as it is to be spiritual, he is still very much a physical part of this planet and needs to give that aspect of his experience more of his attention.

These energy measurements will provide you with valuable insights that you can share with your client, but you should never give your client any information that could be perceived as negative or fearful. Say, for instance, the first center is depleted. Very generally this will tell you that your client is feeling insecure and unsettled and not fully aware of his role in the scheme of things. If this center gives you a measurement that is extremely low and close to the body, it can indicate a genuine unhappiness with being physical or a feeling of having given up all hope. You would not tell your client that the first center is depleted without also saying to him that this has a lot to do with how he feels about being here. You would tell him that your measurements indicate some kind of issue in the first center, and that the first center focuses on survival and the way we relate to our physical surroundings, which include not only our natural environment but the physical body as well.

The second center or spleen area is the seat of creativity and its expression, which can be either sexual or artistic. It is also what we call the birthing center. If your measurement of this center is significantly lower than the aura reading, you will have to determine the source of the problem from the stones that were drawn in the scenario part of the session. If your client has drawn crocoite, obviously you are dealing with some kind of sexual or kundalini disruption of the energy. The presence of calcite or other creative stones would indicate someone whose creativity was squelched early in life and probably feels blocked in an artistic sense. Depletion in this center, especially if it overlaps into the third, can be alerting you to some form of childhood abuse that was either sexual or physical.

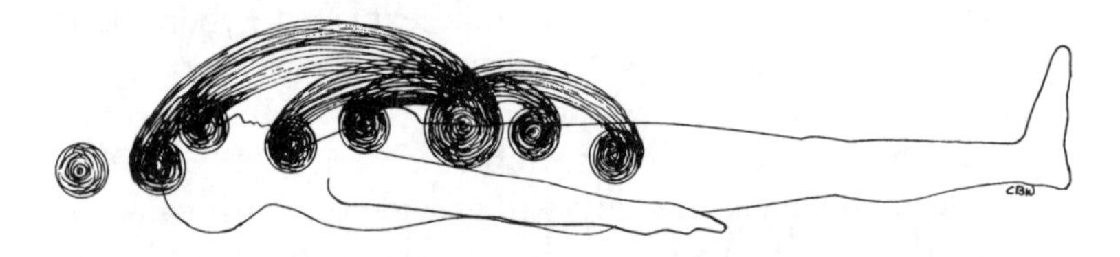

FIGURE 3: *All centers converge in the assimilation\integration center*

The third center of integration, or the solar plexus, assimilates information from the physical environment and energy bodies and integrates it into the light system. This center is pivotal to all the others and ultimately links them together. It is where all the energies from the other centers flow together and intersect. Almost everyone is depleted in the solar plexus because it is so overused. Food is digested and nutrients are assimilated here. If you are angry, frustrated or unfulfilled, this is where you will feel it regardless of the source of the disturbance. Eating disorders, for example, come from emotions that are not being digested. A sexual frustration that is ongoing and chronic, for whatever reason, will eventually upset your appetite. What I call the sagging mattress syndrome graphically describes the energetic appearance of this imbalance, which I have found to be more common than any other in my own clients. The first two centers measure high, there is a sudden drop over the solar plexus and then the energy goes up again.

The solar plexus, the heart and the third eye are the only centers in which I have, on occasion, noticed an excess of energy. A high measurement never seems to indicate imbalance in a center. When all the centers measure high, your client is operating very close to his optimum potential. I have had only one experience with a high measurement in the solar plexus and this was with another crystal healer. The solar plexus is where you absorb, process and integrate everything that happens to you—sensation, thought, feeling, expression—everything. This woman lived from the solar plexus. It was the source of all her energy. She was a very earthy person, a little rough around the edges, but she had no pretense about anything and was an extraordinary crystal healer for people on that level. She was a genius at it. She was not a very ethereal being—there was nothing New Age fluff about her—but she was very good at stirring up this solar plexus energy in other people and seemed to attract clients who needed that connection.

The heart or fourth center houses our feelings and emotions, past and present, and is the place where most emotional wounds settle. Depletion in the heart area generally signifies some kind of emotional wound. Depending on the stones that are drawn, the thoughtform might be expressing the inability to receive love, which is a self-esteem or self-worth issue, or the inability to express love, which could stem from a fear of rejection. If your measurement of this center is high compared to the others, your client has chosen to live and express from the heart in this lifetime, to be "the loving light."

The fifth center of communication can be found in the throat. We present ourselves to the world by word and by example—by the way we walk our talk—as an expression of this fifth center energy. The individual with a depleted throat center usually has something he needs to communicate but, for some reason, is unable to express himself. It might be something personal that he needs to say to a friend or family member or information on a much grander scale that some aspect of his being wishes to relay to the world at large. This kind of energy imbalance could stem from a past life experience which has never been cleared from the patterning and has nothing at all to do with his present day circumstances. If this is the only center that is out of balance and, depending on the stones which have already been drawn, you might ask him to draw some additional stones around, say, amazonite, which would really pinpoint how he feels about expressing himself. Bear in mind that language is not the only form of expression. People express themselves by what they are wearing, for example. Color, fabric and style are statements. When I was bordering on the hippie movement in the 60's, I expressed my views through funky clothes and Birkenstock sandals. It was my way of making a statement and it had impact. My mother would mutter, "Oh my goodness," when I walked into the room. Friends and other members of my family were more tolerant. I am sure they thought it was just a phase I was going through. Little did they know.

Most thoughtforms are located in the mental or spiritual energy bodies, but not always. Occasionally the memory of an event will become lodged in the physical body and the thoughtform can actually be perceived in the affected energy center. This is extremely unusual but it does happen. I had an experience recently with someone who was blocked by a thoughtform that had become lodged in her throat. A client of mine who is also a close friend had, for years, been feeling a lot of inhibition about expressing herself. This woman was held in high esteem by everyone who knew her. Clarity and insight were coupled with such a gentle and approachable manner that people were often encouraged to seek her advice.

When she was approached in this way, however, she found it very difficult to speak out. She was not shy and there was nothing wrong with her voice. She did not lack faith in herself and she was clear about what she wanted to say. The inhibition seemed to be operating very much like a physical reflex. For this reason and because my friend's consciousness is very physically oriented, I decided to look for the thoughtform in the physical body.

When I looked at the energy centers, I could see that the third eye and the throat were blocked. I told her to feel the breath coming up from her feet and traveling through the center of her body to the top of her head. When she reached the throat, it slowed down considerably. The energy was pulsating gently but did not seem to be able to penetrate the throat center. Sure enough, there was the thoughtform—an image of her mother saying that children should be seen and not heard. Even though she was no longer a child and knew that this was not and never had been a truth for her, the image of her mother was still there. And so she simply dissolved it. It was like a throat lozenge that got stuck in her throat. Clearing the thoughtform allowed the energy to rise immediately to her third eye and she was able to access her intuitive abilities directly. A few days later she was surprised and delighted at the wisdom pouring through her when a friend came to ask her for advice.

The last two centers that we use in our measurements are the third eye, or intuitive center, and the crown, or soul center. I have never had a client who has been severely depleted in either one of these areas. Even when clients are truly unaware, they seem to be operating whether they are conscious of these two centers or not.

The spiritual part of you has nothing to do with your dogma or belief system. Even people who come onto this planet to exemplify its shadow, who do not live and act in ways that you would consider to be spiritual, have that light in spite of themselves. A *slight* depletion of the energy in the third eye is not all that uncommon. This is usually apparent in someone who is not using his intuitive abilities to capacity. The intuitive center is the activated universal mind. Sometimes people deliberately shut themselves down in this area if this activation has been frightening or painful for some reason. I have never seen even a slight depletion of energy in the soul center. It has no direct connection to the physical world and so is not as traumatized by the experience of day-to-day living.

There are three other areas which are an important focus for the stones in the layout part of the session—the eighth or holographic center, the knees and the shoulders. They are not, however, used in the measurements. The holographic center, which is located six to eight inches above the crown, is our connection to the soul imprint. The knees represent the expression of what we perceive as our spiritual responsibility and the shoulders, the burdens of responsibility we carry for other people. If, when you are laying out the stones, you feel drawn to putting something on one or both of the shoulders, your client is carrying responsibilities that are not his.

Measuring the energy centers should clarify some of the issues that emerged in the scenario part of the session and give you a kind of picture, or graph, of how your client is doing. Individuals who are more physical in their orientation to the world will register high in the lower triad and show a slight depletion in the centers above the heart. Most clients will have depletion in the third center of assimilation—the sagging mattress syndrome—not taking in information and energy properly, not flowing with life well, feeling blocked or unfulfilled. Spiritually focused individuals will have a well rounded light system with a slight excess of energy in the upper centers.

By the time people become spiritually focused, they should be mentally, emotionally and physically balanced as well. One of my clients was a channel who believed that it was his responsibility to channel fourteen hours a day for the good of humanity. This was the extent of his relationship to the rest of the world and the people in it. "What about your own life," I asked him, "your own patterning, your own soul?" He said that it simply was not important. Our discussion never evolved into a session because he felt that, beyond being an instrument of the cosmos, he had no life of his own. Now here, in my opinion, is someone who is out of balance. The spiritual part of the self encompasses all the other energy bodies as well as the physical body and personality. To be balanced, there must be acknowledgment and expression of all aspects of being.

One important thing to remember in any kind of energy work is that we are all a composite of body, mind and spirit. An overemphasis in any one of these areas means depletion in the others. The athlete who concentrates on exercise and body building to the exclusion of everything else has lost whole dimensions of consciousness that would enrich his physical life. Someone who tries to make sense out of his environment by processing information indiscriminately through the mind will have a diminished physical or spiritual awareness and be able to communicate effectively only with other mental giants who share this same bias. People who have become what we call "space cadets," who spend their waking lives focused on some other plane of existence, are able to function in the physical world only with great difficulty.

When you have finished measuring the energy centers, begin placing stones on the body and around it. Here is where you watch your own involvement carefully. Begin to sense that you are becoming part of your client's light system. At this point, you may be able to see or sense the patterning of the energy bodies. The whole framework of crystal healing rests on the cornerstone of intuition—being still enough, clear enough and trusting enough to effectively interact with the crystals and minerals and monitor the changes they affect in an individual aura. Their energy is subtle. Their message radiates quietly. And their vibration gently penetrates the light system. If the facilitator is receptive and clear, the work will be successful. So allow your intuition to flow freely and be mindful of what you are drawn to do. If your client has created a design or a pattern during the selection process, try to preserve the integrity of that pattern, as much as possible, in the layout. If there is no pattern, just follow your intuition in creating one.

You will be placing stones on the different energy centers and it is important to note which ones go where. If you are drawn to placing an emotional stone on a seemingly non-emotional center, you have to put those two things together. Pink tourmaline on the third eye, for example, would indicate that your client needs to be aware, on a belief system level, that he is a loving, giving person. So the emphasis here would be on a flow of communication between the third eye and the heart. Pink tourmaline at the throat means to communicate that same loving nature to other people. At the heart which is, in a manner of speaking, its true home, the energy would have its most complete expression—living love to the fullest. If you are drawn to placing pink tourmaline on the solar plexus, your client needs to take in love and integrate it into all aspects of being. Someone who is unable to give or be fulfilled in a sexual relationship or who needs to express more love through creativity would be characteristic of pink tourmaline at the second center. And at the root, it would automatically have to do with the understanding that to be alive and physical on this planet should be a joyful expression.

In creating the layout, do not feel that you have to restrict yourself to the stones your client has selected for the scenario. Sometimes additional stones are needed to complete the patterning. Where are you drawn to placing them and why? What changes do they make in the initial selection? Discuss these things with your client as you are drawing and placing the stones. Is there a stone sitting by itself that could use some kind of adjunct? In the next chapter you will find a section on adjunct stones that are especially effective in making the others work—I call them the "A Team" to make the most of their powerhouse qualities. Which energy center, according to your measurements, seems to need the most attention? You might consider creating a mandala design with seed crystals or other small stones. This will intensify the energy in that center by bringing it in from different angles to a central point of focus. It also has a powerful visual impact in the recapitulation part of the session when you have removed the stones and placed them on the floor so that your client can see a three-dimensional picture of his own light body. We call this a totem.

Sometimes it is a good idea to place large generators at the feet and head to set up a movement of energy through the light system. If you do not have generators, you can set up a grid of quartz points around the body or you can use clusters. Observe your placement of these stones. Quartz points that are oriented toward the body will indicate that energy is needed in the light system. When they are pointing away from the body, the client needs to broaden the scope of his vision and consciousness or there has been a build up of energy that needs to be released from the aura. Clusters bring in light from all directions and allow a greater versatility in its expression. Skeletals at the feet will ground your client into the energy that searches his light body for the theme of life purpose. A grid of hematite pieces will facilitate communication with the network of extraterrestrials that are sometimes referred to as the space brothers. Any stone can be used as the basis for a grid.

Try to maintain as much balance in the pattern as possible. Stones on the right side of the body, the active or sending side, should always be balanced by stones on the left or receiving side. This is important to the energy dynamic in creating movement, but if you are drawn to putting them all on one side or the other, then do it. Just pay attention to what you are doing. Your client may be blocked on either side. Place a stone in each hand of the client, if you have not already done this, and be mindful of what you have selected. The stone held by the right hand will tell you what kind of energy your client uses to create an impact in the world. The stone in the left will tell you about the energy he takes into himself.

Sometimes in the middle of the layout, or in the breathing part of the session which comes next, you may want to move or replace some of the stones. For example, if you are drawn to putting black tourmaline at the solar plexus because this client takes in entirely too much negativity, you may want to call his attention to it, ask him to feel its energy, and then replace it with something more soothing. Occasionally the stones will remove themselves—that is, fall off during the layout or the breathing segment. If this happens because a client is breathing heavily, you can replace them. Otherwise, leave them off. They have finished moving energy or actualizing a pattern or whatever it was you were using them for, and they might be overstimulating a center. Sometimes they just jump off!

Now that you and your client are connected, energetically and spiritually, there are a few things that you need to remember. Never lean or step over your client. Always walk around when you need to reach for a stone. You could break the energy field and send a shock to the system. A shock to the system is like a slap. When it happens to me, I feel a sharp pain wherever the break occurs and my aura immediately contracts. Also let your client know when you are about to place stones on the face or around the head area. This space is a sensitive one for most people and they can be startled easily if they are not prepared. Finally, choose your words carefully. Remember that your clients are taking in everything you say on a conscious and subconscious level, even when they seem to be asleep. It can be very disconcerting when they begin to snore, but I usually just keep on talking. This is not an easy thing to do when no one seems to be listening. You have to keep reminding yourself that the information is going in somewhere.

Never leave your client unattended mentally or physically. Stay connected, stay close. Stay in touch with your voice. Check with your client frequently to make sure he is comfortable. If your client has never worked with crystals before, he may be quite unprepared for the energy shifts that are taking place in the light system as you begin to place stones on the physical body. Some people will not feel anything at all as this happens. Others will be hypersensitive to the stones and feel the changes that are taking place in a profound way, emotionally or physically. I keep my voice very low and my manner calm and reassuring as I tell them that I am here, that they are safe, that what they are feeling is not at all unusual. If the distress is physical, and this has happened only once, I just take the stones off and do the rest of the session with the patterning on the floor.

When you have finished placing the stones, ask your client

to visually focus his breathing and scan the physical body. If he is not visual, have him send the breath through the body and sense where he might need additional energy or stones. Is there an area that does not feel complete? Does he feel uncomfortable in any way? Sometimes a client will mention that he is feeling a lot of energy around the heart or throat area, for example. I usually say, "Well, is it a good feeling or a bad feeling?" If he says, "It's very irritating," I look at the stones in that area and either take them off or add something to subdue the energy so it is not quite so annoying. Obviously something is trying to get our attention, so we work on it during the breathing segment.

If your client is relaxed and comfortable, the layout is complete. At this point, I sometimes like to select a stone for myself to hold during the next part of the session. I try to choose a stone that will keep me connected to my client's process. If he is working on an old pattern in his belief system, it might be fluorite. If he is trying to break that pattern, azurite. I take a few deep breaths to get centered and then, together, we begin our journey out into the light system.

Breathing

Step 5

THE BREATHING TECHNIQUE that I use evolved from the color breathing I taught my hospitalized children in the early 80's. It occurred to me that you could breathe focus into the body as easily as color. A massage therapist will often tell you to breathe into a muscle in order to release the tension. I just take that one step further and tell my clients to breathe into the light system, to describe what they see and feel. Any time you are working with visualization, the client is directly involved in what is happening and has control over it. If his attention is on breathing and you are using visualization with the breath to help him find his way through the light system, he becomes intimately involved with the experience. It does not do you any good to have your massage therapist breathe into a sore muscle. It is your breath, your intent that is important. Crystal healing works the same way. The client must experience the thoughtform in order to release it.

The scenario defines the issue and your measurements will tell you which energy centers are depleted or in need of attention. The issue and the energy imbalance are always connected, so it is important to put these two things together when you are making a decision about which center to emphasize in the breathing part of the session. Sometimes issues will surface even during the layout, while you are placing the stones, and you may decide that there is a link between two centers that you had not realized or that the main issue itself is different from what you previously had thought. In any case, by the time you reach this part of the session, you should already have made a determination as to which center holds the wound—whether it is a soul wound, an outdated belief or an emotional trauma.

Unless there is a second center issue of abuse or sexuality or creativity involved, or some kind of heart wound, the solar plexus is the center you will use to guide your client out into the light body. If there is any doubt or question, use the solar plexus. Because it is the integration center, all information is processed there anyway, and there will be a link to the root, throat and third eye centers which your client may find are more difficult to visualize in breathing.

Tell your client to breathe in and out through the energy center you have decided to use as a gateway and to put his vision with his breath. If your client is not visual, just tell him to focus his attention on breathing and remember to frame your questions or comments in terms that deal strictly with feeling or sensation. You may have a few naturals who can slip easily into a meditative state and visualize without any prompting, but most of your clients will need the instructions. If you merely tell them to breathe without giving them a focus for the attention, very often their minds will go somewhere else. As it is, some of your clients will be easily distracted by what they are seeing or feeling and you may have to remind them fairly often to stay focused.

When your client is breathing gently and evenly, direct him to expand the breath, inch by inch, out into the light body, keeping the visual focus or the attention with the breath at all times. About four to six inches above the physical body, the breath and the consciousness of your client will reach the threshold of the emotional body. What does it look like? What does it feel like? Sometimes these are just general observations. It all depends on what has been asked.

If the issue has been clearly defined, ask how the emotional body receives it. Responses will range from a color or pattern to some kind of symbolic reference or a strong feeling. Most of the visual imagery here will be Nature symbols—mountains, a cliff or an abyss, clouds, tornadoes, meadows. Sometimes people will see colors—black, if there is something fearful—or images of a family member. People who are not visual will get some kind of physical sensation, like heat or cold, or experience a wave of emotion.

You will not be spending much time in the emotional body because most of the symbolism here is too reactive to be pertinent. These images tell you how your client is reacting emotionally to the presence of the thoughtform in his light system and while this might be useful to you at some point in the session, it will give you no information about the thoughtform itself. If your client tells you that he sees mountains in the emotional body, for example, he is saying that the issue represents itself to him as a problem he will not be able to overcome, as something he finds impossible to face. The mountains may actually be molehills and his fears may be groundless, but they create an imposing picture in the emotional body. The abyss is a statement of hopelessness or fear of failure. It can indicate confusion or a radical change in perspective. Some clients have seen a dark spiral or funnel that looks like a tornado—feelings of powerlessness or a sense of things being out of control. White, billowy clouds correspond to feelings of euphoria or buoyancy. Your client feels that he can "rise above" the issue, that it is no longer a threat to him. Thunderclouds, on the other hand, hold him oppressively down and obscure his vision so that he cannot "see his way through." Meadows show the emotional body at peace, which is a good indication that the thoughtform is pretty thoroughly integrated into the spiritual patterning.

You will be able to share your thoughts on this part of the experience at the end of the session. Comments at this stage are distracting to the process of opening up this channel of light. Keep the reactions flowing. Keep the breath moving outward and upward. If your client tries to analyze the experience, he will drop into a thinking mode, jerk out of the light body and lose the whole effect. If he seems to want feedback, I might say, "That's good. That's a good observation and we will address it later in the session. For now, let's go on." Be sure your client stays focused. One of my students was standing on the edge of a cliff in her emotional body when she became so carried away by the beauty of her surroundings—the sky and the light and the heavens opening up—that I had to keep bringing her back to why the cliff was there in the first place, something that no longer seemed to matter to her.

Ask your client to move the breath gently, an inch or so at a time, further out into the light system and to let you know when he has reached the threshold of the mental body. Because the dimensions of the emotional body will vary from person to person, there is no standard measurement for how far out you have to go in order to locate the mental boundary. If your client is visual, he will see changes in color and patterning. The images will be more structured. Mountains in the mental body, for example, look like pyramids. They are angular and jagged and, if the thoughtform is very old, deeply layered. Some clients perceive geometric shapes or patterns. If your client is not visual, he will perceive the shift from emotional to mental as a difference in sensation—from hot to cold or vice versa, comfortable to uncomfortable, something along those lines.

When your client has reached the mental body, ask if he can enter it easily. If the answer is yes, have him describe it to you and continue on to the spiritual body. If the answer is no, you will have to stop because there is a block. Ask your client to look around and tell you what is keeping his breath from moving. Again, reserve your comments. If the block seems to be especially intimidating, you might ask how he feels about continuing the journey. "Do you want to find a way to get to the other side?" Invariably the answer is yes. And so you create a crystal bridge or a beam of light that can take you over the block so you can get a better perspective. If you see it from only one side, you are not going to know why it is there or what it means. You need to get to the other side to be able to see where it comes from.

Thoughtforms in the mental body color your beliefs about who you are. The shaking finger, for instance, that says, "You're worthless, you're bad," can influence a whole sequence of lifetimes if the experience was traumatic enough to firmly establish and integrate that thoughtform. Sometimes you will find what I call thoughtforms of wisdom in the mental body. A thoughtform of wisdom could be some philosophical understanding that worked very well in another time and place. You bring it in with you because it is part of who you are, but that does not mean it is going to be as useful today as it was several centuries ago. Strong religious beliefs are like that. One of my clients said to me, "I'm a Jew. I've always been a Jew. In every lifetime, I've been a Jew." That is a strong belief system. I did not say to him that this was an unhealthy thing to believe about himself, because it is not, necessarily, unhealthy. But it can be a good idea to find out why you believe what you believe. Thoughtforms are not necessarily bad things. They hold information that is based on some root, some seed. And these roots are usually in the soul imprint, which is why we go on to the spiritual body rather than stopping to work with what we find in the mental patterning.

One of my clients, a young woman, was unable to go from the mental to the spiritual body because she was blocked by an enormous moat full of bones. She had come to me because, even though she was happily married with children, she did not want to go on with her life. She was only 29 years old. When she got to the other side of the moat, she relived a past life situation in which she was about to be operated on. The doctor turned to his assistant and said, "Don't bother with this one. She's only a woman." She was thrown into a ditch, still alive, and died feeling abandoned, betrayed, confused and angry. Her memory of the experience was so potent that it had permeated her present day life, creating powerful feelings about her safety as a woman and not being important enough even to live. It is interesting to note that when I asked her how old she had been when this experience took place, she said that she was 29.

We worked with this memory. I had her speak to the event by

answering the doctor and she was able to verbalize her anger and deal with the issues of betrayal and abandonment. Eventually she came to perceive the experience as a spiritual event rather than an emotional one. On a soul level, she had made the decision to end that life. How she did it was simply not important. By looking at what had happened from a soul perspective and understanding, as a soul, what she was supposed to learn from it, she altered the patterning of the event in her light body and was able to release her fear and feelings of worthlessness.

These experiences can be quite painful and people sometimes get very emotional. Whenever this happens in a session, I touch my client on the arm or the hand to let him know that he is not alone in the experience, that I am here, that he is safe and that whatever comes up is right for him. I have never ended a session because someone has become emotionally upset. I had one client who sat bolt upright and screamed. He was experiencing his own personal Armageddon which, he said, was worse than his nightmares of Viet Nam. It was a real breakthrough for him and his life changed after that. So it is important to encourage people to release and go on.

Continue the breathing until you reach the threshold of the spiritual body. Again, the distance will vary from person to person and you will need to rely on your client's perceptions, or your own, to sense this transition. Energy in the spiritual body is dramatically different. Some people see what they perceive as an angelic light around themselves—white and gold, gossamer-like and floating. Often there are feelings of euphoria or bliss and a deep sense of peace—peace of mind, peace of soul. The light is unusually vibrant and clear. Even when there are thoughtforms in the patterning, they are surrounded by a kind of radiance. No matter how severe the trauma, how intense the suffering, how wounded the physical body, once you have reached the soul level of yourself you know instinctively that everything has happened according to your own plan. And that seems to cast this warm light over everything. It is like a spiritual "whew!" Everything really is on track. No matter how painful the experience of living, it always seems to have this glow around it .

This is where many people become very emotional. Sometimes they are simply in awe when they see themselves as light beings for the first time. It is like meeting up with the presence of God and suddenly understanding what it means to be spirit. There is no way of experiencing this without realizing that you are spirit incarnate on the planet. You have touched the totality of yourself and your whole sense of who and what you are has been altered.

At the level of the spiritual body, clients are very receptive to the guidance of the facilitator. If you ask them to locate a particular thoughtform, they will hit on it right away. The constructs of time and space no longer seem to apply. Response is immediate. Memory is immediate and unusually vivid. All the senses are heightened, but this is a sensitivity that goes beyond, say, unpleasant noises and sound that makes you shiver. It is not unlike the awareness that you have when you die. When you go through a death experience, colors are heightened and you are acutely aware of sound. You are aware of everything. It is like having multiple visions or experiencing all your lives at once. It is not chaos. You do not feel fragmented, but the heightened awareness gives you a different perspective. If we could hold onto that awareness and bring it back with us, I think life would be much less challenging, because everything would have meaning.

When you restructure a thoughtform, you try to help your client see it from this soul perspective of heightened awareness and correct any misinterpretation or confusion around it which might be creating patterns of behavior or disease in the physical life. What was the reason for the experience in the first place? What did the soul need to learn? Once you have explored the answers to these questions, you need to ask your client if he wishes to release the thoughtform or keep it in its resolved state as a kind of reference point. Very few clients ever dismiss something completely unless there has been a really severe trauma. If there are situations that have contributed tremendous learning and growth, the thoughtforms are usually retained in a healed state. The knowledge will then be available to the individual without the need for experience to regenerate it.

A young woman who wanted to be a healer came to see

me because she was inexplicably afraid to make the decision which would commit her to this profession. Out in her light system we discovered a lifetime in which she thought she had made a fatal error and was responsible for the destruction of the people she had committed to serve. She had been a healer then and worked with stones. One day she was wandering in the valley where they all lived and was attracted by a stone she saw lying on the ground. She picked it up and the whole valley collapsed under an avalanche of rocks.

In her imprint of this experience, there was a connection between picking up that stone and the deaths of all the people who lived in that valley. She had the idea that if she expressed her freedom in exploring new ways of doing things, she would hurt or destroy a large number of people. What we found in exploring the symbolism of this thoughtform was that it was time for an experience of great impact to happen to these people. This was a Lemurian life which probably took place around the time that continent was destroyed. She relived the experience and, by staying with the souls who had chosen to leave, discovered that they had all chosen to be instruments of some greater message.

Once the event has been accessed, it is important to look at it from a soul perspective. The symbolism of an event can be as important as the reality of it. The young woman who picked up the stone did not, in actuality, cause the avalanche. Symbolically, however, it was important for her to believe that she did and to accept the responsibility that comes with being "the messenger." The assumption was that she was in some way part of the collapse of Lemuria, but rather than seeing her role as a liberator she saw it as a destroyer. Lemuria was highly advanced in practical healing techniques and it was the healer in her that felt responsible for the destruction.

It has been my experience that the clients who have the most difficulty visualizing or believing what they see are more often men than women, probably because men are so practical and oriented to "show me the facts" and "let me see this in writing." Sometimes, when the trauma is severe, they are simply too frightened to look at the experience. It is very rare that someone will not have the ability to see or sense anything at all, but it does happen occasionally. At that point, I will usually step in and offer my own perceptions of the experience. This is so rare that I can count on the fingers of one hand the clients for whom I have had to step in and completely take over the visual role.

One of these clients, a man in his early 30's, came to me because he was experiencing emotional outbursts and crying spells, always at inopportune moments, and could not commit himself to a serious relationship with a woman. In going from the mental to the spiritual body, we both suddenly began to feel intense heat. My eyes were closed. I was feeling very warm and started to perspire. When I looked down at him, I could see that he was having the same experience. I closed my eyes again and saw these flames licking around him. The word "suttee" appeared visually in front of me. I saw the letters clearly. This man was so caught up in the end result of his thoughtform that he had no visual abilities at all. I told him what I was seeing. The whole event was so frightening to him that he simply could not look at it or communicate about it. But as I was talking to him and explaining to him what the practice of suttee involved, he started to cry.

Suttee was a ritual practiced in ancient Afghanistan and India. When the head of the household died, the body was placed on a funeral pyre and burned. It was customary for the wife to jump into the flames and join her husband in death. As I was explaining this to my client, he suddenly remembered himself as a woman circling the raging flames around the body of her husband. She was frightened beyond words. A man appeared and whispered in her ear, "Either you jump or I will throw you." When she did not respond, he picked her up and hurled her into the fire.

As the memory subsided, my client began to realize how this event had colored his life. Somehow this experience had affected all of his relationships with women. His fears stemmed from his belief that if he made any kind of commitment to a woman, something terrible would happen to her and he would be responsible. He was reacting to an emotional trauma that had taken place centuries ago and was no longer part of his consciousness. When we had explored what he remembered of this experience, he was tremendously relieved. And in a matter of months, he was able to commit to a serious relationship.

Tearing the veils away from these memories can eliminate what I have been calling a "tug of war" in the light system and remove a great deal of the pressure we experience in our physical lives. When we go into the spiritual body patterning to find these seed events, we eliminate conflict between the different parts of the personality. All these different fragments begin to coalesce into an integrated consciousness and we become more of the totality of ourselves. We become our oversouls. The oversoul is, very simplistically, a collection of these little time capsules—your own individual akashic record of events that have been pivotal in shaping each existence. When your imprint of these events is recognized as no longer being useful, the thoughtform does not need to maintain itself in the patterning and it then becomes possible to resolve or release it.

Sometimes, when I am working with a client, I will see that he is not ready to change, not ready to connect with the thoughtforms or heal the distortions in the soul blueprint. It is at my discretion whether or not to relay this as information. Usually, I do not. If the client has made the determination that the pattern is working for him in ways that I am unable to see, then it is not up to me to tell him that this is a bad thing. So I guide him back into the physical body and encourage him to think about what he has uncovered for himself or about the things I have seen or sensed and shared with him. I let him know that we have choices. He may decide at a later time to use that information to enhance his own healing process or he may decide to use it to make the pattern work. There are many people who want to hold on to their pain. If the pain or the illness is the focus of their life expression or their way of communicating with higher levels of themselves, then it needs to remain as a part of the patterning. Sometimes healing is not the issue. Honoring the soul's choice to see this journey through—whether it is to resolve the trauma or the illness or use it to leave the planet—that is the choice that should be supported.

When you have explored the patterning in the spiritual body and restructured or released the thoughtform which was at the root of your client's issue, bring the breath back down through the light system and lead your client back into his physical awareness. This process does not really differ from taking the breath out, except that you will be asking your client to sense any changes that have taken place since the journey out.

Thoughtforms and symbols often disappear when the patterning is altered and this will be obvious to your client on the way back. Guide him into the physical body through the same energy center you used to take him out into the light system. Ask how it feels to have this issue resolved. Instruct your client to remember these feelings of release and to breathe them into every cell, along with the knowledge that the initial thoughtform has been changed. All the images that you see or sense in the light body are carried on a physical, cellular level and eventually incorporated into the DNA. If there are changes, your client has to experience them physically.

Maintain your link with the client until peace has come to the breath. When consciousness has been returned to the physical body, there should be a release of the effort and concentration involved in the perceptual experience of the light system and a sudden relaxation in breathing, an ending to the process. If you are watching your client, you will see it. At this point, I usually begin to remove the stones and place them on the floor, maintaining the integrity of the pattern. The client will be calm and relaxed and feeling that there has been a major shift. He might not understand it completely, but he will sense that there has been a change. I have *never* had anyone leave a session untouched by the healing process, who stood up, shook my hand and said, "Thank you very much, but nothing happened."

The Totem

Step 6

THE TOTEM is the last step in the healing process. When you remove the stones from the different energy centers and lay them out on the floor, you are giving your client a three-dimensional picture of his light system that will have impact on a number of levels. There will be a visual impact, of course, and many of my clients have asked for photographs of this layout to take home. It is always profoundly beautiful to them because the stones have created a mosaic which is uniquely and personally who they are at that moment. Because they have had a tactile experience with the energy, however, looking at the totem or a photograph of it will reactivate the centers and the energy bodies, which will speed up the integration process.

During this part of the session, I try to bring my client into a full awareness of what has happened and have him recall, by putting words to his experience, what it feels like to be *consciously* free of the old patterning. I bring in my own impressions and interpretations of the session and answer any questions he may have.

What happens in the light body when a pattern heals? Well, what I see is sort of like a domino effect—except that the geometrics are not falling over but shifting to create a new pattern. When you transform or eliminate a thoughtform that has been dictating the circumstances of a lifetime, or of many lifetimes, the entire light body has to change. The mental body will shift because the beliefs are no longer there. The emotional responses to the encapsulated drama have been changed or eliminated altogether. In bringing the breath down through the light system and making your client consciously aware of these changes, the physical awareness gets the message as well.

It takes about three days for the patterns to really shift, and so I usually tell my clients to be very aware of thoughts and feelings that are surfacing during this transitional period. A major shift like this one is going to affect the external environment as well as the inner life. Relationships may change and opportunities for expression may open up in other areas. Or the changes may be very subtle. I encourage my clients to apply what they have learned to the current situation, whatever that may be, and to be willing to alter their behavior in accordance with the healed pattern.

Sometimes this process is like peeling back the layers of an onion. One session may clear a distortion and alter the patterning but not reach the original thoughtform underlying an issue. The session will, however, initiate a process that, over time, ultimately results in access to that thoughtform and the healing of that seed pattern. The time it takes for an issue to completely resolve itself will vary from person to person. Sometimes the resolution happens immediately, sometimes it does not happen at all, and sometimes you never know if it does. When your clients walk out the door, you never know if they are going to accept what you have offered them and allow it to make changes in their lives. Very rarely will you ever hear back.

Occasionally the time factor involved may not lend itself to a gentle, gradual healing. Someone with cancer, for instance, or someone in crisis who is suffering intensely may require more frequent interventions. It is a good idea, however, not to see people too often. It takes time to assimilate changes of this magnitude and you do not want to work on a new issue until the energy around the old one has been cleared completely. You also want to avoid creating a dependency. What you are doing in these sessions is giving your clients tools that they can use to heal themselves. Even if they do not have the stones, they have the visualization and breathing techniques. They know what the energy bodies look and feel like and what the energy feels like when it changes. When you are reviewing the session, you encourage them to recall the experience in a way that is both visual and tactile. Remember how it feels to be balanced. Remember how it feels to be free. Because that is what will help to heal them the next time.

I would like to say a final word about responsibility, which does not end when your client walks out the door. It is important that you not allow your clients to leave until they are completely recovered from their journey. Be sure that they are fully conscious, that they are not starry-eyed or off in a dream somewhere. You can get some real space cadets who enjoy being out of body and are difficult to control with your voice and your guided imagery. Looking at the stones and talking about them during the totem part of the session will drop your client into a thinking mode and give you a chance to evaluate his condition. You do not want to put anyone behind the wheel of a car who might drive into a tree. This happened to one of my students who went into a meditative state during one of my sessions with her and was unable to get completely back before she left. She lost control of her car on the way home, went off the road and ploughed into a young tree. Her car was a heavy old clunker and the tree was small, but the circumstances could have been quite different.

Once the sessions are over, try not to hold onto them by mulling over your clients and their problems or reviewing the layouts. I tell my clients that when they walk out the door, their issues go with them. I do this for two reasons. One—the sessions are always deeply personal and elicit a lot of information that should be kept confidential. Your client needs to feel that his process is respected. Two—it is a matter of my personal, psychic survival to let these issues go and not try to second guess the scenarios, the layouts, the summations. Did I give my client the information he needed? Did I do the layout right? That, to me, is second guessing. One of the first messages I received when I started channeling years ago was "give what you are given and let it go." And so I have. And so should you.

FACET IV

Shaman Tool Box

Stones of the Trade

A BRIEF PERSONAL NOTE. *In reviewing this material, you may find some similarities between my information and what was presented by Katrina Raphaell in her books—*Crystal Enlightenment, Crystal Healing and The Crystalline Transmission. *Katrina and I channeled the information for her first book together. We meditated on each stone and discussed it at length while we were preparing our work for her publication. Some of this information appeared in her last two books as well. We have been friends for years and have great respect for one another, although we do our work quite differently now. In the years to come, I hope that my students will carry on the tradition we began by creating a literature of their own and composing variations on our healing methods and ideas. It is the desire of every teacher to see her students shine with their own light.*

TODAY WE WORK with crystals and minerals in much the same way traditional shamans use power animals to facilitate healing. The different kinds of animals seen while journeying are indicators of the type of "medicine" carried by the seeker and symbolize strengths as well as weaknesses. The direction from which the animal enters the vision, whether it appears as an enemy or an ally or whether it changes form at some point during the journey all say something specific about the individual. These animals are the tools of the shaman's trade. They are powerful archetypes. Each one has an energy or vibration as well as a distinct personality of its own and can be read just like we read the stones in a scenario.

Crystals and minerals give a different perspective to this kind of healing. Traditional shamanism as it is practiced by the American Indians is a very heavy discipline. They travel to the dark side of the soul, into the underworld or what Jung has called the collective unconscious, and use the power animals to somehow bring about a balance between the shadow side and the light. Crystal shamans travel out into the light body and penetrate the shadow of the imbalance from a soul perspective. Both are valid approaches to healing. Traditional shamans are born to the office—to the gift, as it were—and are trained by someone in that same lineage. Not many people have access to the training. Crystals, on the other hand, are physically available to most people and, for that reason, seem to be easier to teach. You can access the energy of a stone by meditating on a photograph of it, but it is much easier to become familiar with that energy if you experience it directly.

Since crystal healing has become more respected as an alternative healing method, a number of books on the subject have appeared and each one seems to have something different to say about what the stones mean and how they should be used. I would like you to read through the interpretations given here, work with the stones yourself and make use of any information, from any source, that feels appropriate to you. That I use a certain crystal in a certain way is not in itself a reason for you to restrict your own view of a stone's potential.

Over the years, I have implemented many changes in the classification system that Katrina and I created initially. We began, as I have said, by assigning the stones to the chakras according to color. It was not so much that the color system of classification was wrong, but that I found it limiting. We had limited placement of the stones to the chakra system itself, root through crown, and we used the stones only where they had been assigned. I played around with a broader interpretation of the chakra system, renaming the chakras energy centers and studying the energy of each one. At that time I decided to reclassify the stones according to the affinity they had for the energy in a particular center. Strangely enough, this did not seem to affect the color distribution all that much. Black tourmaline and rhodonite were moved to the solar plexus, which I was calling the integration center, but most of the other stones were in the yellow to gold range as before. I moved chrysoprase to the third eye or control center with the deep violets. Some stones, I felt, belonged in more than one center so I had amazonite in both the second center of creativity and the throat. This system worked for a while but it was still too complex for beginners so I tried to simplify it even further by leaving the centers out altogether and focusing exclusively on the energy of the stones themselves. Some were movers and shakers. Others told a story and had no energy of their own, to speak of. They were quite inert. Others were clearly high spiritual vibrations. We all had great fun with this information and it was good, in a way, for people with no prior crystal knowledge because it forced them to relate to the stones energetically at the outset. However, it does require a great deal of sensitivity to the stones which is not always there at the beginning. This is something that grows and intensifies with time and exposure to the energies, but it was asking rather a lot from most beginners.

My older students must have been very confused at this point, but they heroically worked along with me and allowed me to take great liberties with the information I was giving them. Though the changes were frequent and at times radical, they greeted each new system with interest and enthusiasm and we spent many stimulating hours arguing, organizing and experimenting with the new material. I owe so much to my students and to the clients who have come to me over the years, each one giving me the opportunity to learn, to grow and to delve even more deeply into this work.

One day it occurred to me—out of the blue, so to speak—

that I could classify the stones according to the energy body they seemed to impact the most. What a revelation! It was just too simple. I had been classifying my clients this way for years—this is a very mental person, this one is emotional, this individual is very physically oriented. So I plunged into this new idea and the system has worked so well that I am still using it. I have presented it here but if, for some reason, it does not work for you, by all means throw it out and come up with something that does.

As you are reviewing the stones as they have been organized by energy body, you will probably begin to wonder what has happened to some of your old friends. Press on. You may find them included in the section on Families—tourmaline or calcite, for example. The Families have been presented separately because of the unique configuration of their energy, with as many as eight variations on a single theme. Or your favorite may be one of the Indicators, a stone that tells a story but has no energetic impact. Or it could have been assigned to the Adjuncts because it has a talent for making the other stones work.

Of course, there are some stones I have not included simply because they are very rare or because they are not in my collection and I have not worked with them. I usually encounter one person in each of my classes who challenges me with a stone that is not included in the material or wonders why I am not aware of every mineral on the planet. My brain cannot hold any more crystals—there are over 150 varieties in my collection and I max out just about there.

It has taken me years to put all of this material together but it is important that you not be intimidated by it or limited by anything I have said. Take from it whatever works for you and throw out the rest. It is your own agreement, your own relationship with the stones, that will make you effective as a facilitator. We are all pioneers in the field of crystal healing!

Physical Body Stones

Amazonite

THERE ARE CERTAIN STONES which have come to exemplify central themes or common denominators in the lives of my clients and are pivotal to the reading of any scenario in which they appear. Amazonite is one such pivotal stone. Whenever it appears as part of a scenario, it is putting you on notice that your client is struggling with one or more issues around the central theme of self expression. This can involve verbal or written communication when there is something that needs to be said to a friend or family member, a message on a much grander scale to be presented to the world at large, or a pattern of suppression that has affected a whole series of lives. Amazonite can stimulate communication at all levels of being but, like all of the physical body stones, it is primarily a physical expression. The communication does not have to be verbal. Your lifestyle, your manner of dress, your movements and gestures, your facial expressions, are all ways in which you interact with the world at large and creatively construct the window through which you allow other people to catch glimpses of who you are.

Amazonite is the stone that activates and enhances ego expression and its emphasis is on the persona which is developing in the current life. The current life expression, however, is a like a sum total of the expressions of other lives. When amazonite appears in a scenario with stones like apophyllite, dioptase or kyanite, the issue exists as a thoughtform in the soul blueprint and has been reinforced as a pattern in at least one other lifetime. If it appears with mental body stones like fluorite or lapis, something in the belief system is probably telling your client that his very survival depends on keeping his thoughts and feelings to himself. Moonstone would indicate that there is something your client knows on an intuitive level that needs to be expressed in a physical way. If amazonite appears with, say, kunzite, which is an emotional body stone, it is telling you that your client's physical and emotional balance at this time in his life depends on being able to freely express his feelings to others.

When I am using amazonite in a layout, I often put it on the throat because it works better than any other stone in releasing blocks to the flow of fifth center energies. Communication is the keynote of fifth center expression, but if there is a thoughtform in the soul blueprint that is at the root of the problem, I try to determine which center is holding the wound and I place the amazonite on or near that center—on the heart, for instance, if the block has originated in a heart wound. Like most of the stones which will be covered in this book, amazonite can be used anywhere.

Bloodstone

BLOODSTONE, or heliotrope as it is sometimes known, is a dark green form of chalcedony with red flecks of iron oxide. Roman soldiers wore it as a charm against hemorrhage. During the Middle Ages it was thought to have magical powers because the red spots in it were believed to be drops of Christ's blood. My own experience with bloodstone has been that it stimulates the flow of what we call life force or prana throughout the light system and, over a period of time, seems to act as a kind of blood builder that restores vitality to the physical body. I have found that people drawn to bloodstone are very often anemic. Many of them are suffering from what we call "burn-out." They feel physically tired and emotionally drained. If they consciously work with the bloodstone energy by meditating with the stone or putting it under a pillow and sleeping with it, the anemia sometimes turns out to be temporary rather than permanent and the overall physical condition improves. However, I have not had tests run on any of my clients and I cannot give you specifics as to what it is that physically changes. Because the *symptoms* of the anemia disappear, I am assuming that the blood is affected. The physical body holds much more mystery for me than the light body, where I can clearly perceive these changes taking place.

Bloodstone in a scenario always indicates that your client's issue, regardless of what it is or where it is coming from in the light system, is affecting him physically. If sulfur or malachite occur in the same reading, then the physical problems are intensified and your client needs to give them some attention. In a layout, place bloodstone either in the first or seeding center where the energy begins its flow throughout the physical system or at the third center of assimilation, where the body and aura exchange energy. Bloodstone is one of the healing stones that does require the client to work on their issues following the session until their physical conditions improve. A client that comes to you for a session must be made aware that crystal healing will not solve all their problems. They will have to work on the issues that come up on their own.

Blue Lace Agate

I HAVE WORKED with blue lace agate primarily in the form of cabochons, but I have seen it also in crystalline form as part of a geode. As a rule, the more clear and crystalline the stone, the more refined its energy, the faster it moves through the light system and the more subtle the effect—especially at first. The more density a stone has, the closer it works to the physical body and the more physical its effect. Unfortunately, I have not had much opportunity to work with blue lace agate in its crystalline form, so the information I am giving you necessarily comes out of my experience with the cabochons which have a very calming effect on the physical body. Blue lace agate acts directly on the nervous system to alleviate physical tension. My clients often comment on how calming it is. It is not selected all that often, but the people who seem to be drawn to it are usually in a pretty agitated state.

When blue lace agate appears as part of a scenario, the stones around it will pinpoint the source of the tension. If it occurs in combination with fluorite, your client may be experiencing what I have described as a tug of war in the belief system which needs to be looked at and resolved. With sulfur, the digestion is affected and your client is probably so stressed out that he is not able to eat or assimilate nutrients properly. Emotional body stones, of course, indicate emotional tension. Tourmalines would suggest that he has overextended himself in relationships, continually sacrificing his own needs to meet the needs of others. This pattern tends to be compulsive and very difficult to break, even after you realize that you have it. Believe me, I know.

In a layout, blue lace agate belongs at whatever center the scenario stones indicate the stress to be held. I usually add it to a layout regardless of whether the client has selected it, especially in cases when a client is nervous or excitable. Don't be shy about adding your own stones to a layout, but be sure to tell the client where and why during the totem part of the six steps. This calming blue stone should be playing a more important role in these stressful times.

Boji Stone

BOJI STONES are a relatively new discovery for most crystal healers and there has been a lot of speculation on how they work and what it is, exactly, that they heal. They are a dense black mineral, with a surface that can be either smooth to the touch or covered with small, rough ridges. It has been suggested that the two different surface expressions of this mineral, the smooth and the rough, represent the feminine and masculine polarities of human sexual balance and that if you work one form without the other, you will have imbalance. In my own work with this stone, the question of gender or sexuality has never even come up. I do not understand how the densest mineral on the planet has anything to do with sexuality!

Boji stones come from a southern state, on an Indian reservation near a pyramid shaped mountain. For years their secret was held close to those who found them and how they are used by the Indians is still not known. Bojis appear following heavy rains when they surface and are gathered only by select members of the tribe. These intriguing stones have stems attached to them that are removed in a ceremony before they are taken off the reservation. They are thought to have been seeded here, but by whom and why remains a mystery.

I have a hand-size, ridged Boji that weighs two pounds and shows no preference for one gender over the other. When I sit with it in meditation or with any of my other Boji stones—small or large, rough or smooth—what I sense has to do with determination and resolve, with how my physical balance is in counterpoint to the dynamic of my light system and how I am affected as a composite being by the choices I make on a physical level. I have a sense of being solid on this physical planet, of being focused on earth existence and on my own destiny as an earth expression.

To work extensively with the Boji stone will ultimately result in bringing your choices more in line with your destiny and effectively balance your own master plan or life script with the destiny of the earth as a planet. Choices that are made with this kind of conscious focus are always in line with your destiny. We only get confused when we start second guessing ourselves—"I shouldn't have said that" or "I should have done this." Balance is not a balancing act. Sometimes our options seem to be very limited, but reasoning stops with the mental body and the suffering which is not always a graceful physical experience, but may be a tremendous catalyst to the growth and expansion of the soul. This, in itself, is a matter of choice—not on a personal level, of course, but at the soul level where we are not bound by the restrictions of time and space and where our consciousness is pure light and energy. To take conscious responsibility for that choice is to live from a soul perspective. To experience that perfect sense of proportion and cooperation enjoyed by all aspects of the balanced, composite being, you have to be able to trust in yourself and in your sense of your own destiny.

Boji stones are rarely selected other than by those who already know what they are. Because they are so dark and dense, most clients tend to stay away from them and other black stones. When they first appeared on the healing scene, the mystery surrounding them left a wide interpretation for their meaning, so even those that think they understand them will select a boji. In a scenario the presence of a boji indicates the need for a greater perspective of balance. Notice the surrounding stones for any clue as to the location of the seed of imbalance that may assist the boji in its job. In a layout, I have placed bojis around the feet along with generator crystals or other stones that tend to pull energy down into consciousness. Rarely are bojis put along the energy centers unless at the integration center where they bring their essence of proportion into the body. Boji stones are making their way into crystal healing slowly, with the same determination that lies within their energy.

Carnelian

WHENEVER you sit down to do something creative, you are connecting with the creative energies you sense as inspiration and allowing them to flow through you. Carnelian works from the light body levels to bring those energies into the physical consciousness where they can be focused and expressed in a physical way. It is not the lofty thought that counts but what you do with it. How do you put it into that piece of sculpture or onto that canvas? Any area of your life that can be enriched by inspiration falls under the auspices of this stone—whether you are creating a sculpture, planting a garden or building a business from the ground up. Working with carnelian will break up any blocks that are inhibiting the flow of that energy.

Carnelian is not selected as often as it used to be since the orange calcite became so popular. Perhaps people are drawing their creative spirit from a higher vibration of their light and carnelian is too dense for them now. But I still use it in my grids with hematite and seed quartz when I really want to design a creative dynamic for myself.

Carnelian usually appears in a scenario as part of a group or configuration of stones. Very rarely will it stand alone or serve as the primary focus for a reading. The stones around it will pinpoint the source of the creative block, if there is one, and suggest a means of dealing with it. Depending on the scenario, carnelian could be indicating that the energy is flowing well and the emphasis then would be on how it is directed and utilized, especially if there is no azurite present.

In a layout, carnelian can be used anywhere. I allow myself to be guided by information gained from the scenario and the energy center measurements and, as always, I use my intuition in placing the stones. I have used carnelian on the intuition center for greater insight into more creative ways to access personal spirituality. I use it on the throat or communication center along with sodalite for more creative expression. Carnelian lends itself to any center that needs a creative boost.

Chrysocolla

THE BOULDER FORM of chrysocolla, as opposed to gem silica which is an evolved form of the same mineral, activates the feminine persona that exists within all of us as a powerful archetype, the goddess or the earth mother, and awakens from far memory a relationship with the earth that is primitive and instinctive, that changes with the seasons and fully responds to its rhythms and signals. Chrysocolla uproots and soothes old memories rather than offering a healing energy that alters patterning and is good for people who have lost their earth connection with the feminine. Men who are drawn to it seem to feel some kind of connection to the earth as mother which derives from affiliation with earth-based cultures and religions—like the Native American, for instance. They tend to be a little rough around the edges, the man who needs to recognize and acknowledge the feminine in himself. Women who identify with this kind of energy are trying to understand the archetype. Many of them are reacting to a collective pattern of repression and persecution of the feminine nature that has been more prevalent in some societies than others, but has existed in one form or another for centuries. They tend to be feminists and openly express the desire to become the living embodiment of that archetypal energy.

In a scenario, regardless of which gender selects it, chrysocolla offers the client the opportunity to look closer at their feminine energy and how it plays out in their life. A man came to me looking for ways to find his life partner, not a question usually asked of crystal healing, but when I asked him to draw stones about the kind of woman he was looking for, chrysocolla was among the eight he selected. I smiled and told him he was looking for an 'earth-mother' type, well connected to her spirituality, yet strong like the rock of boulder chrysocolla and comfortable being a woman. Oh, and several fluorites around that told him she had to be very mental as well! I wonder if he has found her yet? In a layout, chrysocolla belongs in the lower energy centers, close to the earth and physical energy centers. In the first center of seeding of consciousness this stone stimulates the soul memory of the feminine. In the second center of birthing it would align more with sexual manifestation.

Crocoite

CROCOITE came into my life some years ago as a gift from a friend who had picked it up for me on her travels. This woman was very sexually focused and when I established my New Age counseling center in Newport Beach, she jokingly volunteered to be my expert on psychic sexuality! When I asked her why she was so attracted to this stone, she laughed and said that it probably had to do with something sexual.

Surprisingly enough, this turned out to be true. When my clients select crocoite for the scenario, I know that we are dealing with the second center type of energy disruption that could indicate sexual abuse in childhood, blocks to the expression of that energy in adulthood, or a very active, rising kundalini. Kundalini, in Hindu philosophy, is a liquid energy that moves up the spine from the first chakra or energy center to the crown at the top of the head. Controlled by meditation, this energy is the sacred path to enlightenment.

To interpret several indications of crocoite, much will depend on who is sitting in front of you, the other stones that have been selected, and the question that has been asked. If your client is eighty years old and draws crocoite for the scenario, chances are that sexual expression is not an issue. If one or more spiritual body stones are present, you are probably dealing with a manifestation of the kundalini energy—in which case, you need to explain to your client what the kundalini is and how it is operating in his life. If your client tells you outright that he has difficulty expressing sexually and then he selects crocoite, then you have an automatic validation that the energy disruption in the second center is, indeed, at the root of the problem and you would use that center as the basis for your explorations.

If he has difficulty expressing sexually and selects, say, amethyst, then you know that your client has entered into a phase of life in which sexuality is not really as important to him as he says it is and he needs to spend some time getting to know the spiritual part of himself. If your client is a ten year old boy, it is up to you to decide how far you wish to go with your explanations. Children standing on the edge of puberty are just beginning to wake up to themselves sexually and to experience their first sexual impulses, but this session may not be the time or the place for such a lecture.

I would like to reiterate my words of caution on the subject of sexual abuse in childhood. If this comes up in the scenario and your client remembers the event on his own, then you can explore it together and resolve the issues or the thoughtforms which have developed as a result of the incident, or which triggered it in the first place. It is not advisable to even mention it as a possibility if your client does not bring up the subject himself. Some clients are extremely suggestible and you may be planting seeds of doubt and suspicion that could create needless conflict and even destroy an entire family. The issue may have nothing to do with sexuality. Crocoite in a scenario might be telling you that this particular kind of energy has been focused in another direction—into a creative expression, for instance, if your client is an artist—especially if it occurs together with creative stones like jasper or calcite. If it is surrounded by mental body stones, then your client probably channels most of it into ideas. Spiritual body stones, as I have said, would indicate an active kundalini. If the energy is manifesting primarily in the emotional body, as indicated by sodalite or gem silica or rose quartz, then you need to determine whether the emotional experience of this energy is a source of frustration to your client, or whether the emotions are simply his way of relating to the world.

In a layout, if crocoite wants to be at the first center seeding of consciousness, the indication of a spiritual opening or expansion would be enhanced by this stone. Placing crystal points going up the body or tabular quartz to connect to the higher centers would force the energy to rise up through the energy centers as far as it needs to go. A word of caution here, do not lead a client with such an energy too fast or out the top of their heads. Your role here is to be the guide and allow the client to be in charge of the raising of that kind of vibration. If crocoite is on the second center of birthing, where sexual issues reside, smithsonite is a good companion, the color of which to coincide with the gender of the client. Mica lepidolite would help to peel away any layers of emotion that may surround the issue at hand. If the client has a sexual block, make a mandala of stones at the second center that include energies pertinent to your scenario discoveries. You may want to include black tourmaline if there is negativity around the issue, or aventurine for emotional stress. Any time you create a mandala of stones it should be at the center that is the most important to the healing session and the breathing should be directed there as well.

Garnet

GARNET IS ALWAYS CONNECTED with winter in my mind and I often refer to it as the winter stone. Not only is it the birthstone traditionally associated with the month of January, but its ability to move and circulate energy would seem to be needed most in the middle of winter when the physical energy tends to be lower than at other times of the year and we are less physically active. As I have worked with this stone over the years, it has become clear to me that the functions of bloodstone and garnet are closely related and, to a certain extent, dependent on one another.

Where bloodstone works to strengthen the physical body by stimulating the flow of energy we call life force, garnet circulates that energy through the light system. Activity, then, enhances circulation in the physical body. In other words, it is the kind of jump start bloodstone gives you initially that enables garnet to do its work. You would expect these stones to be selected together fairly often, but this is usually not the case. The problem generally seems to relate to one or the other.

In the early years of my death and dying work, while I was still counseling critically ill children, I had a young client, a little girl, who was very drawn to garnet. Jenny had renal failure and working with the garnet energy helped her to feel that she had some control over the progression of her disease. As long as she could keep that energy moving, she did not need to succumb to the fear of shutdown that is a part of every waking moment in the lives of most people with kidney failure. Her sister, Heather, who was very close to her in age, liked bloodstone. Heather was physically and emotionally depleted by Jenny's illness and there was a part of her that was trying to build up her sister, strengthen her and make her well. Bloodstone seemed to build Heather up physically giving her the stamina she needed to cope with the emotional situation at home. I worked with both of them for two years, at which time Jenny died. The garnet was not able to keep Jenny alive, nor was that my intention when I gave it to her to work with. My intention was to make those two years easier for her, to give her a sense of purpose and a certain amount of control over her environment by allowing her to participate in her own treatment. There have been several books published which make claims for these stones that I consider to be quite unrealistic. The stones can help, but they are not miracle workers and there are limits to what they can do. They focus the energy of your own intent. They can do nothing in themselves that you would not be able to do on your own.

Most of the garnets in my collection are rough cut or tumbled specimens, and I have worked with the red, green and pink varieties primarily. The colors are not as clear and vibrant as they are in the faceted stones and their energy is perceived as being profoundly physical. When garnet is selected for the scenario, your client is telling you that something in his light system is preventing the circulation of energy through the physical body. The stones around it will clarify the issue and tell you where it can be found. Red garnets focus on the type of energy that is initiated by bloodstone—physical energy, life force—and will act as a tonic on the circulatory system. I have a pink variety of almandine garnet that seems to catalyze a physical experience of the heart energy by circulating self love and appreciation throughout the entire system.

Green garnet also works with the heart energy and its presence in a scenario would indicate that your client needs to use that energy to heal himself. It carries the message of the healing heart to all parts of the light system and to every cell in the physical body. I do not have much experience with the violet tinged variety of rhodolite garnet, but my assumption would be that, depending on the other stones in the scenario, there is mental or spiritual body information that needs to be circulated. Orange garnets would help to break up physical lethargy by moving energy through the solar plexus.

In a layout, I place garnets on the physical body wherever they correspond to the areas of density I perceive in the light system, with the intent of moving energy through those areas and breaking up the stagnation. If you are not visual, just use your intuition in placing the stones or focus the energy on a center that, according to your measurements, seems to need building up. If the problem is physical, you may want to use garnet in conjunction with bloodstone if it has not already been selected for the scenario. When I first started using garnet as part of a layout it was predominantly a second center stone but now I use it wherever there is a need for circulating energy.

Howlite

WHENEVER I TOUCH into howlite during a session, I become aware of a subtle but definite spiralling energy. Howlite is not a very forceful stone and its energy is too gentle to impact the light system to any significant degree on its own. However, it has been very successful in focusing the energy of other stones and I now use it primarily in grids or layouts where I wish to create a spiralling effect with the energy. Howlite is an enabler. It creates a spiral pattern or helix which enables the energy and information in a layout to be assimilated at a physical, cellular level. The spiral is the most basic energy format that exists on our planet. The DNA double helix, for example, carries the physical blueprint of existence that we share with every other earth lifeform. So what we have in howlite is a gentle reminder that earth is at the center of our beingness and it is time to realign ourselves according to the priorities of earth life.

In a scenario, howlite would indicate that there is some very basic information that needs to be assimilated by the physical body at a cellular level. Perhaps there has been a shift in the patterning of one of the energy bodies that needs to be physically acknowledged. Perhaps your client needs to bring his consciousness down to earth for a while. The stones which appear around howlite in the scenario should all be incorporated into the layout. The solar plexus is the best place to set up the grid because it is the integration and assimilation center, where the energies from all the other centers flow together and intersect before being redirected throughout the light system. However, as I have said before, there are no hard and fast rules in this work and it is important to follow your own intuition when placing the stones.

Jasper

JASPER CAN BE either quartz or chalcedony and is relatively dense, though I have seen some beautiful specimens that come very close to being translucent. For me, jasper is the "back to Nature" stone. It is like a physical translation of that creative energy or inspiration that comes from the experience of living very close to the earth. In Nature there are resources available to meet every need that we have, no matter how fundamental or how exalted. Food, shelter, tools, medicine, inspiration and beauty—if you were able to strip your life of all that is superfluous and unnecessary and begin it over again with only these essentials, you would eliminate the need for distraction and escapism on a physical level and be able to function at a very high level of spiritual as well as physical health and awareness. Jasper holds in trust for us the assurance that the earth is, after all, the mother of all lifeforms and the source of all nurturing and nourishment. You have everything else you need within you to recreate your world.

I have worked primarily with the red and green varieties of jasper, though it occurs in a multitude of colors and there seems to be no limit to the designs created by the bands and swirls and flecks of color which inscribe the surface of each stone. Jasper is so richly creative and varied in its expression that I was not surprised to find that the clients most attracted to it were artists. Red jasper especially seems to draw the attention of people who like to work with earth tools—clay, stone, pieces of wood, fabric created from natural fibers—as opposed to synthetics like acrylic or glass. In a scenario, it would indicate that your client needs a creative outlet for his energy and should consider exploring one or more of these natural mediums. Perhaps he simply needs to eliminate distraction from his life by finding a natural setting in which to work. Green jasper, on the other hand, is telling you that your client has lost touch with his creativity altogether and needs to go "back to Nature" for the inspiration which would make it possible for him to reconnect with that sense of himself as "one who creates." The green crystals and minerals we use in this work are very often active healers and green jasper is no exception to this not so very hard and fast rule. Healers attracted to this stone are also primarily interested in working with earth tools—herbs or crystals, for example. Sometimes it draws the attention of people who need to explore these alternatives in order to heal themselves.

In a layout, jasper functions primarily as a second center stone, though a creative block can originate in any of the centers. Red jasper serves primarily to eliminate distraction and focus the attention on the creative energy. Sometimes this is all that is necessary to create an outlet for it. The green variety rekindles inspiration to the creative center.

Lingam

THE LINGAM has been around for centuries, yet crystal healers are just now beginning to discover it. Lingams come from the Narmada River in India where it has a strong sexual identification. Seen as a phallic symbol, local priests long ago used the lingam as a propaganda to increase the population of their villages. Lingam is Sanskrit for phallic and is likely why the sexual meaning came along with the stones. These river rocks come in an elongated egg-like shapes, dark gray and brown earth tones with streaks of red that circles around them. They are found with a rather rough finish, but are polished to a shining smoothness by the local people.

On one hand they are a phallic symbol and on the other myth has it that lingams came from the moon and were originally used by women in childbirth. The red markings symbolized the blood of the birthing process. Somewhere along their evolution into healing stones, they came to mean balance between male and female. Man and woman coming together to create life or unification. And there is definitely a feeling of coming together with lingams, like a gravitational pull to their center, but I do not sense the gender aspects as much as I do the unification.

Most everyone who is drawn to lingams treasure them as something special. If you ask these people why, rarely do they understand what it is about lingams that makes them so endearing. When you hold one, there is a sense of coming together and a nurturing that makes them comfortable to be around. I have always sensed nurturing from lingams as if I were receiving an energy from the earth that fed right into my lower energy centers. From the seeding of light to the birthing of light in the second center, lingam's vibration does its work. It is here that lingams unify these centers, bringing them together to fill a void.

There have been so many of my clients who lacked the proper love and nurturing in their early formative years, never bonded with their parents and were left with a vague sense emptiness at the core of their being. Their very foundation of living was shaky which led to a feeling of not being able to accomplish a great deal even to the extent of being dysfunctional. How lingams fill this void is beyond me, but my personal and professional experience has shown me that there is a unique frequency emitting from these stones that goes right to the lower energy centers and the result is a feeling of well being and nurturing that many of us missed out on from our beginning.

In a scenario, the presence of a lingam can open a pretty good discussion about early nurturing. One client, who had cancer, went right for a lingam that was quite a distance from the other stones. The story of her early childhood went along with the lingam story, there was no sense of unification in her life or the coming together of a loving and supportive family. In my opinion a lingam in a scenario becomes the pivotal stone of the session and regardless of the initial question or issue the client came in with, the direction of healing should begin with lingam. In a layout, it should be placed right between the first and second energy centers with appropriate physical and emotional stones along its side. If the early abandonment left a severe mental problem, I would use chrysoprase with the lingam for courage to see the early experience and how it effected their life and following your session suggest to the client that further psychological counseling is advisable. These are deep seeded issues effecting the foundation of our living and likely will not be fully addressed or healed in one or two crystal sessions.

Malachite

IF YOU KNEW that you were going to be stranded on a desert island for a year and could take only one stone with you to meet any crisis of health or spirit, malachite would be your best bet. Malachite has been classified with the physical body stones because it is so useful in physical healing, but it can alter the patterning of any of the energy bodies. It isolates the distortion or shadow in the light system that is responsible for a particular physical manifestation and actually draws the energy of the disharmony into and through its own energy vibration. Like a loving mother, it takes the pain into itself—which is why I call it the mother earth stone. It is the only stone in your collection that needs to be cleansed after using it in a layout. You can smudge it with sage, wash it in soapy water, or use your intent to clear and surround it with light. Other crystals and minerals are able to clear themselves and will return to their original pristine state in a matter of hours. If you have clients scheduled back to back, of course, you will want to smudge your crystals after each session. Malachite, however, will hold onto pain which is why in early days of healing, it was called a negative stone. If you try to use it without clearing it first, you will find that it very quickly becomes warm, or sometimes even hot, to the touch and will literally jump off the body when you try to place it on one of the centers.

Malachite likes to buddy up with chrysocolla, turquoise and azurite and it has always been interesting to me that these stones, which are fragile and sometimes even brittle on their own, are considerably strengthened when bonded to malachite. Malachite works well with all other stones and can be a useful adjunct to the energy of any layout or stone configuration. When it appears as part of a scenario, it is telling you that the problem has become a physical issue, that your client is physically affected by it, and that he needs to shift or possibly even reverse the pattern of that energy in order to heal himself. If you look closely at a cabochon of malachite, you will see the markings of deep green move throughout the stone and the pattern completely reverse itself in a very short distance. Change is the key to malachite, healing is change. If your client selects it, then they must be willing to change, on whatever energy level malachite shows itself. In a layout malachite can go anywhere there is a need for movement or change to take place. Around the integration center, malachite energy keeps the energy in flow and heals the breath that is directed to the thoughtform in the light body needing healing. It is truly the universal healer.

Obsidian

OBSIDIAN is a powerful indicator of deep, hidden emotions or repressed thoughts that need to surface to consciousness. The energy stems from the volcanic source of this mineral and can literally erupt painful memories from the core of your being that need to be re-examined and resolved. I have classified obsidian with the physical body stones because it seems to focus on memories that have to do with your physical presence on this planet—that is, your incarnational focus—and on memories that have been physically incorporated at a cellular level. Whether these memories are from this lifetime or any other, the body is still reacting to them and reliving them can be painful. Some of my clients sense this instinctively and will go to great lengths to avoid even touching this mineral. Others will avoid it just because they fear the black. Hopefully the days of the sinister black are ending and we can now respect the powerful energy black has to heal. So, all you people out there who are afraid of the dark, go and hug an obsidian! You will feel much better.

Obsidian has been one of my biggest helpers over the

years. It reminds me of those American Indian storytellers who bring legends out of the past and weave tales around tribal secrets. From the depths of the earth to the depths of your soul, it allows whatever is hidden in the darkness to come forward into the light of your own conscious awareness. People who select this mineral feel a need to get in touch with these deeply buried parts of themselves. Fear is not the only thing which may be lying dormant in the unconscious. There may be powerful resources and abilities that are not being utilized, even though they are available to the current life expression. In a scenario, obsidian would indicate that your client is ready to touch into some new aspect of himself or that he needs to become aware of the next step in the earth script or master plan. In a layout, obsidian is usually placed at the feet of the client, where the energy flow through the centers really begins. Surrounded by quartz that enhance clarity when the issues come up, obsidian can really uproot a hidden issue.

You will normally see obsidian in black spheres or because it comes from hunks of volcanic glass. People who are drawn to the black are committed to face the shadow side of themselves, which is a landmark or milestone that is reached sooner or later in every shaman journey. There is a certain point beyond which you cannot travel if you are still carrying illusions about yourself. Mahogany and snowflake obsidian are not uncommon, but the pieces I have in my collection are not selected as often as the black. With mahogany obsidian, there is emphasis on viewing the incarnation from an earth rather than a soul perspective, whereas snowflake obsidian, or Apache tears as the American Indians call it, seems to be the American Indian answer to the Oriental yin/yang theory of duality.

At my New Age counseling center in Newport Beach, among the many metaphysical offerings, we sold crystals. One day a woman came in who worked as a counselor with some of the feminist groups in the area. She was very attracted to an obsidian sphere that was sitting on my shelves. She asked about it, so I explained the energy to her in great detail and told her about the kind of effect it would probably have on her light system. I even mentioned that many people were afraid to work with black stones because they considered the energy to be negative. She insisted on buying it, however, and took the stone home with her. Three weeks went by before she called me in a panic. The obsidian was now in a box, hidden in one of her closets, and she wanted to return it immediately. She simply could not deal with the issues that were surfacing as a result of the energy.

It is interesting to me that some of fastest growing spiritual communities and healing centers in the United States—Santa Fe, Seattle, Hawaii—are obsidian-based from once active volcanos. Santa Fe is sitting on top of a mountain of it and it is no coincidence that those people who move here, or come for extended visits, often find themselves doing a lot of "processing," getting in touch with hidden issues, healing themselves or becoming healers.

Onyx

ALL THE ONYX in my collection is black because this is the variety that I have found most useful for grounding, which is the way I use it in my sessions. Onyx occurs naturally in the form of a layered chalcedony that is a kind of white or off-white material on a black or brown base. The white onyx is often dyed to simulate the appearance of other more expensive minerals like sugilite or lapis. When you are working with stones in a healing capacity, it is important that you keep the energy clear by avoiding specimens that have been dyed or treated with certain types of chemicals. Epoxy, for instance, which is used in making jewelry, changes the energy of turquoise though it does not seem to affect quartz. Chalcedony, which is a quartz precursor, would probably not be affected by epoxy, but you need to be aware that this is a factor when you are working with the stones in this way.

Onyx often appears in the scenarios of people who are living hectic lives with too many irons in the fire. It is the kind of grounding energy that I call "rocks in your pocket". It brings the energy back into the physical body and focuses the consciousness on the physical, earth plane. I use it in my own grids when I feel that I need to be walking the earth in a more conscious manner. When your client selects onyx, he is telling you that, at this moment, he is feeling scattered and somewhat overwhelmed, and that being physical is something of a struggle for him.

Onyx seems to work more effectively with the energy of the individual than with the energetic configuration of the stones in a layout, so if you need to bring the energy or information in a layout into the physical body so it can be assimilated, howlite or smoky quartz might be a better choice. When I use it in a layout, I place it at the first energy center where most of us need to feel grounded and fully present on the planet. If you are feeling "spaced out" and you need to bring your energies back into the body, onyx will exert what can be immediately perceived as a steadying influence. Steadying is a good word for this stone—carry it with you and it will keep your moccasins straight.

Peridot

PERIDOT became popular in wartime, during World Wars I and II, when the world was in a great deal of physical pain. Most of the jewelry during wartime was made of peridot.Its color is an interesting green, light with a cast of yellow. I have found peridot most useful in physical wound healing. You can put it in your mouth to alleviate the pain of a toothache and I have put it in water and given it to people to drink when they have been physically ill with a cold and flu virus.

A client who selects peridot for the scenario probably has some kind of physical wound or illness or disability, but my specimens are very small, tumbled stones and, because they are so small, they are not often selected. It is not that the larger stones have more energy, though this can sometimes be the case, but most of my clients simply do not see the smaller ones. Because peridot seems to accelerate the healing process, I will use it in layouts, when I know that my client is experiencing physical discomfort or pain. Often I will make a circle of small peridot around the affected area or energy center with appropriate healing stones in the middle pertinent to the issue brought out in the scenario.

Rhodonite

RHODONITE, with an abundance of deep pink mixed with gray, has always been considered a heart stone, pink and love and all of that. For years the rhodonite eluded me, it just hung around my crystal cabinet with the other heart stones and was rarely selected. And, as usually happens, once the true meaning of a stone is revealed, clients suddenly take notice! My first specimen of rhodonite was from a museum collection, very old and rather small and dark. I did not care for it very much. When I found a brighter, more transparent piece, the colors came alive and I began working with it more seriously. I followed along its journey that led away from the emotional body and the heart straight to the integration center and the physical body. It was there that rhodonite taught me that compassion is not an emotion, but a physical action of creating change, something you do rather than feel.

For me, compassion is far more profound than merely feeling sorry for someone. It is a commitment that cames from deep inside of all of us, an active physical expression rather than a passive emotional feeling. Compassion came to mean 'with passion', putting feelings into action. You can be sure that my insights are met with much discussion and controversy. To take compassion out of the emotional body is difficult for heart centered folks, who think of it as pity or leniency. The really compassionate person is one who acts on their feelings.

Rhodonite has become quite a popular stone these days now that its message has come forth. In a scenario it will always bring up the topic of compassion and suggest that the client may be ready to act on his feelings. It is not enough to just emote feelings and opinions anymore, this is the age of action. Rhodonite says it is not enough to be disappointed or feel badly about people or situations, it may be time to do something about them. The client may be overwhelmed by his surroundings and think he cannot make a difference.

Look for other physical body stones near the rhodonite to bring greater clarity to the scenario. Malachite, for instance, would surely indicate the need for change, energy is moving and needs direction. In a layout, rhodonite belongs at the assimilation center where compassion as an action can be a part of the breath and taken right into the body. Putting citrine around it enables the rhodonite to integrate without undue emotion. Creating a bridge from the heart to the solar plexus with a double terminated quartz would surely direct compassion from a feeling to an action. Rhodonite requires a great deal of thought on your part, to identify with compassion in your own way.

Smoky Quartz

THERE IS a well-known crystal healer in California who claims that smoky quartz is extremely negative, that to work with it is dangerous, and that to work with it at all you have to be absolutely clear. Smoky quartz is, to me, one of the most beautiful and powerful members of the quartz family. When I hold it, I feel focused and clear but on a very physical level. When I use it in layouts, I see that the energy of smoky quartz penetrates shadows and areas of density in the light system much more readily than the clear quartz points. Perhaps it is the grounding element, staying focused on the earthplane, in smoky quartz that makes it so effective as a healer. Clear quartz seems to be primarily an amplifier. It will enhance the vibration of anything it happens to be physically or psychically close to, whether this is the vibration of another stone or the personal vibration of a human individual. Smoky quartz, on the other hand, has the ability to give focus to that clarity. In a scenario, it would give emphasis to any configuration or group of stones in which it appeared—sort of like a symbolic exclamation point.

Smoky quartz is not as popular as it used to be and is not selected all that often. I attribute this partially to the fact that there are so many more interesting, brightly colored, faceted stones to choose from now and partially to the fact that so many people have lost touch with the importance of being physically centered. People who are drawn to select smoky quartz for the scenario seem to be making a conscious effort to stay clear and focused on a physical level. In a layout, I usually place it on the solar plexus with the point towards the feet. It then has that sense of pulling energy down into the body, thus allowing to be collected and assimilated on a physical level. Smoky quartz will ground the energy of an entire layout into the physical body. In other words, it is able to focus that energy for distribution throughout the light system.

The only note of caution I would like to introduce in regard to this stone has to do with the darker specimens which have been irradiated. In the mid-1980's I had a small growth on my knee that was bothering me. A friend gave me a smoky quartz to work with that, I learned much later, was irradiated. Within a month, it was cancer had doubled in size and had to be removed surgically. Now, I am not saying that the irradiated crystal created the cancer, but I do suspect that it accelerated the growth to a more serious stage very quickly. You need to be very cautious about working with irradiated specimens. These crystals hold radiation for several years and if you are projecting the energy of the quartz into somebody's aura during a healing session, you are also projecting the radiation. Whenever you buy a smoky quartz specimen, ask your vendor whether or not it is ir- radiated. You are much safer, however, if you can sense the radiation on your own by holding the specimen in your hand. If you feel a vibration from the quartz, then it should be alright, if it feels inert and inward like a black hole, then do not purchase it. A jeweler friend of mine went to a lecture about precious stones and someone asked the expert how to determine whether gems are genuine or treated with dyes or radiation. 'Simple', came the answer, 'hold them and see if there is any energy there!'

Sulfur

SULFUR is the most simple and straightforward of all the physical body stones. Whenever sulfur appears in a scenario it is telling you that the issue, whatever it happens to be, is affecting your client physically at the level of his digestive system. Either there is something wrong with the diet or your client is unable to assimilate nutrients from the food he does eat. One of my students drew stones for a layout during class that consisted of sulfur and amber calcite, almost exclusively. I did not know her very well then—it was the first time she had attended one of my classes. The presence of amber calcite suggested that there was information from the life script not being assimilated on other levels in addition to the physical digestive problem indicated by the sulfur. When questioned about this, she admitted that she had been forced to take drastic measures to deal with a severe weight problem and so had her stomach stapled together. She was unable to assimilate any nutrients at all from her food.

The best place for sulfur in a layout is, of course, the solar plexus because this is the area where digestion and assimilation take place, but again you have to look at the problem from the perspective of the entire light system. If an emotional problem is causing the digestive disturbance, you might consider placing sulfur on the heart to encourage assimilation of the emotion that is not being "digested" and turquoise on the solar plexus to neutralize the distress signals that are upsetting the digestive processes in the stomach. Because the solar plexus is the integration center where the energies from all the other centers flow together and intersect, a distress signal from any one of them will throw the digestive system out of whack. We all know from experience that when we are emotionally upset or off balance in any other way, we can compensate by developing an some kind of eating disorder. Either we compulsively overeat or we become compulsively anorexic. The digestion is always affected. I often take sulfur with me when I travel to foreign countries where I am forced to make sudden changes in my diet and eating habits. I stay healthy much longer than my travel companions, as a rule, and almost never get sick!

Sunstone

SUNSTONE is one of those special minerals that has been around forever, but recently 'discovered' as a healing crystal.

It is much like its cousin moonstone, with iridescent qualities of light, but differs in energy and color. Moonstone reflects light, sunstone creates light. Moonstone is a milky bluish white, like the full moon in a midnight sky. Sunstone is a bright orange/yellow with a slight cast of pink that looks like the sun on days when the sky is clear and shining. Sunstone activates the sun center of our bodies, the integration center located at the solar plexus area. This is our most vital center, alive with energy that flows from all the other centers, and the entire light body system, assimilating experience and thought. Sunstone radiates its light through the sun center to facilitate the free flow of energy, penetrating any density accumulated there.

In a scenario, sunstone tells you to play close attention to the assimilation center, energy there is not flowing properly. Note the surrounding stones to see where the lack of movement is coming from. Usually it is the emotional body that creates a sluggishness in the sun center, emotional stress of any kind can bind up energy that can severely block the energy flow at our most important integration center. If an abundance of emotional issues arise, then the session should focus on clearing those as much as possible and let the sunstone vibration re-stimulate the energy center. This is the one center that if overloaded with stress and emotion will shut down and create all kinds of problems physically. So in a layout, sunstone belongs exclusively to the sun center. It keeps the energy flowing and clearing a path for the breath to get out to the emotional and other light bodies that may hold the troublesome thoughtform.

Turquoise

NOT MANY of us can say that we have experienced peace in a deeply personal way—at least, not over an extended period of time. When you look into a piece of turquoise and get lost in that ethereal blue, you become very peaceful—for a brief moment. When you meditate, you have a few more of those moments and sometimes you can sustain the experience for a few hours, perhaps even as long as a day. When the peace that you feel in your meditations permeates every area of your physical life and consciousness, you will have a true sense of the healing potential of this stone. Turquoise is the peaceful, physical expression of your soul's energy and purpose when there are no blocks, no stops, to that energy. Working with it over a period of time will bring "the peace that surpasses all understanding" out of the realm of ideas and into your experience of day-to-day living. It is no coincidence that the American Indians, who have been making it into jewelry and putting it into their medicine bags for hundreds of years, are becoming the New Age messengers for world peace.

Most of my clients recognize turquoise for what it is and because it is so familiar, they tend to overlook it in favor of stones that seem to promise a newer, more exciting, unfamiliar experience. Another reason that it is not selected very often, I think, is because peace is not a high priority in the lives of most people. Many of us thrive on excitement and enjoy being constantly stimulated, so we live very hectic lives. Those individuals who are at peace with themselves and the world do not usually seek out crystal healers, so when I see turquoise as the predominant stone in a scenario, I usually interpret it to mean that my client is feeling a lack of harmony in his life or is not at peace with his choices. When turquoise does not dominate the reading but seems to be functioning in a kind of subsidiary capacity, it is usually identifying a gift or a talent that wants to express physically. Amazonite, for example, would indicate that this person is very close to becoming a professional communicator, that he is probably very drawn to a career that involves writing or speaking. Fire opal would point out that latent qualities of leadership are very close to manifestation in the physical life.

In a layout, turquoise can be used with benefit on any of the centers where the energy flow is perceived as being too strong or too harsh. This can happen when a mandala, for instance, focuses energy on a center that has been blocked. The client often experiences tension or discomfort in that area when the center is activated and turquoise can relieve this kind of pressure immediately, so at times I will include it as part of the mandala as a kind of relaxant. I have used it to alleviate headaches and, in conjunction with sulfur, it can soothe an upset stomach. The energy of turquoise will soothe smooth out all your rough edges, especially where they seem to involve the interaction of the physical with the emotional body.

Variscite

THE NEWEST GREEN on the scene is variscite. As if to appear out of nowhere, this remarkable healing green mineral comes a long at just the right moment to heal the first energy center, the seeding of consciousness. Often confused with green aventurine because the color tones are so similar, variscite has created its own purpose in crystal healing. It never occurred to me that the first energy center would be in need of healing until I began working with a new computerized radionics program which measures energy flow through our entire physical and light bodies. With every one of my personal experiments, my first center was consistently reading lower than all the others. It was more than not being grounded or fully present in consciousness, which many of the first center stones address themselves to, it was a deep seeded unhappiness with my being here at all.

When you work in healing and counseling for many years you become increasingly more sensitive to the world around you, problems unresolved, potentials unrealized. I was loosing touch with my planet, seeing only frustration and confusion here and feeling powerless to make any difference. There comes a time for all healers when we hit the wall and begin to question and doubt our abilities. I remember standing in front of a huge cancer hospital where my friend Eric was dying. It is an experimental facility for patients in the last stages of cancer with little chance of a cure. Hundreds of rooms filled with patients that would never survive and not one counselor or therapist to help them or their families to cope with what was happening. With tears in my eyes I silently asked how one small person like me could possibly make a difference in an institution like this and heal those sad souls. The answer was simple, one person at a time. That is really all we can hope to accomplish as counselors and healers, but we must not lose faith in ourselves or our special talents. Variscite, with an earth green that warms your heart, rekindles your love for this planet. The vibration is soft, the movement is subtle, but it does heal deep seeded sadness we carry at the root of our energy system, at the core of our being that threatens our very spiritual foundation, our reason for being here.

In a scenario, variscite becomes a reminder to the client that is life living is important and how he relates to this planet is vital and that he must not lose sight of why he is here. Now, many clients will say they do not know why they are here, so as the facilitator, look at the stone surrounding the variscite for clues. If there are other physical stones, watch for their message. Amazonite or carnelian indicate the creative attributes to be explored. Mental stones, like fire agate that may lead the client to consider some role of leadership in his community or personal life. Spiritual stones, such as clear apophyllite indicate the need for the session to go out to the spiritual light body for information important to how the client relates to the earth. In a layout, variscite is usually placed at the first energy center and can be surrounded by stones that ground energy such as black onyx. Adding gold fluorite along side brings the mental body into play and assists in bringing new insight into the realization that this life is a choice, this planet is a choice. The vibration of variscite revitalizes the seeding center with a healing energy that can clear away the emotional or mental obstacles to the question of why we are here. Those of us who get pretty far out with this crystal work find variscite a valuable companion. As my friend Melinda says: living in these earth suits can be a challenge!

Emotional Body Stones

Aventurine

IN THE EARLY DAYS of crystal healing, green aventurine was the only deep green stone that we had to work with, aside from green tourmaline. You must remember that not too many years ago the many varieties of crystals and minerals we use in this work today were simply not available. Because the heart had two chambers, we had assigned two colors to this center—pink and green—and two stones. It was thought that rose quartz and green aventurine epitomized the heart energy. I used to wrap them in cloth bundles and sell them as "heart center stones." If you carried them with you, they were supposed to attract love into your life. Well, what can I say? That was all we knew then. Life was relatively uncomplicated. Each energy center had a color and the stones were assigned to centers by color. We had so few choices. It was easy to have a crystal collection that covered all the bases, or so we thought.

As other green stones became available, the heart center became a bit more complicated. Heart wounds, loving relationship issues, self-esteem, and the ability to give as well as receive love crept into the healing picture. All these areas of concern required subtle energies to heal them. Green aventurine was at the top of the list and it soon became obvious to me that its healing vibration did more than merely express the loving heart, which is actually the province of green tourmaline. It was clear that emotional stress was an important factor in the lives of many of the people who came to me for healing and its source could not always be found in heart issues. What we needed was a stone that could alleviate stress so that the real issue could surface, and green aventurine seemed to operate very well in this particular role.

Any emotional problem will eventually create stress in the physical body and this fact has long been recognized by the traditional medical community. High anxiety has always affected us physically. It also flows in the other direction and will sooner or later work its way into the mental body patterning as a belief—"I am a highly-strung or uptight person" or "I always have difficulty in relationships." The soft, gentle tones of aventurine seem to settle into an emotional block no matter where it is in the light system and regardless of which center holds the issue. It clears away the emotional static and prepares the way for a greater depth of perception into the experience that created it.

As the blue and orange forms of aventurine became available and I added them to my collection, I began to respect the healing abilities of these other two members of the family. Orange aventurine is a fairly recent discovery of mine. It is very similar in appearance to carnelian and the two stones are often mistaken for one another. Orange aventurine neutralizes the physical effects of emotional stress and also works specifically with the energy of the second center which may hold tension in the form of sexual confusion or dysfunction. In a scenario, it is telling you either that your client is physically stressed out or that sexual dysfunction is the issue, especially if crocoite is also present. Blue aventurine, on the other hand, indicates that emotional stress has created a lot of mental confusion in your client. He may believe that he has no capacity to feel, that he is untouched by the situation at hand, or that he simply has very little emotional capacity.

In a scenario, any member of the aventurine family is putting you on notice that the emotional reactions to a specific issue are obscuring it. Your client needs to set his feelings aside so that he can take a closer look at what is really bothering him. The other stones in the scenario will clarify the approach you should take in dispersing these emotional clouds. Aventurine with malachite, for instance, is letting you know that the energy needs to be moved through the system so that the problem at hand does not affect your client physically. Aventurine with sulfur signifies that the situation is interfering with your client's ability to assimilate nutrients. People who are too upset to eat or who compulsively overeat need the aventurine vibration to neutralize the confusion that keeps them from responding to the natural rhythms of the physical body.

In a layout, aventurine can be placed anywhere on the body, near any center that seems to require its soothing vibration. It works well alone or as an adjunct to the energy of other stones. You may want to use it in the layout even when it does not appear in the scenario. Any kind of emotional stress should be given your immediate attention, whether the effects are mental or physical. The more of it we can neutralize by taking responsibility for creating and healing it in our daily lives, the healthier we can be.

Chalcanthite

MY FRIEND CATHERINE gave me a small piece of chalcanthite to work with a few years ago. We were both fascinated by the color as neither one of us had ever seen a stone that came close to being such a vibrant—almost electric—royal blue. As luck would have it, my clients and students headed straight for it as soon as I had placed it in my case. "This stone is so inviting," was an early comment. I am always glad when this happens because it helps me to learn about each new piece. Chalcanthite was "the new stone on the block!" So many people were drawn to it that I knew we would soon be able to reach a new plateau of understanding in relation to its potentials and possibilities.

Chalcanthite heralds major shifts in consciousness which

require leaps of faith and radical changes in belief. Anyone who commits to the shaman journey knows all about the period of void which precedes any major shift in consciousness, a time when you let go of everything that feels solid and familiar to make room for the unknown. Whether you are changing religions or lifestyles or ending a relationship, there comes a time—usually mid-point in the transition—when you feel shaky and unsupported, no matter how enthusiastically you make the initial leap. This is my Grand Canyon story. Whenever we drastically change direction in our lives, we are jumping across a wide canyon. You have to take your foot off one side in order to reach the other. You must leave behind everything that no longer serves the new direction. And what a leap that is! You take off graceful as a gazelle and suddenly, in the middle of the jump, you see that there is nothing between you and the rocky landscape but air! You must have faith that your direction is true, that what lies ahead is right, and trust that you will, indeed, land on the other side.

Changes of this magnitude are not easy to process. Certain patterns in the mental body are breaking up or fragmenting and the new patterning has not yet coalesced. The emotional body usually reacts to this kind of fragmentation with fear. If the physical environment has drastically changed—if you are between jobs, for instance—you may feel that your survival is physically threatened. The emotional body reacts with more fear. Chalcanthite acts directly on the emotional body to alleviate fear and clear away any other emotional static caused by fragmentation of the mental patterning. It creates a kind of emotional bridge between the physical consciousness and the mental body that supports the new ideas, the expanded vision, the changes in lifestyle, until you are comfortable with them.

When I first moved to Santa Fe, I found myself in the middle of the biggest change in my life. We left a well-established network of family and friends in California to come to this relatively small town where we knew no one. My husband and I had both decided that we wanted to live here, but he had no job prospects at all the first year and so the period before he decided to go into business for himself was a very uncertain time for both of us. I often found myself wondering what obscure destiny had pulled us away from the security we had and the loving support of people we knew. It was a difficult time, but we had not been here long before my own work took off in a new direction. We soon had a new circle of friends and our children and grandchildren enjoy their visits with us. Chalcanthite came along just after my experience, but it would have been very useful in processing the internal changes that were happening as a result of the move and the alternative lifestyle that came out of it. I saw my gazelle self leaping over the canyon and what a relief it was when the other side finally came into view! I now understand that we should welcome these periods of void and uncertainty. What a joy it is to realize that life does not have to be rigid and confining.

When your client selects chalcanthite, you can be sure that he is heading right into the void. He is probably already experiencing the fragmentation and the anxiety that goes along with it. The other stones in the scenario will clarify the kind of transition that is manifesting in the physical life. Emotional body stones are telling you that a crisis may have been precipitated by the ending of a relationship. Mental and spiritual body stones indicate that the belief system is changing to accommodate new ways of thinking and a more spiritual focus. Chalcanthite is a great conversation piece and a good introduction to those long discussions about all the changes that come out of change.

In a layout, chalcanthite can be placed on any of the centers. It lends itself well to mandalas. If you feel that more clarity is called for, you may want surround it with quartz points or seed crystals. Chrysoprase would bring out the courage needed to complete the journey. Lapis would be helpful in dispelling any illusions your client may have about himself that are keeping the process from completion.

A WORD OF WARNING. Chalcanthite is highly toxic and should never be made into elixirs or, in a layout, placed on or near the mouth. The energy, however, is not toxic in the least.

Charoite

CHAROITE COMES FROM Russia and has not been available very long as a healing tool. It is often confused with sugilite, which has similar violet tones. It is fragile like turquoise and until it was bonded with plastic or glue it was considered quite useless. Now it is polished and carved into wonderful triangles and diamond shapes. It can even be made into jewelry and is becoming useful to crystal healers as another energy that is very helpful during major transitional periods. Making serious transitions in life is difficult at best, and clearing the way for those transitions is nearly impossible unless we get a boost from our superconscious self that says it is not only all right, it is to be encouraged.

I really like this stone. Charoite lets you know that your client is ready to confront the emotional blocks that are keeping him from his mental or spiritual path. Now, here is a vibration that is helpful. Without fail, clients who pick up this stone are saying, "Yes, I am ready to confront my issues now." Some of my clients have a little too much enthusiasm. "Am I ready to confront! Oh yes!" If those issues involve other people, I suggest that they learn the difference between confront and assault. It is important for your client to understand that it is never helpful to create a battleground for these confrontations. Blazing guns only create more confusion and can lead to anger or bitterness. Explain to your client that true confrontation involves the use of reason. It means facing whoever or whatever stands in his way with spirit in mind—in other words, being truthful but gentle with himself and others.

Charoite is a pivotal stone. It speaks to the spirit in all of us and assists in peeling away the layers of emotion that keep us from knowing what our true direction is. When it is selected for the scenario, the focus of the entire session is on confronting personal issues that stand in the way of progress. And usually those issues are emotional—feelings that range from abandonment to anger, fear to hopelessness, situations or people that keep us from moving forward in our lives. The stones around it will help to define the problem. Variscite would indicate that the way your client feels about being on this planet should be readdressed from a soul perspective. Any of the spiritual body stones would be telling you that perhaps the issue which is standing in the way of spiritual growth is coming from another life expression, especially if kyanite is also present.

In a layout, charoite belongs wherever the issue of confrontation appears to be. This is usually near the assimilation center where the power of change resides. All energy passes through this center for integration before it is redistributed throughout the light system, so any kind of confrontation or challenge will draw heavily on the solar plexus. During the layout, it might be helpful to create a mandala for this area or use some of the heavy hitters, like citrine or apatite, to build it up.

Citrine

CITRINE WAS ONE of the very early stones in crystal healing. It has been a major contributor in the area of emotional assimilation—pulling together whatever needs to be ingested energetically, especially emotionally, and infusing it into the light body system. Citrine still plays an active role in my work because so much of what we are processing emotionally needs to be sifted through and sorted out before we can take in any new feeling. We are the therapeutic generation, delving into our present and past lives and processing what we find there. This is a great deal to take on and when we are dredging up old emotions, reactions and pains, we need to carefully select what to hold onto and what to discard.

Citrine keeps the doorway to assimilation open and clear, strong and selective. I love this stone. I have it in my collection in a variety of forms—clusters, points, and simple polished pieces. I usually carry it with me when I know that I will be doing a lot of processing. It is particularly helpful when traveling to far-off lands where ancient memories or emotions may surface at any time. My friend Gail, in California, tapes small citrine pieces to her navel whenever she travels or feels vulnerable. Might be worth a try!

When a client selects citrine, it puts you on alert that he may be experiencing an emotional trauma of some kind that he is finding difficult to digest or assimilate, that he needs to decide what aspects of the experience are worth holding onto and which ones need to be discarded altogether. Lessons learned from emotional trauma are valuable to keep, just throw out the bad parts! Citrine clearly indicates that the emotional experience needs to be re-evaluated. If malachite is present, then these emotions have already begun to affect your client in a physical way. He may, at the very least, be losing sleep over them. Rose quartz would indicate that the issues of self-esteem and self-acceptance are trying to get your attention and need to be explored. With rock ruby, there is a heart wound that most definitely requires attention.

In a layout, citrine can be placed just about anywhere, but it usually ends up around the solar plexus, the assimilation center. Often I make a mandala out of citrine points surrounding a pivotal stone like black tourmaline which neutralizes the negativity in excessive emotionalism—anger, fear, etc. I recommend that you gather together as many citrine points as you can for your collection. They are invaluable aids to the digestion of any emotional energy. A word of caution here—many citrine pieces are heat-treated or even irradiated to intensify their deep yellow color. Be sure to test your new pieces for clarity by silently asking to feel the energy that resides in the stones before you buy them. The heat-treated variety are not as distorted as the irradiated specimens, but it is always good to know what you are working with. Citrine is a good friend. It lends a hand whenever emotional upheaval is present and disrupting your life. Its deeper tones of gold, yellow and brown remind me of sitting next to a cozy fire, warmed and comforted by its glow.

Gem Silica

WHEN I FIRST saw a specimen of gem silica, I was enchanted. My first crystal friend, Gary Fleck, sold me a small diamond-shaped piece set in gold wire. I felt wonderful when I wore it that day and said to several friends that it reminded me of deep ocean water—powerful and purposeful in its flow and direction. Every time I closed my eyes, I saw water. "What a revelation," I thought to myself. "How empowering and stimulating is the feminine." Water and flow have always meant feminine to me. That very evening, while racing my small sailboat at the local marina, over I went, keel straight up in the air. I was groping through the dark waters, holding onto my new stone friend, and when I came up for air, I was laughing uncontrollably. "You silly stone," I said. "All that water, eh? Well, here I am, wet with power." I felt strong and empowered all right, as I was pulling my Sabot sailboat around and climbing into it full of water. The sails were as sopping wet as I was. But I finished the race, determined and stubborn, to the whoops and wails of the men on the dock. Feminine empowerment, indeed.

Believe it or not, gem silica is not selected very often—even in this age of women finding themselves—but once it has been discovered by a client or a student, it is usually treasured. I feel that this evolved form of the mineral we know as chrysocolla will be coming into its own very soon. However, not until all the emotional layers have been pulled away from the issue of being a feminine—not just for women but for men who are trying to reconnect with the anima in themselves—gem silica will probably remain a bystander in the process of healing the feminine. Usually a man will select smithsonite when confronting male/female issues, because it has more to do with the sexual expression. Gem silica, as feminine empowerment, awaits our attention and respect as a major factor in the evolution of role consciousness. How can we instill the idea of empowerment as a possible way of life in those who feel that powerlessness is the real issue here?

I do have one small triangular piece of gem silica that is inside a crystal pyramid and this combination is selected more often than gem silica alone. It usually indicates to me a past-life experience of Egyptian initiation, which the individual failed. And being a woman was the reason for that failure—in the seed thought. Indicators like these can be important to a scenario, so it is good to have an assortment of stones and talismans that can represent some of these other civilizations.

Gem silica, then, points to the path of empowerment—to honoring the feminine in yourself and others. In a layout, it can play an important role as a heart or solar plexus stone. With chrysoprase, it instills the courage it takes to stand up and be counted as a woman or to recognize the power of the feminine, say, in intuition for a man. Gem silica brings its subtle vibration into the Women's Movement as empowerment and into the Men's Movement as permission to express feelings from the heart. Emotional it is, the energy of this watery, blue/green, captivating stone that draws you into its fluid motion and gives you permission to *feel*.

Larimar

SINCE LARIMAR entered the scene, just a few years ago, more clients are reaching for it with a slightly puzzled expression. "What is this stone anyway?" I can almost hear them thinking. If ever there was a welcome addition to the healing stone family, it was larimar. It literally takes the trauma we experience as a part of transition out of the process altogether and what a gift that has been to us all! This soft, blue, flowing stone, usually found in cabochons, energetically puts you back into the flow of life. What better way to go through change than to be supported and flowing along with this soothing vibration? We are always going through changes—some of them are subtle and some are brutal—but the major transitions in our lives seem to take quite a bit of time and energy away from living day-to-day. We can clothe the transitional experience in so much emotion that we can miss the point of the change altogether. What good is a transition if we do not recognize it for what it is? To assist in the elimination of all undue and unnecessary suffering, larimar comes along to make our way easier and calm any ensuing emotional storms.

When you find a piece of larimar that speaks to you, hold onto it. Keep it as an important addition to your collection and do not hesitate to use the energy, even if it is not part of the original selection. Emotional trauma seems to be everyone's middle name these days. Hardly a day goes by that someone does not call me up on the phone, overwhelmed by one crisis or another. So keep this energy alive in your mind and heart as you listen to the dramas unfolding in your sessions. It is important that we all lift ourselves out of the suffering modality of "poor me" and get on with our lives. Suffering has inflated the emotional body until it is out of proportion to the rest of the light system. In suffering, we become the victim, inundating ourselves with self pity. If people are unable to pull out of their patterns of self-destruction, there is little hope of healing. The emotional burden can be too great, too overpowering, to make the transition possible. The mind set that is created by "oh, you poor dear," is not helpful or healing under any circumstances. Look your client right in the eye and talk about transitional periods and the need to grow. Introduce larimar as the soothing agent that will enable him to meet the challenge of change.

In a scenario, larimar can indicate where transition is affecting your client the most. If it appears with other emotional body stones, the change is being felt emotionally. Mental body stones will direct your attention to the beliefs that are being challenged and spiritual body stones will indicate that the blueprint needs attention as your client shifts his spiritual focus. Rather than dwell on the inevitable confusion and emotional turmoil, use larimar to gently lead your client into a new perspective on spirituality.

In a layout, larimar can actually alleviate physical discomfort. I block energy in the throat, for example. I go into coughing spasms which make it difficult for me to breathe. Larimar placed on the throat almost immediately restores my breathing. It is very like malachite in the way it moves energy to soothe and heal the effects of any transition—physical, emotional, mental, spiritual. Larimar can be placed anywhere on the body to help clear an energy pattern that is resistant to change or growth. It calms the stress or tension that is surrounding an issue so you can see it clearly and accelerate your own changes. Is it any wonder that we are all so fond of larimar?

Lepidolite

LEPIDOLITE is a powerful stone. It is already respected by the medical community as a precursor to lithium, a mind balancing drug. Once considered a discard from the tourmaline mines where it is most frequently found, it can be appreciated now for its energetic and anaesthetic qualities. When I first discovered lepidolite, I used it on clients who had arthritis, placing it on areas that needed to be anesthetized before they could be more deeply probed for the source of the discomfort. It actually numbs pain, physical or emotional. Sometimes the pain is so great that your client is not able to reach the source of it because he simply cannot feel or think about anything else.

A new form of lepidolite that has become popular in this work very recently is the mica lepidolite. This stone is a deep pink color that occurs in shining layers and there seems to be a special light around it. People who select mica lepidolite are so layered with patterns of emotional pain and mental confusion, generated over time by a particular seed thought that they are unable to react to life in a spontaneous manner. Sometimes the wound goes so deep that the conscious mind does not know it is there. Mica lepidolite in a scenario is always alerting you to the presence of such a wound and the stones around it will tell you whether it has been registered in the physical body as illness or disability, in the emotional body as hypersensitivity or sadness, or in the mental or spiritual body as a thoughtform.

Lepidolite numbs the emotional pain around an issue so that it can be seen clearly. Some of my clients who select lepidolite or mica lepidolite are not even aware that they have this pain because it exists at such a deep level. Those individuals who have had many marriages or dysfunctional relationships may not realize that they are acting out the pattern of an event that has been deeply buried and long forgotten. Mica lepidolite enables you to peel back the layers so you can get to the root of the problem. When an issue is this heavily insulated, resolution will probably not happen in one session.

You might suggest to your client that he keep a journal or meditate on some of the insights that come out of the healing process until he is able to see the actual course of events that actually precipitated the layering.

If your client selects the azurite/malachite/cuprite combo along with the lepidolite, chances are that you will be able to uncover the issue in one session because these stones indicate that he is ready to see it. It is rare, however, to have this much emotional layering fall away easily. In working with this kind of problem, timing is very important. Even when you see the course of events that formed the initial seed thought, it is up to your client to acknowledge and recognize them on his own. You can lead him visually to the thoughtform in his light system but it is important that you let him decide what it means and whether to accept it. You do not want to dissolve the layering—remove the insulation—unless both of you agree that this is desirable. I cannot stress this enough. It can be extremely traumatic.

In a layout, lepidolite or mica lepidolite may be placed wherever the pain registers or near the energy center that holds the wound. I would recommend that you also use chrysoprase for courage to see the real issue and green aventurine to alleviate the emotional stress around it. You might want to put a quartz point on top of the lepidolite specimen for clarity and focus on the problem. Be ready to deal with some pretty extreme emotional reactions—they are part of the healing process—and use your energy and insight to help your client restore balance and harmony to his light system. Lepidolite is, indeed, Nature's gift to us, allowing the heart to heal by neutralizing the pain of a deeply felt wound.

Rock Ruby

OF ALL THE emotional body stones, rock ruby is the least known and recognized. Rock ruby allows the heart to breathe through emotional pain. Years ago, we knew nothing about the technique of processing pain or anything else through breathing. Color therapies introduced us to the breath as a vehicle for transmuting pain into passage to and through the pain. I used it effectively even with blind children who had never seen color and could only imagine what it must be like. I remember one young boy who had fallen in a bus corridor and was panic-stricken because he did not know where he was and did not understand fully what had happened. I picked him up and whispered in his ear, "Quickly now, what color is your sore knee?" "Red," he answered, responding to some instinct, I guess, that red is the color of cuts and blood. "Okay," I said, "breathe into it and tell me what color it will be when it is all better." After a couple of seconds, he said, "Beige," and smiled. We held each other until he said, "My knee is beige now. It doesn't hurt anymore." And he skipped down the aisle. I knew then that the breath was a way of keeping any client involved in their healing process, whatever the problem happened to be. Years later, Katrina gave me a beautiful piece of rock ruby for my birthday. I was thrilled to discover a new tool for breathing in my crystal work.

I notice that more people are selecting the rock ruby these days. They are willing to face the pain around some of these heart wounds and resolve it once and for all! Red is such an energizing color. It activates all the energy centers, but rock ruby, in particular, belongs to the heart. This is where emotional trauma usually registers in the physical body though, energetically, it originates in the solar plexus through which all experience flows and is assimilated. In a scenario, rock ruby alerts you to the presence of an emotional trauma and focuses the reading on the heart area. In a layout, the best place for this stone is the area right between the solar plexus and the heart.

Rock ruby says, "Breathe through me. Breathe through the blocked energy in the heart and allow healing to take place." This process will reactivate the wound, briefly, and there may be a sudden, forceful release of emotional energy, but your client will feel wonderfully free and relieved afterwards. I love this stone. I guess I have said this quite often in my classes and in my writing—how much I love and appreciate the stones that have given so much of themselves to the healing process. Rock ruby actively participates by showing us how to let go of our emotional pain—bless its heart!

Rose Quartz

ROSE QUARTZ is the most popular member of the quartz family. Everyone knows rose quartz. It was the second half of the green aventurine/rose quartz love duo that became such a fad in the early days of crystal healing. Rose quartz was thought by many to epitomize the energy of the loving heart—to open the heart, to attract love to the heart, to do all those loving, heartfelt things that, in my work today, fall within the province of pink tourmaline. I went along with this for years, but then I began to realize that rose quartz was more powerful than a love amulet and that it had a greater role to play in the healing of the emotional body. The energy of pink tourmaline seemed to be more representative of the open, giving, loving heart. The more I worked with rose quartz, the more it had to say about self love—you must be able to love yourself before you can love others or allow love into your life. Suddenly those little packets of rose quartz and green aventurine tumbled stones took on new meaning. To love another, you must love yourself first, and love should not be a painful experience that generates a lot of emotional stress. There has to be room in the heart for love to be able to flow into it and through it. If you do not feel worthy of another's love, you block the flow of love into your being and it is impossible for you to flow it outward to someone else. Delving deeper into the issue of self-esteem, I discovered that a lack of self-respect or self-love usually had its roots in some mysterious past event that generated shame or self-recrimination and closed the heart to receiving. Rose quartz has the ability to heal that shame.

Feelings about loving, giving and receiving and are all recorded in the emotional body patterning and rose quartz is most assuredly an emotional body stone. In a scenario, you need to assess its position in relation to the other stones present and allow the story to unfold. They will clue you in to which aspect of the heart is being portrayed. Orange calcite, for instance, will tell you that the creative flow has been impeded by a lack of self-esteem or self-worth. Azurite indicates a limiting belief around the issue of receiving love—"I am not worth loving" or "I do not deserve a loving relationship."

Rose quartz also can be found in crystalline form as clusters, though these are relatively rare. I have one exquisite specimen of crystalline rose quartz and whenever it appears in a scenario, it holds so much light that it eclipses the energy of the other stones. Whenever this piece is selected, I look to the higher forms of love—spiritual love, cosmic love, the love of the Creator that is rejected just because the individual feels unworthy. How many of us, when given a compliment, respond by saying, "Oh, it was nothing"? In periods of deep meditation, when we sense the skies opening up and light rushing in to greet the expanding light body, we often shut down because we instinctively feel that we do not deserve such light and wonder. I know this reaction well. For many years in my meditations I turned away from the Light and the presence of love for the same reasons. I guess all the rose quartz around me wore down my resistance, and I now accept it most willingly. A little unconditional loving from spirit can go a long way!

Rose quartz is becoming increasingly important as, more and more, people are opening consciously to the higher self—to realms of light beyond the physical that love and support us. Let me say here that the love the spiritual realms send to earth is a love of acceptance, of respect and honor, not the kind of love we find in physical loving relationships. More and more, we are accepting the energy of unconditional love into our hearts and minds and souls. To shut out that light and refuse that energy would turn us away from the spiritual path or stop our growth altogether.

In a layout, I do not use rose quartz exclusively around the heart area, though it would seem most natural to place it there. If the issue of self-worth has penetrated the mental body and the vision is clouded, the third eye would be appropriate. If the energy depletion is primarily in the solar plexus or the second center of creativity, then rose quartz can be placed there. Rose quartz deals with the issue of receiving on all levels and can offer assistance in any stage of the crystal journey. Any center that suffers from the inability to assimilate or take energy in would derive some benefit from working with rose quartz. It would greatly assist in opening and clearing that center and increase the flow of energy through it.

Rose quartz has many lessons to teach about loving. It is not a miracle cure for all love issues, but it plays a significant role in bringing that pink, healing light deep into the inner being. With enough light, the root of the problem can be brought to consciousness, explored and healed. With enough light, we can see ourselves as the loving beings we truly are, and set the loving self free to love. Many crystal healers disagree with this assessment, so I invite you to work with it for a while and see for yourself how rose quartz participates in the loving heart.

Sodalite

SODALITE facilitates expression and acknowledgment of the emotion that has come to stand for personal truth. Sodalite is often confused with lapis, the blue tones are nearly the same. They are similar in appearance, but their energy is quite different. Sodalite has more to do with the expression of the personality, while lapis enables you to reach beyond the illusions you have about yourself to find out who you truly are. Lapis is a mental body stone. Sodalite encourages you to speak from your feelings, and this is definitely part of a current trend which invites even small toddlers to express through temper tantrums. It is no longer considered appropriate to suppress your feelings. We encourage those around us to speak from the heart. This is all well and good, but not everyone is able to do that.

My husband and I have been married for many years. Whenever I asked him how he felt about something, very early in our marriage, his response was "I don't feel anything" or "I cannot put my feelings into words." I was really surprised by this. What a struggle it is to try to pull emotion out of someone who simply is not used to expressing this way—men are conditioned from childhood not to respond with feeling. It was frustrating for me because I did not fully understand this at the time, but I kept at it. Most people would have given up, but not good old tenacious Capricorn me! I doggedly kept after him to express and feel and speak from his heart, and put sodalite in his closet and sock drawer, and he finally gave in. He joined a men's group and I am happy to report we are at last communicating on a real heart level. I was delighted when these perky blue stones appeared to be a catalyst for this kind of expression.

Many clients are telling you, when sodalite appears in a scenario, that they have difficulty expressing themselves and are not comfortable with feeling as a medium of expression. They need some sort of permission to explore this side of themselves in a totally new way. If you can give them this permission, it often results in an outpouring of emotion that has been bottled up for years. I had a client recently who showed a preference for sodalite in her stone selection—she picked several pieces along with some lapis, azurite and malachite, and a couple of transition stones. She was a quiet, introverted woman and a powerful light being. She was unable to sense this aspect of herself and had never been particularly expressive. The abundance of azurite and malachite in her scenario indicated that unless something was done soon to break up the pattern of suppression, which had extended over several lifetimes, the limitation could express as some kind of physical illness. I carefully communicated my concern and she understood me very well. We covered a lot of ground in that session and as we addressed the issues, one by one, her true nature began to emerge. By the time the session ended, she was convinced that a new woman, long dormant, was waking up and actually becoming visible. Look out world! Together, we laughed and chanted, "I am Woman!"

In a layout I find sodalite works best at the throat area of communication. Here is where this energy is the most useful.

Often I surround it with turquoise or larimar to calm any resistance to feeling this centers release. You will find sodalite a welcome member of your healing stone collection, it is easy to find and the vibration very useful.

Tempest Stone

NEVER BEFORE has our planet been in such chaos, or so it seems. In the darkest of past times—during the two world wars, for instance—chaos was not as visual in a global sense or as emotionally charged as it is today. With cameras alongside guns in natural disasters and wars, we are thrown directly into the experience, no matter where it is happening in the world. We sense the impact of world events in a much more personal way. We feel the anguish and the pain of those who are suffering, but do we process it? More than likely it becomes a thoughtform in the reactive emotional body under the label of "world pain I can do nothing about but feel personally involved with." These thoughtforms eventually congest the emotional body and when there are enough blocks to our light and understanding, we become numb to what is happening around us.

A relatively new stone on the crystal healing horizon, tempest stone—or Pietersite as it is more formally known—has come to represent the movement and chaos that break up those energy patterns particularly resistant to change. When the heart and mind are not on the same frequency, it creates a kind of furor, chaos, in the light body which is reflected by the personality. It is, essentially, energy in conflict. Tempest stone gathers all the emotional reactions to a pattern of events, planetary and personal, past and present, and hurls them into a new perspective. The energy of this stone is very forceful. It literally jolts us into change, personal change. You could say that it creates a kind of orderly chaos, dismantling the thoughtforms so they can be sorted out, mentally and emotionally.

In a scenario, tempest stone indicates that your client is in a transitional period that he probably experiences as chaos.

This energy is especially characteristic of people I call "cosmic eggbeaters." Their personalities are intense and forceful bundles of contradiction. Their lives are always in a state of flux. When they walk into a room they are an energy vortex all by themselves, and the collective energy of an entire group of people can be focused—or rather, unfocused—by this dynamic. You may have noticed this in business meetings where a lot of strong statements are made but nothing gets accomplished. When your client selects tempest stone, chances are that he is feeling some pretty intense emotions or feels his life is in a state of turmoil. Suggest that he view this transitional time as an opportunity to break up some emotional impaction. My crystal class loves the tempest stone because it is a clear indication that change is coming. It may not be easy and it will certainly be full of emotional challenges, but it need not be painful. If you consciously decide to ride out the chaos, you can use the energy constructively to stimulate you into action. You can even enjoy the ride.

In a layout, tempest stone works most effectively on or near the solar plexus, where the flow of energy leads to assimilation and integration of experience and where you will find most of the resistance—right in the path of breath and life! Especially when the congestion extends beyond the emotional body, begin with the solar plexus. In the midst of chaos, the eye of the storm is the safest place to be. We all create hurricanes in our lives—emotionally, mentally, even physically. Tempest stone will keep the chaos level high until a new perspective can emerge. Walk into the fire, face your challenges, and come out on the other side with greater insight, emotionally free.

Mental Body Stones

Amethyst

AMETHYST is the alchemical stone that develops the intuition and facilitates meditation. It was part of the spiritual resurgence that began in the middle 70's, when the color purple first became popular. Most people do not remember what it was like to live without purple. I have always loved it and I was wearing it long before it became stylish or acceptably avant garde, so to see people wearing purple on the street and actually looking for it in the shops delighted me. I was drawn to amethyst initially because of its color, but then I noticed that when I wore it, my third eye was constantly being stimulated. I was able to perceive etheric patterns and colors and intuit things about people and situations. I began to experience the clairvoyant visions, the CV's, that I mentioned earlier. This is how amethyst worked for me but I discovered later on that, for most people, amethyst opens up an initial channel of communication to the higher self. Moonstone is actually a better choice if you want to get in touch with or develop your psychic abilities.

Except in a symbolic sense, true alchemy has little to do with the transformation of base metal into gold. The value of the alchemical process is in the ability we have as human beings to change, which, as I have said before, is an essential part of the healing process. We facilitate change by altering our concepts or patterns of belief about ourselves and the world we live in. A change in belief will catalyze changes in awareness, and when the new awareness predominates in our physical lives, we have a different experience of the world. You can begin this process at the physical end of the continuum by working with the manifestation first—by acting out what you would like your experience of the world to be—but, to me, this is like putting a bandaid on a wound before you know how deep it is or whether there will be repercussions to the injury. Where did it come from? What does it mean? And, perhaps most important of all, could it happen again? You have to eliminate the problem at its source.

Amethyst did most of its work in the early crystal days—we wore it, we carried it, we used it in our work—but the group consciousness, the planetary consciousness, has evolved since then and people today seem much more aware. Amethyst is not selected very often now and the people drawn to it sometimes seem to be expressing love and appreciation for an old friend. They will pick it up because it looks familiar and they feel comfortable with it, but they do not necessarily use it to develop the intuition they already have. People are picking the clusters now rather than the points, which I find interesting, because it gives emphasis to a broader perspective, a kind of globalism, for the intuition, instead of a single focus. The amethyst points were more popular in the late 70's and early 80's when the emphasis was on going within and accessing higher dimensions of the self. People who work with amethyst clusters will have a wider reach in their meditations—more contact with the group consciousness.

When amethyst appears in a scenario and your client is not another crystal healer or someone who has enjoyed having amethyst around for years and feels affection for it, he is probably just beginning to understand what the intuition is and how it is operating in his life. Amethyst is the stone of initial change—it signals the first spiritual awakening. Your client is learning how to access his higher self through meditation and is working with some basic metaphysical precepts—like, for instance, "energy follows thought". Amethyst is one of those windows to the soul that people talk about, but once that window is open, it has pretty much served its purpose and will not expand the intuition any further, though it can be a useful adjunct to some of the other stones.

In a layout, I often use amethyst with people who are just beginning to open up spiritually, or who would like to open spiritually, and I place it on the third eye to focus the energy of that center. I usually suggest that they work with this crystal on their own by using it in their meditations. Sometimes amethyst will be part of a scenario but the issue will have nothing to do with developing the intuition and, if this is the case, I use it to enhance the energy of the other stones wherever a third eye focus might be useful in unblocking a center or breaking up an area of density in the light system. Its action is very gentle and can be effective with people who are hypersensitive to the stones and easily thrown off balance by sudden shifts in the energy bodies. It works quite well in conjunction with malachite.

Azurite

AZURITE is the pattern breaker. It carries a vibration that dissolves limited concepts. Azurite occurs in crystallized form as blue-violet nodules and in a boulder form that is rough in texture and usually bonded with some malachite. The differences indicate whether the limited pattern is in the mental or spiritual bodies or the denser azurite shows it closer to a physical living experience. It works directly on the mental body patterning to break up thoughtforms which are, essentially, patterns of limitation. Thoughtforms in the mental body that limit us usually develop from beliefs about the self that are the result of misunderstanding or misinterpreting an event that took place early in our present life or another incarnation.

I had a client recently who selected several pieces of azurite and placed them around a Dow crystal which was at the center of her scenario. It was clear to me that a thoughtform in her spiritual body was directly responsible for her ideas about the kind of person she was. She had a very low self-image which centered around the belief that she was not a spiritual being—could not be a spiritual being—because she was unworthy. She had also selected dioptase, which indicated that the thoughtform had been created by a soul wound. The emotional body was still reacting to the initial event. She was deeply depressed and felt that she simply could not cope with life. We found the initial event in another lifetime and re-examined the drama that was held in the thoughtform. She was able to see the misunderstanding from the point of view of this life and was able to change the belief about herself in a very short time.

Azurite appears as part of the scenario whenever there is a pattern of limitation in the mental body that ultimately impedes the flow of energy to the physical body and creates an imbalance in one of the energy centers. The gem-like nodules indicate that the limiting concept or belief has already been integrated into the spiritual body patterning and is blocking spiritual growth and expression. In that form it can also indicate a thoughtform in the mental body that is affecting your client emotionally. The more dense form of azurite, a paler blue and an earthy texture, means the limitation is physical, your client feels confined or even powerless to take a next step. The other stones in the scenario will enable you to be more specific as to how the limitation is playing out in the physical life and consciousness. It is interesting that, unless it is bonded with malachite, azurite is a very fragile, very brittle, mineral. This intense fragility says something significant about patterns of limitation or limiting beliefs, that they can be changed or broken fairly easily.

In a layout, I place azurite wherever I perceive that a thoughtform of limitation is blocking the flow of energy through the light system so that there is a measurable energy depletion in one of the centers. If I have a client who is blocked in the third eye, for example, because he believes that he is not intuitive and not visual, I will use both azurite and amethyst—azurite to break up the energy that is blocking the vision and amethyst to focus the energy of the center. If the limitation comes from fear, chrysoprase would be a good partner with azurite.

Chrysoprase

WHEN I FIRST started working with this stone, I experienced one of my CVs in which I saw Alexander the Great with an array of stones on his breastplate, and chrysoprase was clearly the predominant mineral on that template. It was much later on that I happened to read about chrysoprase in Pavitt's book on gems and talismans, where he says that it actually formed the amulet of Alexander the Great. At the time, however, I had no knowledge of the connection and I assumed that the message was more symbolic than factual. I interpreted it to mean that chrysoprase puts us in touch with the same self-mastery and courage that inspired the conquests of Alexander the Great, and who exemplified both of these qualities.

I have several specimens of boulder chrysoprase which is so different in appearance from the gem quality variety that for a long time I did not believe it was the same mineral. Boulder chrysoprase in a scenario indicates that your client probably experiences life as a tremendous struggle, that it requires a lot of courage for him to physically walk this earth plane. Those of us who feel more at home here do not realize how much we take our health and our balance of mind and spirit for granted. Gem quality chrysoprase, which is a deep translucent green, symbolizes the courage it takes to acknowledge and evolve into an awareness of ourselves as composite beings. I have called chrysoprase the avatar stone partly because of the connection with Alexander the Great who conquered and mastered the self before he conquered the world, and partly because we are all living exemplars of spirit, each of us representing a unique pattern in the overall configuration of group consciousness. To become the avatar we need only to accept the totality of ourselves, to live consciously so that we are able to make conscious choices, and to have the courage to act on our convictions, assuming that our convictions are based on what we know to be truth. And truth is a highly individual revelation. Each person will perceive it differently.

Chrysoprase does not need other stones to describe and clarify it in a scenario. The issue is always courage—not so much the lack of courage, but your client's need to recognize that he has it and to view his life from an experience of strength rather than powerlessness. If the gem variety has been selected, your client needs to embrace his own spirituality and acknowledge all of his potentials and abilities in that area. Many people who are drawn to chrysoprase simply need permission to be themselves. Once this has been communicated to them, and this often happens during the scenario, the whole demeanor changes. They begin to smile, even to laugh, and you can see that even though the physical circumstances have not changed, the perspective is different and there is movement in the light system. Healing is now a possibility and the physical changes may be able to manifest at some point in the future.

When we get as far as the layout, I use chrysoprase on the third eye, the heart, the throat and above the crown. Most of the mental body stones can be used most effectively on the third eye because that is the center of intuition that accesses the mind. The boulder chrysoprase works with the root and solar plexus energy, primarily, though it can be placed on the third eye if you feel that your client needs a more physical orientation for his vision. Chrysoprase has been one of my most exciting discoveries, and working with it has been an uplifting and enlightening experience, for my clients and myself.

Halite

HALITE is rock salt and it is mostly available in small clusters, the colorless and pink varieties being the easiest to find. Blue and violet halite are more rare and they can sometimes be found in specialty shops, although the gem and mineral shows seem to have the best specimens. I use halite to crystallize new patterns in the light system. Sometimes at the end of a session, after a thoughtform has been accessed, evaluated and resolved, I will use my tuning forks or Tibetan bowls to set the new patterns with sound. Not all clients are comfortable with this technique, however, especially if they have never worked with crystals before. Halite is a less conspicuous means to the same end. It works the same way. I can project blue halite into the aura at the end of the session, before the client begins his journey back into the body, and this will crystallize the new mental body patterning. When you are resolving or releasing thoughtforms, most of the time you will be altering the geometrics of the mental body. When you are working with the actual blueprint, the violet would probably have a more profound effect, but the information will eventually reach the level of the spiritual body no matter where it comes from in the light system. If you do not have violet halite, you can work with the blue or the pink. Pink halite works primarily on the emotional body to facilitate the release of patterns of reaction to resolved thoughtforms. It seems to bring the awareness of the release or change into the emotional body so that there is less confusion directly after a shift. I do not have a specimen of the white or colorless variety in my collection, but my sense is that it would work most effectively in assisting the physical body to assimilate the information in the new patterning.

When halite is selected for the scenario, it is telling you that your client has been going through some energy shifts on his own which have not been communicated to all parts of the light system. Halite helps the energy bodies to energetically realign so that they are all functioning as an integrated network. Some people, for instance, advance so quickly on a spiritual level that the physical body has a hard time catching up with the changes and there can be a period of void that lasts for hours or months, depending on how drastic the shift has been. Occasionally people will decide to accelerate their spiritual growth on their own and get heavily into different techniques and meditative practices that cause the energy bodies to develop at different rates. This is less likely to happen in a crystal session where your whole consciousness is focused on triggering these changes and then assimilating them.

When pink halite is selected for the scenario, it is telling you that there is an inappropriate emotional reaction to a seed thought. Usually this happens when there has been a shift in the mental body patterning that, for one reason or another, is incomplete, so that the message of change has not reached the emotional body. The emotions are still responding to the old energy configuration that exists side by side with the new patterning, kind of like a warped record that plays the same musical fragment over and over again. Pink halite indicates a need to readdress the issue so that the message of change can be consciously acknowledged and incorporated into the emotional body, where it can be perceived by the physical. Blue halite would suggest that these new pathways need to be set into the mental body patterning. Violet halite is telling you that a thoughtform in the spiritual body needs to be readdressed—not healed or resolved—but consciously acknowledged so that the residual effects of the old thoughtform can be cleared and the blueprint can realign itself to the new patterning.

Hematite

HEMATITE has been given the name "iron rose" by mineralogists because some of its specimens appear flowerlike in their formation, but most of the specimens you will see in rock specialty shops are tumbled and polished until they have a shiny, metallic luster. Of all the metals, hematite is the one I have gone way out on a limb to interpret and use. I have called it "the galactic stone" because it seems to bring us into contact with the network of extraterrestrial energies that we have come to call "the space brothers." There is an otherworldly vibration to this stone that seems to act as antennae that reach out to beings from dimensions outside this planet or into the genetic coding that identifies you with the energy of your planet of origin.

I have tried to work with this stone in many different ways. I started out by using it as a blood purifier but that never felt right. One day my friend Raven brought a large box of hematite specimens to my center. "How do you work with these?" he wanted to know. This led to my first experiment with hematite. After almost everyone had left for the day, I asked my friend Therese (who later married Raven, by the way) to work with me on these new stones. I had her lie down and I created a hematite grid that extended from her forehead to her lower abdomen. I asked a friend to sit at her feet with a large crystal generator and I sat above her head with another. What followed was extraordinary and fortunately I got most of it on film. Therese had just closed her eyes when they popped wide open. Her small voice, which no longer sounded familiar to me, boomed with authority: "This is quite cumbersome!" We were talking to a space being! Part of his message had to do with hematite. Answering our unspoken question, he said that hematite called in the ships in the area to make contact with those who were ready. 'His' head turned towards the video camera as I asked if it had been all right to tape this encounter. "Quite archaic, isn't it?" he said, to which I replied: "Well, it is the best we have!" You can be sure that I never again used hematite as a blood purifier again.

Whenever hematite is chosen for the scenario, I know immediately that my client has some kind of association with other-worldly dimensions of light that serve not only this planet but the entire galaxy. Sometimes my client simply needs to recognize that these dimensions exist also within himself. In a layout, I usually place hematite on the third eye with other stones that will enhance this connection—sugilite is a good hematite partner, to the clear light body and insure a freer flow of energy. I have used hematite many times in personal grids along with variscite, seed crystals and onyx to bring the two light polarities of myself—earth and sky—together. You will enjoy working with hematite, especially if your a 'space cadet' like me!

Lapis

LAPIS, also known by its gem name Lapis Lazuli, has been a part of crystal healing since we began. When Katrina and I sat with these stones early on in our work, the information on lapis was pretty sketchy. The definition we knew then was 'penetrates illusion of the mind', but I must say that it was not until recently that this description made complete sense to me. We knew about the deep blue of lapis having its history as far back as Egyptian times when the color meant royalty, as depicted in the gold and lapis statuary still vibrant today. In those times gemstones like lapis and malachite were worn as amulets or ground into poultices to be taken internally as elixirs.

Through the years in my work, lapis had become a bit of an enigma, clients were not selecting it and I did not know why. Where did the energy of penetrating illusion belong, on the intuition center or placed on the throat area? Should it be surrounded by turquoise or sugilite to ease any congestion in the communication center? Is who we are who we think we are or how we present ourselves to others? It was becoming apparent that our true self is hidden somewhere amidst all the reflection of everyone around us.

From the time we are children we are inundated with the opinions and projections of others, and we take their information into our mental body patterning. Somewhere in all of those beliefs is our truth, but often so difficult to find. Lapis can lead us on a personal crystal journey through the illusions of the mind and put us in touch with what I call 'mental body pollution'. All of the input gathered over the years clouds our beliefs until we hardly know who in the world we really are! Lapis says: have a mental garage sale and throw out those beliefs that no longer fit!

In a scenario selection, lapis indicates the need for the client to take a closer look at who they truly are and that perhaps it is time to clear away a lot of the debris in their mental body patterning. There are likely several cloudy issues surrounding the lapis so look for emotional stones to tell you that mental body pollution has effected their feelings about who they are. And here is where a problem with self esteem will show up. If rose quartz is nearby, you can be sure that much of their reflection has been negative. Inundated with remarks such as: 'oh, you think you are so smart', 'you are so dumb', 'you will never amount to anything' and the like, the client has impacted their thinking and feelings around the input from others and see themselves through their eyes. Any emotional stress surrounding the input would be indicated by green aventurine. With any of the emotional or physical body stones, lapis will tell the story of how the pollution is affecting the client.

In a layout, the cleansing attributes of lapis will make its way through any of the energy centers that carries the illusion. Is the integration center congested and unable to process issues of self identity, or are they carried like a wound in the heart? Is the client so confused that he is unable to express much about who he truly is? Placed on the third eye area, lapis, along with amethyst, will help the client to better intuit their truth. With azurite, lapis will assist to penetrate any thoughts and feelings of limitation. Lapis has revealed its true light and vibration just as crystal work went beyond physical and emotional healing and began to penetrate the mental and spiritual light bodies.

Moonstone

I DISCOVERED moonstones with my friend Mel, who was my travel companion on much of this inner journey. Mel and I had started our psychic explorations together but I was moving faster than she was. I could see energy around people and intuit things about them, and I was channeling everyday. Mel was always with me. She wrote down everything I said in longhand because we did not have a typewriter or a tape recorder. It was a very long and tedious process, I will tell you. We read over the material everyday and I copied her notes. One day she was talking about how frustrated she was because she could not see what I could see or do what I could do. I had some moonstones so I said, "Let's try these." I created a grid for her third eye with the moonstones and some clear quartz points and put another one just like it on her throat. "How do you feel?" I asked her. She said it was like having a door open. Suddenly she could see all these colors in varying hues of blue, green and violet. She still sees them today and associates them with healing. She feels that when she sees these color tones, she can project them to others as a healing vibration.

Moonstone in the scenario is a sign that your client is ready to expand into the psychic realm of the inner senses. It does not mean that this expansion will be instantaneous. Mel's experience was unusual. Apparently her readiness to move into this next dimension of awareness coincided with the session we did together. Moonstone is suggesting that this is something your client should pursue in his studies or in his work—that he should be open to clairvoyant, clairaudient and telepathic kinds of experiences. Everyone has these abilities, but they may be dormant if their expression is not a part of the soul's purpose in this lifetime. If their presence does not facilitate growth, they are not always an active part of the experience. Whenever moonstone is a part of the scenario, however, these abilities are latent and waiting to happen.

In a layout, I use moonstone almost exclusively on the third eye. The third eye is where the vision is. I put it with chrysoprase, with sugilite, with lapis, with whatever is going to move the energy and make that connection available. I will use it on the throat occasionally because it facilitates communication—the perception of your inner voice, say, or telepathic experiences with other people. I have never put it on the heart or the solar plexus or any of the other centers. Psychic ability is strictly a mental thing.

Opal

THE DIFFERENT VARIETIES of opal that I have used in my work—the blue Australian water opal, the white opal and, to a lesser extent, the fire opal—all seem to be variations on the theme of movement and flow. The opal flow of energy has an ethereal quality about it, more like a spiritual apparition would look, floating yet contained. Malachite movement creates a real change in patterning and affects the client physically and emotionally. Sugilite movement is keeping the core of light that threads through the light body uninhibited. Opals have always been considered a feminine stone because of their high water content, but I believe that they are more representative the evolving androgynous consciousness than of the emergence of the feminine.

If there are barriers that exist to the merging of masculine and feminine polarities in consciousness, they originate within the constraints of a belief system rather than in any kind of emotional response or even biochemical dichotomy. The aggression or, rather, the assertive approach to life that comes so naturally to men is conditioned out of women at a very early age just as men are conditioned to sublimate their sensitivities and suppress their feelings. On a soul level, we are both male and female and the physical differences, which are structural and hormonal, do not seem to play a large part in the formation of the personality.

When opals appear in a scenario, the masculine energy is unable to blend and flow with the feminine. Australian water opals are opaque white stones with a bluish tinge, usually small and quite dense with no iridescence. In a scenario they indicate that energy is not flowing, that there is a block somewhere in the light system that has to do with the feminine expression of energy on a physical level, though the density of my particular specimens may have something to do with this. Water opals that are more translucent may have more impact on the light system. I have used these stones in conjunction with gem silica on women who are experiencing menstrual discomfort or the cramping which sometimes follows amniocentesis. My conjecture was that the pain in both cases was caused by energy that was blocked on some level, physical or otherwise, and that if we were to get it flowing again the pain would disappear. This treatment is usually effective—not always, but usually—and I have found that malachite is another useful adjunct for these types of problems. I have never had a man select this stone, but if it did happen I would have to assume there is a strong feminine influence in his life that may require greater scrutiny and understanding.

Fire opals will often appear in the scenarios of people who are passionate about their beliefs. It seems to be opposite in polarity to the water opal and has a movement that is more forceful and fiery than flowing and receptive. The fire opal seems to catalyze qualities of assertiveness and leadership in people, and both men and women are drawn to this stone though, as a rule, opals are not selected as often as, say, malachite or sugilite, other stones that move energy through the light body. Someone who selects fire opal for the scenario is probably a natural leader who is struggling to stay out of the limelight.

The white opal activates the universal mother energy which exists within all of us as an archetype, of unification and, in my opinion, is neither masculine nor feminine. People pick it up with a kind of reverence. Of all the stones in my collection, this is the one that they will hold in their hands for a few minutes, as if they are reluctant to put it down.

More women than men are drawn to the white opal, but when men do select it they tend to be highly evolved, spiritually focused individuals. One of them in particular had tears in his eyes when I explained to him that this stone represented the universal mother and that it was making a statement about the way he related to the earth and to the cosmos and that it was probably an important part of the work he had chosen to do here. Whenever I see white opal in a scenario, I know that we are dealing with issues that are collective or global in their application and that the people who are moved by it are functioning very close to their optimum potential on this planet.

In a layout, opals belong primarily in the upper energy centers, it is far more ethereal that the other mental stones. Even though their presence may effect the client physically, I still find opals stimulate the mind and the spirit first. I have used small mandalas of opals, herkimer diamonds and lapis at the intuition center and they have opened the inner vision pretty well.

Selenite

RECENTLY, I realized that although selenite is very popular with the students in my classes, the majority of clients, even those who are spiritually focused, tend to overlook it when they are making a selection. The striations are like threads of light that link the conscious mind to a superconscious perspective. This stone can be used like a scanning device by facilitators who are not visually oriented to get an overall view of the light system and examine the thoughtforms in each of the energy bodies. It expands the aura out to the very limits of the light system and focuses the intuition beyond it, sort of like a mental catapult, so that it is possible to look back and see the entire light body. You have to be able to interpret what you see and this takes practice, but the potential is definitely there. You can use selenite to view your own light body, or you can direct the energy toward your client by physically pointing the stone in his direction and then mentally aligning with its vibration to examine each of the energy bodies and the thoughtforms that are contained within them.

My own experience with selenite came as something of a surprise. In the past, I used it to experience that enlightened perspective that comes with total clarity and the sense of being consciously aware on all levels of perception. It seemed to facilitate an experience of totality—of being multidimensional and, at the same time, integrated—and I used it in layouts with clients who had come very close to that experience on their own. It gave them the energy boost they needed for that final leap. I was working with selenite one afternoon in the company of one of my students who had come to spend the day. We had just gone into a meditative state when I suddenly found myself zooming outward and upward. I looked back from what seemed like a great distance and saw a sphere of white light with shadows moving across the surface of it. It was like viewing the earth from space and just being able to make out the continents through the clouds, except that there was so much movement on the surface. The shadows were constantly shifting.

I realized that I was seeing my own light body from a perspective that was outside my light system. I mentioned this to my friend and she asked me what I thought the shadows were. As I examined them, I understood that each one represented a thoughtform or an issue that had not yet been resolved and that I had the ability to call them up individually for a closer look, evaluate each one, and release them one at a time while still maintaining my perspective of distance. I could view the energy bodies as a composite or experience each one separately. I sensed feelings in the emotional body but from a state of total objectivity. I could see where they originated and how they were manifesting. I had a sense of the physical body also, but as light and form and movement. It was like being in a crystal session which had been concentrated or compacted so that you could experience all aspects of the light system simultaneously.

A lot of information came out of this session. I found that not only could I use the selenite to examine my own light system in minute detail, but I could focus on my friend's light body and scan hers in the same way. She picked up the stone I had been using and was surprised to find that she was able to visually scan my light body as well as her own. She does not consider herself to be a visual person, and yet she had no difficulty in visually orienting herself with the help of this stone. The energy that runs through it, an electromagnetic energy that seems to follow the path of the striations, is part of a two way movement that takes your consciousness out beyond the envelope of light and energy that contains you in the earth vibration and simultaneously pulls it back so that you are able to maintain both viewpoints. It is kind of like a yoyo that goes only so far, but you are not aware of the movement.

Selenite is a powerful tool but intent seems to be necessary in order to activate this particular capacity. Holding it or sitting with it in meditation may not have as much impact if you are not accustomed to working with the energy or using it to focus your attention. If you choose to work with selenite on a regular basis, however, you need to be grounded enough not to be disoriented by the experience. Under no circumstances should you try to activate this stone if you have been exposed to any mind-altering substances within the last forty-eight hours or if, for any reason, you feel physically off balance. If you want to use this energy in a layout, be sure that your client is as clear and balanced as you are. Selenite is strictly a facilitator's stone, in my opinion, and its abilities should be respected.

Smithsonite

FROM THE MOMENT of conception we take on a gender identity, a masculine or feminine expression that determines how we perceive ourselves and, to a large extent, the world. We forget that, even though we experience ourselves physically as a male or female, on a soul level we are both. On a soul level the distinction does not even exist. And so people who are not at peace with both of these expressions are in conflict with an essential part of themselves—fully one half of their total expression.

Sometimes there has been a traumatic experience in a past life that has caused the individual to become alienated from one sex or another and the imbalance has become apparent because it needs to be resolved. The difficulty or alienation stems from a pattern in the belief system which creates expectations about what it means to be male or female. Depending on how those expectations have been met in the past, the emotional body reacts accordingly.

Most of the problems between men and women have to do with mental constructs. If we could allow our bodies to respond to one another, simply and physiologically, there would be no problems. When the personalities get involved, the mind and the emotions get into the conflict and that's when we have issues. When the issues have been resolved and we can let go of our ideas about what it means to be male or female, balance and harmony are restored and we come much closer to the soul experience of androgyny.

Smithsonite activates the mental body patterning that has to do with gender identity and relations between the sexes. In bringing those issues to consciousness, it highlights the perspective that needs to be incorporated and brings the two energies into harmony and balance with one another. Blue smithsonite in a scenario indicates that your client needs to get in touch with the masculine point of view. Pink smithsonite would highlight the need for a feminine perspective. In both cases, you will probably find that your client has experienced mental or physical abuse, neglect, and/or intimidation in all relationships with the members of one sex throughout the current life expression—so that all the relationships with men have been affected or all the relationships with women—and that this is a pattern that has been evident since childhood.

There is a form of brown Smithsonite which seems to attract the attention of people who are already androgynous in their orientation, even though they may not be consciously aware of it. When it appears in a scenario, I know that I am dealing with someone who is perplexed as to why these questions no longer seem important to him and why he does not feel sexually polarized or even interested in participating in this kind of energy exchange. I am careful about approaching the subject of androgyny and try not to give it too much emphasis. Many people are uncomfortable with it—is so different from what they are used to—and so I usually just give these individuals permission to allow these issues not to be important and tell them that this is a very forward way of thinking.

In a layout, I use Smithsonite at the second center of creativity or at the solar plexus where its energy will be easily assimilated and integrated because, even though the source of the imbalance is in the mental body patterning, it is perceived as emotional and physical distress. Sexual impulses, which are generated and perceived physically, are tied to the sexual orientation which is as much mental as physical, so that any impediment to the flow of that energy is felt as a physical and emotional frustration. Smithsonite can be used on the third eye if it is only the mental body that is affected.

Spiritual Body Stones

Apophyllite

APOPHYLLITE is the stone that introduced me to soul level healing. It is a member of the fluorite family and is probably like an evolution of it in our terms—like the way chrysocolla has evolved into gem silica. A friend gave me a beautiful piece of green apophyllite years ago. When I held it for the first time, something shifted and caught my attention. I remembered the enigmatic message I had been given years before when I asked about the direction my own work would take—healing, but not in a way that was familiar to me or accepted at that time. The minute I had it in my hand, I knew that this stone was a soul level healer and I had the glimmer of a thought that it would lead me to other stones in the same category.

At that time, I was working with stones in what I think of now as the traditional manner—in the "Crystal Enlightenment" way—allocating the different crystals and minerals to the various energy centers. Katrina and I were still focused on physical healing at the emotional level and I had only just then learned how to access the mental body. Apophyllite was altogether different from anything I had worked with before.

It has been my experience that when new stones come onto the scene they will, if we let them, function as way-showers that guide us to the next step in the evolution of our personal and planetary consciousness. That is how I thought of apophyllite. It gave me insight into who I was on a soul level and what my capabilities were. It opened up a channel of light into that dimension of myself. I knew that apophyllite was in the fluorite family, and fluorite was helping me to actualize the healing potential of the mental body. In working with apophyllite, I just took my understanding of the mental body one step further.

Apophyllite puts us in touch with the knowing and inner wisdom we experience on a soul level, as opposed to the knowing and instinctive wisdom that is a perception of the mental body. The mental body is like a computer chip or databank and the knowing we experience there is information that we draw on as we live our daily lives. This knowledge is focused on our survival as physical beings and its presentation is relatively businesslike and orderly. The knowing that we experience in the spiritual body is much more surreal. It is coded into symbols that are metaphorical or archetypal in nature and presented, as I have said before, as a series of pictures in vignettes or filmstrips. There is clarity in one sense—the images themselves are clear and vibrant—but there is less definition.

The thoughtforms that you would normally find with green apophyllite generally have to do with beliefs that are no longer useful to the present life expression but still remain an active part of the patterning. In most cases, they do not carry the kind of wound or emotional suffering that would be indicated by dioptase, for example. They do sometimes create what we call problems in living—failed relationships, mental attitudes that develop from outdated self concepts, or misplaced fears that sabotage success in business or any other kind of creative venture. Such patterns can eventually disrupt the entire light system and, after forming what I have come to call pockets of disharmony, can create a channel into the physical body that could manifest as illness or disease. Illness does not have to be caused by a soul wound. It can grow out of any confusion or misunderstanding that creates a thoughtform strong enough to block the flow of energy through the light system.

When green apophyllite appears as part of a scenario, it is telling you that either there is a thoughtform in the spiritual body patterning that needs to be addressed or, depending on the stones around it, your client has the ability to be the soul level healer. This is the most difficult part of working with the stones. With green apophyllite, you have two possibilities. One or the other could be true of your client, or both—which gives you a third option. The thoughtform may be blocking his ability to realize these capabilities in himself and express them in a physical way. This is why the scenario part of the session is so important. It is impossible to assign absolute or unequivocal meanings to any of these stones. You have to note where they appear in the overall picture and focus on the question that has been asked.

With white or clear apophyllite, the emphasis is on perception and recognition of the patterning, rather than healing. There is something in the soul blueprint that needs to be consciously experienced and integrated—it may be that your client needs to see or feel his own light and acknowledge, from a soul perspective, his purpose in being here. Sometimes clients who select white apophyllite sense that they are expanding into new dimensions of themselves but are not sure what direction to take with this information or what their next step should be. That next step has already been incorporated into the patterning. White apophyllite can help you to access the information or it can help to activate the patterning itself.

The scenario will establish that there is an issue in the spiritual body that needs to be addressed. Using either one of the apophyllites in a layout will take you directly to the part of the soul which holds the patterning of that issue, whether it is a thoughtform that needs to be a healed or a truth that needs to be realized. When the thoughtform has been recognized, you and your client together can project the color of the green apophyllite, an icy green, into the thoughtform in order to heal it. This will transform the shadow or distortion into a point of light and your client can then decide whether to release it completely or keep the experience in its resolved form. If you are working with the white apophyllite, whatever it is that you perceive in the blueprint requires acceptance rather than change.

One of my clients came to see me because she was having trouble in her relationships with men. She had been married several times and was continually marrying or being pursued by the wrong kind of person. When we got out to the spiritual body, she remembered that she had been a goddess once who had some kind of interlude with a commoner that affected her ability to be the goddess from then on. That was her perception of the experience. In other words, she was a light being who had some kind of energy exchange with a physical and, as a result, lost her freedom to move back and forth between dimensions. The imprint had registered as, "Any relationship I have with a man is going to hurt me, somehow. Any relationship I have with a man is going to be detrimental to me as a woman."

Green apophyllite in her scenario indicated that here was a powerful thoughtform that needed healing. She needed to understand the experience as the expression of her destiny in that particular dimension of consciousness and not as an imprint that was supposed to color all her lives to come. I pointed this out to her and, while she was not sure she wanted to accept this interpretation unconditionally, she was willing to consider it as a possibility. When an issue is not resolved in the session, the client will often leave with piles of homework. The session can be the catalyst that sets the stage for the real work which your client will do on his own. If this is the case, encourage your client to go home and think about what has come up, to look at how this issue has affected his life and make some kind of determination about where to go from here.

Sometimes information accessed through the soul blueprint is uncomfortable or it is contrary to a current state of belief. You might consider altering that pattern in the same way you would change a core belief in the mental body. Recognize it as being out of harmony. Realize the lesson that needs to be learned from it. Affirm that this pattern no longer suits your consciousness and that you have the right to change it. If free will exists anywhere, it should exist in the spiritual body where you have the most freedom and, ultimately, the most responsibility. In all my years of counseling, however, I have never known the patterning of the blueprint to change. You can heal the thoughtforms and eliminate the shadows in it, but I have never seen the blueprint itself altered in one of these sessions.

Suppose you access the patterning of your spiritual body and you discover what you believe is a stamp of poverty on the blueprint. What is it teaching you? How are you responding to it? Can you create a fulfilling life around a soul pattern that says you will never have a million dollars? It is possible that at some point in your life, the patterning will change on its own. I have never seen it happen, but it is possible. Even if the patterning does not change, however, you still have options. Your beliefs about the issue, your emotional reactions to the way it is manifesting in your life, your ability to make peace with that part of yourself will create the life you are living from moment to moment. My experience has been that there is no disputing the blueprint, which is the geometric configuration of your own soul's purpose in this lifetime. As the architect, you can move a few rooms around but, to the best of my knowledge, you cannot change the structure.

Celestite

CELESTITE represents the shamanic transformation of the spiritual warrior into the spiritual knower. Over the years, I have come to see the shamanic warrior as the stalker who diligently seeks his path by exploring and testing the alternatives around it. The spiritual knower, on the other hand, accepts himself according to his patterning, once that pattern has been realized. The idea that celestite represents the emergence of a new kind of strength came out of a conversation I had with Katrina over lunch at the Pinon Grill in downtown

Santa Fe. I had just given her a small clear point of celestite as a gift and she asked how I used it now. She touched on the subject briefly in *The Crystalline Transmission.* My own work with celestite has developed and expanded this original concept until, for me, this stone has become a metaphor for the spiritual transformation that is now taking place in planetary consciousness.

If we assume for a moment that the purpose of this physical drama is to move us into a dimension where we can become spiritual beings, then we have to realize that the whole warrior concept or consciousness that has been with us throughout the history of our planet has evolved into an exercise in futility. Becoming the spiritual being has to do with perceiving, acknowledging and expressing who and what we are.

This is what makes up the spiritual blueprint. The spiritual knower, to me, is someone who lives from that blueprint. We have had thousands of years to be warriors and are only now beginning to realize that wars and battles are not getting us anywhere. We have not learned from harshness and conflict and struggle. Now spirit seems to be saying, "Let's learn from softness. Let's learn from the beingness of who we are."

Beingness is one of my buzz-words. We are all in beingness because we are all acting on the patterns that exist in the spiritual body as a blueprint or template, in the mental body as our beliefs about that template, in the emotional body as feelings or reactions to those beliefs, and in the physical body as their manifestation in the external world. Celestite is about raising our consciousness to the spiritual dimension of ourselves and allowing that to be the focus and the energy behind our expression. If everybody on the planet lived from this soul perspective, without all the emotional tags and the ego, we would never have another war.

In the mid-80's I established a center for consciousness in Newport Beach which I called The Edenic Light Center. I did my crystal work there, taught classes and held channeling sessions in the evenings. The archangel Michael always came through for a few minutes at the end of each group channeling to balance the energies, set the pattern changes and seal the group. There were forty or so people present one night when he said that it was time to replace the sword of the warrior with a flower from the earth. Spiritually he placed a flower in front of each person there. Many of the flowers were swordlike in appearance, like a calla lily or iris, with long stems. So his message was carried by the image of a sword but with the softness of the flower and the gentleness of the blooming earth spirit. Ever since then, I have associated the celestite with Michael because of the substance of that message, the ethereal blue that I perceived in his light at the time, and the similar transformative quality of the vibration.

Celestite speaks for the light of soul that is present in each individual consciousness. Consciousness was seeded here along with the sword that symbolically indicated a kind of battle for survival. This imprint played itself out in our history. It was the warrior spirit that sustained physical consciousness on this planet and ensured the survival of light in its physical form. The time has come for a major shift to occur away from the physical/mental form of existence we have been leading up until now to a higher vibration of spirit manifest on earth. To be a part of this transformation, we have to live consciously not from the perspective of one's personal self, but in the awareness of total being. To express not as one physical life form, but as the oversoul in its entirety. The time has come to put down the sword and take up the light of spirit. It is more than peace on earth that we are striving for—it is peace of soul. Peace on earth can only come with peace of soul.

For the few who have glimpsed the potential of soul light on this planet, it would seem to be taking a great leap of faith to say that peace on earth can really exist. The idea that our ultimate spiritual goal as a planetary consciousness is to become perfectly unified, to become one mind, is misleading. Yes, we are all one, but we are all individuated and we will have to get in touch with our individual oneness before we will be able to reach our collective oneness and the understanding that if we shoot somebody, we are shooting ourselves. This realization is partly what is softening and transforming the consciousness of the planet—a process that began here in the 60's with the flower children who were preaching peace and love, harmony and joy. And so few really got it. How can you have these things if you are not willing to fight for them? Now each one of us can say, individually, that yes, I can have these things because I am touching into my oneness which is this light, this presence. I am becoming the living spirit, the creator that I have come to know and to recognize as myself.

In a scenario, celestite is telling you that here is a warrior spirit who is ready to access the spiritual dimension of himself and live from that blueprint. He is ready to express as a soul—freely, openly and lovingly. The spiritual warrior expresses himself in action. The spiritual knower expresses simply through being. In a layout, celestite assists in this transformative process by bringing the clarity of soul expression into the physical consciousness as a seed of light. Where that clarity already exists, it assists the individual in going within to the integrated oneness of total being, the oversoul which is the true inner teacher, the gentle spirit behind the inner voice. To enable that gentle spirit to become the expression of the physical consciousness is the celestite empowerment.

Dioptase

DIOPTASE is the only spiritual body stone that does not carry a message of softness, and I have come to regard it as the most pivotal of the stones in my collection. It is the one stone that can cause an entire scenario to fall into place if no definite pattern seems to be emerging from the selection process. When dioptase appears as part of a scenario, it immediately alerts the facilitator to the presence of an ancient wound in the spiritual body patterning—literally, a soul wound. The suffering around it is usually so deeply ingrained that the pattern repeats itself in lifetime after lifetime, while maintaining the intensity of the original experience. The wound always registers in the heart and can sometimes be perceived as a shadow in the heart area. In the soul patterning it looks more like a fracture than a distortion and can extend into the other energy bodies as well as the physical body where it can manifest as mental or physical illness. The emotional body, particularly, is affected. It continues reacting to the trauma as if it had happened five minutes rather than five centuries ago, and your client may be having emotional outbursts or experiencing feelings of deep sadness, anger or anxiety that seem to be either free-floating or out of proportion to the cause.

In a layout, dioptase seems to provide an instantaneous connection to the original trauma that can be felt on any or all levels—physical, emotional, mental, spiritual—and its energy can be used to heal the wound. The deep dioptase green is projected directly into the fracture until you see that the patterning is whole again or you and your client experience a sense of release. It is very important that you allow your client to be a part of this process so that he is able to have a sense of closure or completion where the trauma is concerned. I will often help my clients to visualize the fracture or I will say to the non-visual ones, "Fill the part of yourself that has been holding the pain with the deep green of this stone and allow yourself and the centuries of reaction around this wound to be healed."

I would like to mention here that whenever a deeply felt wound is brought to consciousness, there are always other players involved in the scenario and it is important that everyone who is connected in any way to the original trauma be energetically released from the patterning, whether or not they are actively participating in the current drama. As long as the intention is clear and honest, healing and loving, the others involved in the original drama will be spiritually released. Whether or not they learn their lessons will remain in their light system until resolved.

One of my clients came to me saying that she felt she was not fulfilling her spiritual obligations, though she did not really have a clear idea of what those were. She was still mourning the loss of a relationship which had ended two years previously. Dioptase was the last stone she selected. Three major players emerged in her past life scenario—a druid priest who was also one of the elders of the community, the reckless young woman she had been in that life, and a young man who belonged to a different religious sect and with whom she had a relationship. The young man soon abandoned her and she was still mourning him when she died in the arms of the religious leaders of her community. That was the experience at the core of the wound. The gentle, forgiving druid priest became the father she dearly loved in this lifetime who was no longer alive to protect her. The young man was the present day relationship she was still mourning. She was able to resolve her connection with him by realizing that he had played a key role in many of her lives and that he was karmically linked to her sense of disappointment and her inability to create a new life for herself. However, she also needed to release the soul of her father from his role of protector which had likewise repeated itself throughout a sequence of lives. Each person involved in the original drama needed her to say, "I fully understand the role you played in my life then and now, and I release you from the pattern we created together and perpetuated." The pattern has not been resolved until all the participants have been released from it.

Such a high percentage of my clients today select dioptase that I have come to perceive it as a signal going out that these soul wounds have to be healed before we can advance any further as an individual or collective consciousness.

Herkimer Diamond

SECOND ONLY to a Madagascar quartz in clarity and light is the Herkimer diamond. Found in only one location on the planet, Herkimer, New York, these tiny quartz specimens, all of them double terminated, are a wonder to see. It is like holding stars in your hands their light is so bright! Most herkimers you will find are quite small, rarely larger than a dime, however, I do have a larger one but it is filled with inclusions and doesn't seem like a herkimer at all. It is the tiny clear ones that find there way to the spiritual light body. At first I used to call them the jewels of our crown, as if they would light up when we reached our true spiritual awareness. But intuitively I knew they were much more than a jewel. Surely they must have a special story to tell.

When we talk about crystals and stones being 'seeded' on the earth, it means they are not part of the original plan of energy on the planet. Star systems and planets that migrated souls here, often preceded their coming by implanting an energy on the planet that would literally draw their light like a magnet. Mostly this high vibrational energy came from crystals and minerals for they could hold the light that would not diminish in time. I have experienced an energetic time capsule far beneath the land I used to live on here in Santa Fe, and was 'told' that many such time capsules were placed here at the first seeding of consciousness. They were carefully planned in accordance to the energy vortexes of the earth and their information would be released telepathically to those people whose vibration exactly matched the capsule when it was time for major growth in a civilization. It was called evolution.

Well, if this wasn't interesting enough, the Herkimer diamond reveals a similar phenomenon. The deposit of Herkimers was also carefully orchestrated, one location in the 'new world' would carry a vibrational frequency so high that even years after their discovery, there was little known about them. They too were a time capsule, but rather than single cylinders of information, they would spread their light throughout the land and wait for the right time to release their information and vibration. They are a signal for the beginning of the next root race, the enlightened ones, the evolved souls. The signal has sounded. Herkimers are beginning to sing in our hands and hearts.

If a client selects a Herkimer diamond, they are just like the rest of us, sitting on the cutting edge of a new age of light and awareness. We are all the precursors of this coming time. The client will need to know that and understand, too, the role he is to play in the coming unfoldment. Herkimers may just well be the jewels of our crown, but they are more than a beautiful adornment. They are the signal we have long been waiting for. In a layout, Herkimers belong above the top of the head, between the crown and the 8th Ray center. It is there that their light must shine and signal the entire spiritual light body that it is time to be clear. It is the wake up call for us to take responsibility for our spirituality and heal ourselves and this planet.

Phenakite

PHENAKITE IS the most subtle of the spiritual stones. Once the patterns in the spiritual body have been activated and the thoughtforms examined and resolved, phenakite can step in and say, "See, this is really a gentle process." Phenakite functions as sort of a bridge between the spiritual energy body and the physical consciousness—if you can think of a bridge as being a type of energy and not a structure or fortification. When the shadow or distortion of a thoughtform has been reduced to a point of light and the patterns in the light body have shifted, the emotional and mental bodies are in balance. At that point phenakite can act as a kind of catalyst which blurs or softens the boundaries that keep the energy bodies separate from the physical awareness and from one another. These different areas of consciousness coalesce and fuse together, allowing the physical awareness direct access to this part of the soul patterning. The more issues we can face and resolve, the closer we will come to being physical expressions of the light we have come to recognize as the essence or substance of who and what we are.

My belief is that our goal is to become these physical expressions of the spiritual light. The mind and the emotions are like a kind of washing machine turmoil in the middle of these two very different types of energy vibration. In a roundabout way, they try to link the physical awareness to the spiritual consciousness by creating drama in the physical life that elicits feedback from the spiritual body and at the same time keeps it separate. We do not see ourselves as composite beings. We experience life from the different parts of ourselves.

"Here is how I act, this is what I feel, this is what I know." With phenakite, there is no need for the confusion created by the mind and emotions. It gives us direct, conscious access to all parts of the light system and we are able to experience ourselves as composite beings.

It is interesting that phenakite is not selected very often. Whenever I get a new stone and put it in my case, invariably the first client who walks through my door will pick it up. This did not happen with phenakite. And except for the students in my classes who enjoy working with all of my stones, people still do not seem very drawn to it. There are other stones that will give you conscious access to the spiritual patterning—kyanite, apophyllite, dioptase. These are the heavy hitters and they will work whether or not you have thoughtforms, energy blocks, shadows or areas of density in the light body. But for phenakite to work, you have to be perfectly clear. In a scenario, it would indicate that your client has that kind of clarity at the very beginning of a session, before you ever have a chance to do any work on him The emotional and mental bodies are perfectly balanced and free of static. There are no thoughtforms of significance in the spiritual body patterning. In a layout, phenakite can be used on the third eye to bring awareness of the soul blueprint to consciousness. It will rarely appear as part of a scenario, so you would normally use it toward the end of a session, after the issues have been resolved and the thoughtforms released from the patterning.

Rhodochrosite

WHEN I FIRST found rhodochrosite in a gem show years ago it reminded me of malachite, with patterns of white moving throughout the stone the same as the deep green flows of malachite. They seemed similar in vibration, but rhodochrosite was a higher frequency that aimed its energy to the spiritual light body. I often refer to rhodochrosite as the New Age Trinity stone because of the three colors within its range, especially in the gem quality crystals. Gold for wisdom, orange for creativity, and pink for love. When I think of the real possibilities for this planet, these three definitions come to mind. Surely when we evolve to the next plateau of consciousness and our true spirituality unfolds, wisdom will be at the top of the list of our potential, tapping into our personal and collective wisdom. Creativity drawn from our highest perspective will interact with the planet with imaginative vision. Love as we have never experienced, unconditional love from our spirit to our consciousness, untouched by intrusive thought and undue emotion will be abundant! Rhodochrosite is all of these things and energetically brings them into awareness from our highest levels of understanding. As a talisman for the New Age, this remarkable mineral, heralds the coming age of enlightenment.

Rhodochrosite is the color and frequency of the newest color ray upon which advanced souls are entering this earth plane. This is the first new ray for many hundreds of years and it comes at a time when higher vibratory rates are accessible to our consciousness. These new souls are coming from great distances and most of them for their first incarnating cycle. They are experiencing the same spiritual traumas that the angels did when seeding early consciousness here. But they have an advantage over the angels, they have enlightened souls already present here who can assist their journey and destiny. We are the precursors to the New Age, each of us who work with crystals and healing can aid these new lights by sending them the energy of rhodochrosite in our meditations, prayers and projected telepathic thought, most especially when we are around children. Many of them are having a difficult time and do not stay physical very long. We can help them to feel safe and secure here on earth, console their spirit and give them a sense of well being.

As a scenario selection, rhodochrosite informs the client that he is put on notice to take his spiritual tasks to heart. He is likely one of the precursors to the New Age and there is work to be done! Move ahead with spiritual development and share light with others. It is time to bridge to the 8th Ray of consciousness for a greater perspective of life and spirit. If there are mental stones along with the rhodochrosite, they point to the light body for information to impart. Fluorite especially will assist in tapping into that innate wisdom. Emotional stones say to rise above an emotional reactive state and reach for a higher awareness. Usually when a client selects rhodochrosite, they are enamored with the color, it is bold, yet gentle, moving yet silent. There is a spiritual quality about it that stirs your soul. In a layout, I usually place this mineral between the integration center and the heart to act like a bridge to connect our active and passive polarities. The solar plexus is the center of action, the higher vibrations of the heart and soul are more passive. I like rhodochrosite in the middle to remind the body to connect with spirit.

Scolecite

IT IS IMPOSSIBLE to look at scolecite and not feel some kind of welling up of wonderful joy and appreciation for this planet. Scolecite looks like a fountain of light and its energy expresses as ecstasy—the perfect merging of love and joy into all aspects of experience and levels of perception. Scolecite seems to activate the joy of being spirit on earth. There is a tremendous amount of laughter and rapture and sheer playfulness in that dimension of ourselves which does not view the earth as a school of hard knocks but as a playground full of rides and slides and wonderful surprises, representing all the opportunities for learning and growth, experience and change, that are available to us as physical beings. For the soul, love and joy are components of a physical experience. There is no emotion in spirit and there is no medium of perception or expression which can carry the experience of emotion through nonphysical channels.

In a scenario, scolecite indicates a tremendous capacity for joy and appreciation that may or may not be activated. It is, however, part of the patterning and the individual who is drawn to scolecite has the potential for a rich emotional life expression that could translate very well into works of art, music and mysticism, the lifestyles of ecstatics or saints, or any creative endeavor which provides an outlet for the experience of ecstasy. Scolecite really puts the ball in your court, spiritually speaking. The root of the pattern is based in joy and being that wonderful fountain of light and allowing that light to flow through you, but you can create a reality based on joy or any of its polarities. And the capacity that you have to feel joy is capacity you have to feel fear or anger or deep sadness.

In a layout, scolecite would be most effective placed between the solar plexus and the heart, which is the strongest link between who we are as physicals and who we are as spirit. There it would provide a physical, tactile experience of light surging throughout the body. But wherever you sense a block in the flow of energy for self-appreciation and joy, that is where it should go.

Scolecite really does represent choice to me. I can work in harmony with universal law, flow with whatever life has to offer and use that energy to live joyfully on the planet, or I can use that same energy to be miserable. The older I get and the more contact I have with what I call spirit, the more detached and simple everything becomes.

Tanzanite

SEVERAL YEARS AGO in a meditation, a series of images came into my vision showing large tapestries hung on gilded frames that I could flip through like a book. They looked like a series of lifetimes in picture form held together by a thin silvery violet thread. When I reached this present life I saw a merging of the fabric, as if it were time for me to see one whole aspect of my life expression was completing, while a new one emerged on the same canvas. Seeing my living as a totality instead of scattered experiences was a remarkable sight! Some time later I was introduced to tanzanite, the most beautiful stone I had ever seen, periwinkle blue/violet and I suddenly remembered the tapestries. It was not the violet of amethyst I had seen after all, it was the blue/violet of tanzanite, a much different direction of intuition than I had originally thought. Amethyst takes the mind and vision inward, like a portal of light into your soul. Tanzanite can takes the mind and vision out to see life patterns of all the life expressions as easily as this present one. It is a most incredible experience and not easily forgotten. To see your life coming together like the merging of your cosmic fabric and to glimpse into your totality, ever moving and expanding is beyond description.

In a scenario, tanzanite tells the client that this journey is possible for them to take during the healing session and that there is valuable insight to be gained from their tapestry. There is little question that the presence of tanzanite in the selection makes it a pivotal stone for the session. Whether the client has asked for this kind of crystal journey or not, tanzanite makes it available. And for this journey place the tanzanite either at the third eye intuition center or above the head in the area of the 8th Ray center. Surround it with the clearest crystals you have along with Dow crystals and clear apophyllite for accessing the soul patterning. Tanzanite is the needle carrying the thread of the cosmic fabric, pulling the tapestry together when it is time to be seen.

Families

I HAVE RESERVED a special section for minerals that occur in a spectrum of colors, each of which represents a variation on a single vibrational theme. These families have a unique contribution to make to the field of crystal healing. As a group energy they have considerable impact and they are significant indicators in a scenario when two or more members of the same family are selected. Not all family members have been given space here, however—some of them are rare and either very difficult to obtain or prohibitively expensive. When this is the case, I have mentioned them briefly by name but have not included a description of the energy or an explanation of where and how to use them.

Families deserve special recognition in this work. I guess I figured that if Nature went to all the trouble to give us so much variety within the energetic confines of a single mineral, then we should honor the gift by exploring the multidimensional facets of its expression. When I first began to experiment with these minerals as a group energy, I found that certain groups were especially compatible with one or another of the energy centers. Topaz and tourmaline are both heart stones, for example, whereas calcite is a particularly creative stone with an affinity for the second center. Even today, when a client selects more than one member of the tourmaline family, I look for heart center issues—even though I no longer use the energy centers as a way of classifying any of my stones. The colors within the family spectrum are the same colors that we had assigned to the energy centers in the early years and are still used, to a certain extent, in interpretation. Many of the blue stones still work with the energy of expression, for example, which is a throat center issue. So, in keeping with the suggestions I have given you so far, there are no hard and fast rules. As always, you are free to establish your own agreements with the stones and to create your own system.

Beryl Family

THE BERYL FAMILY represents the soul level heart. All of the energy centers are represented in some way in our spiritual patterning. The beryls collectively bring us information about the heart of the soul and offer a very high frequency of light and sound to heal energy that is stored there. The soul level heart stores feelings, memory, trauma and love not unlike our physical body heart that holds the same things. Each member of the beryl family has to do with one aspect of the energy held by the spiritual body in the heart of the soul. There are, of course, many emotional thoughts and feelings we experience on all levels of our light body system, but for the spiritual body there are six categories that the beryl family represents. The presence of a beryl in a scenario or layout can trigger ancient memories held in the etheric heart center, memories now ready for resolve, change or enlightenment.

What is interesting about this beryl family is that no two members seem remotely alike. Placed together they would not appear to be related in any way, yet, their combined energy when used as a harmonic blend of light and sound can influence our spiritual light body. Most of the beryl family is relatively unknown, morganite, heliodore, bixbite and goshenite are beryls that have largely been ignored in most crystal healing. Those members of the mineral kingdom that stay silent in the background, do so usually because their message is waiting to be revealed or their energy has not been intuited because their vibration rate is so very high. Rumor had it years ago that the beryls were seeded here and not indigenous to this earth, but I suspect this is the case with many minerals. They are quietly waiting for our vibration to catch up with theirs! When we first began healing with crystals, aquamarine was the only beryl around and they were so pale they seemed unimportant. Emeralds were far too expensive so the entire family took a back seat to the more substantive stones. After all, we were more concerned with physical and emotional healing then. The spiritual body was not even in our realm of possibility!

Now the six beryls have stepped out of the background to show us the heart of the soul and make their patterning and information available. Emerald, aquamarine and goshenite reveal and heal the traumas the soul heart holds. The rest of the family, bixbite, morganite and heliodore, deal with patterns of feelings, memories and love. The etheric heart energy found in the spiritual blueprint now wants to gain our attention in order to heal any old wounds long held there. Our soul light patterning is not exclusive to this life expression. It also contains holographic imprints from our oversoul that govern all of our incarnating lives.

Aquamarine

AQUAMARINE IS the most known of the beryls, it's pale turquoise tone is attractive and soothing. Of all the beryl family, this gemstone has been used over the years as a healing stone far more often than the others and it is far more powerful than what it was originally used for, communication. As soon as the beryl family revealed the role it plays in the heart of the soul, the soothing vibration of aquamarine seemed to take on a new light that showed its real purpose to calm the trauma of an awakening soul.

Imagine what it must be like for a new soul to awaken on this planet. Following a long journey through energy fields and physical birthing, it suddenly finds itself in a three dimensional world that is harsh and confining. The awakening trauma begins at the moment of birth and registers in the soul heart as shock and disbelief, confusion or dismay. There is a birthing canal within the planetary light body of this planet for all souls entering our atmosphere. Visually it is not unlike our physical passageway for birthing, a funnel of light that narrows as it approaches the earth plane. It is filled with small lights coming and going from our dimension. Early visionaries who saw these small lights likened them to birds flying to and from the planet and called them angels.

Not all incoming souls are shocked into trauma at their birthing but many are and especially those 'angels' who came here at the time of the early seeding of consciousness on the planet. People who are drawn to aquamarine are those souls whose spiritual patterning holds a memory of the awakening trauma, from past or present life birth experience. Aquamarine heals this trauma.

I used to call aquamarine the 'earth angel stones' because everyone who selected them related to the awakening trauma of angels coming to this planet, stunned at their birth that imprinted on their soul patterning. The result on an emotional level was that this planet was not safe. My first aquamarine story came from a client who came for a session, a formidable woman, business with a businesslike air who selected this beryl right away. A small light appeared in her light body that glowed each time she picked up the aquamarine to hold, and the story unfolded.

At the time of the first seeding of consciousness on this planet, many souls out of love and dedication to this earth came like great flocks of birds to alight here. It was not an easy destiny for some who found the density of this planet very difficult. As time went by, souls from distant star systems and planets arrived and the conflicts began between light and darker forces. The delicate angels, fearing for their very existence, tightly wrapped their energetic wings around themselves to protect their light. For many, their soul destiny was put on hold, and they would come back, time after time, until the vibration of the earth was compatible with their own. Only then could they safely unfold their wings and be free once again to radiate their loving light.

Tears came to my client's eyes as the small light in her aura told her story. She was safe enough now to let her light be seen and free enough to fully express her hearts desire. She no longer needed to hide behind her austere personality and appearance, her 'wings of self protection'.

Aquamarine in a layout seems best at the heart where the emotional reaction to early seeding traumas are usually held. However, for those who need to breathe through any blocks around those feelings, the integration center would be best. On the intuition center, or the third eye area, aquamarine with chrysoprase for courage would help to see the past and release it from the present.

Aquamarine not only opens a channel of light to the soul level heart to reveal the awakening trauma, its high vibration and light heals the original wound that is energetically held in the patterning. This beryl is making a profound difference for many clients who need to re-awaken their angelic roots and heal any trauma that surrounds them. Aquamarine is my best story teller.

Bixbite

BIXBITE IS ONE of the lesser known beryls, a deep magenta mineral that is usually found in very small specimens. In the heart of the soul, bixbite has to do with emotions, the feelings and reactions to life experience, feelings that create memory held in the soul patterning. As a healing color, magenta is called the emotional equaliberator, bringing balance to an abundance of reaction and responses found in the emotional body.

In the soul heart, the reactive heart of physical experience is stored energetically and needs now to be recognized and healed of any distorted feelings. If bixbite is selected in a scenario, the client is telling you precisely what area of the light system to go to and specifically what to look for, the thoughtform in the spiritual light body that houses emotional trauma. In a layout, bixbite belongs at the heart area, surrounded with clarifying stones such as seed crystals or clear points to connect the living heart with the spiritual heart and release any emotional trauma held there.

Emerald

EMERALD is the most recognized member of the beryl family, a deeply profound green in its gem quality with an almost unbelievable light. In most healing stone collections, emeralds will likely be the less expensive specimens and far more opaque. Emeralds in any form play an important role in the heart of the soul by lending its vibrant healing green light to the healing of soul level transitions. Any major leap of consciousness can create trauma in the light body. If a client selects emerald, chances are that the spiritual heart center is calling for attention and possibly a healing of traumatic scars found there.

You may want to question the client about any recent changes in belief, or major life direction shifts and if there are any, the emerald indicates the need to heal those blocks the soul heart is holding. If the client has no awareness of change, then emerald is telling him that a major shift of some magnitude is coming soon and preparation needs to be made so that the change flows easily without creating problems for the light body. If he has selected moonstone as well, then a psychic opening is imminent and that can create a shift in consciousness. Amethyst nearby indicates an alteration of spiritual awareness like an acceleration of intuitive abilities is at hand. However the transitional trauma shows itself in this lifetime or is held over from a past experience, emerald carries the message of some disharmony and has the high vibration to heal it.

Emerald is the one healing stone that requires an intention to accompany its healing journey. The activation of this intention can be done with a projection of thought or as part of the breath. Emerald heals by its sound, visually seen as a diamond shaped double cone that resonates a sound throughout the spiritual light body, much like a Tibetan bowl sound radiates its vibration through the light system. Emerald's sound is like a tiny bell whose tone is far beyond our hearing range and it heals any transition trauma held in the heart of the soul. Intention releases the sound. In a layout, emerald plays best at the heart center and is especially empowered with crystals such as clear points that add clarity, or with rock ruby that brings in the ability to breathe through any pain held there.

Goshenite

GOSHENITE is the clear member of the beryl family, so clear in fact, that eye glasses used to be made of this mineral. Next to the diamond, goshenite is the most pure of all gemstones with no distortions or inclusions. Of all the transitions a soul makes, experiencing birth and death is perhaps the most traumatic. To go from a light essence into physical form can create a shock to the soul. Some say that the trauma of birth is greater than the trauma of death, but from a soul perspective, they are about the same. Birthing onto this planet is a painful and stressful experience on a physical level and is stored in soul memory. Many new psychological therapies, including hypnosis, take a client back to their physical birth of this lifetime to re-experience the trauma and release it from memory.

Our soul memory houses not only this life's birth but also the emotions of all the others. The impression this kind of trauma can make in the heart of the soul can be profound, especially if a difficult experience is repeating over and over again. Physical death, although it is not physically painful in any way, is also a drastic alteration of consciousness and soul projection. It can be as traumatic as birthing in terms of the transition from physical form to light essence again. Anyone who dies and is not spiritually prepared for the experience will have a very difficult transition adding to the trauma of soul transition.

Goshenite assists in the healing of the birth/death trauma by creating the clearest perspective possible of the ultimate transition a soul can make. As an evolving consciousness, we are now able to experience our birthing and scenes or lessons from our other soul projections as well as the collective unconscious. We are developing spiritual skills that enable us to see our 'before and after' and explore our super conscious self, mend ancient wounds and heal soul patterning. All of this has become available in a relatively short amount of time.

If a client selects goshenite, he will likely have no idea what it is. But the message is as clear as the stone itself, there is a birth or death trauma that necessitates further exploration and healing. Goshenite in a layout would do best at the intuition center located at the third eye area where vision is focused. Clarity is the key to goshenite and to the ability it has to bring enough light to a soul heart impairment to make a healing possible.

Heliodore

HELIODORE is a beautiful golden gemstone of the beryl family that holds its light and color even in the smallest of specimens. When I first discovered heliodore, not knowing what it was, there was a warm glow about it and an immediate attraction. Polished or faceted, heliodore's golden light beams out with great intensity and vibration. Heliodore in the heart of the soul holds the memory, all memory of traumatic experiences. Not only does this beryl hold the insights of the memory, when accessed with the light of intention it reveals the memory patterns so they can be dealt with. The wisdom held in the experiences, the lessons, the teachings break away from the trauma and become resolved issues.

Held in the heart of the soul is also the memory of our soul home, the roots of our soul projection. I have noticed that among new age people, the more they uncover their past life expressions, the lonelier they become. A friend of mine, tears welling up in her eyes, told me how separate she felt in this life, that something was missing or incomplete. I gave her my heliodore to hold for a while, telling her I thought she was homesick! Her trauma manifested as loneliness here, feeling she was not doing her destiny thing, a bit overwhelmed by our planet, unable to see she was making any difference. We have our life script, and we are all on schedule, but when we do not realize it, we long to return to where we are from. It is not a matter of deep depression, there is just a lingering feeling of homesickness. Some of us are very far from soul home.

In a scenario, heliodore tells the client that he is reaching for the memory that holds a wisdom or insight into a traumatic situation held in the heart of the soul. Watch for stones around the heliodore to see what light body carries the impact of the memory; aventurine that says the memory creates negative or hurtful feelings, azurite indicates a residual limitation from the memory.

Always look for clues, not only in how the stones are placed before you, but also which ones relate to the core issue. If the heliodore conveys a message of loneliness, stones such as larimar assist in taking the trauma out of the transition of soul to earth. Chariote says the client is ready to confront the memory straight away. In a layout, heliodore would be good at the heart or feeling center, where traumatic memory would likely be held in the physical body. Wherever the heliodore finds itself in a layout, there will be a warm and gentle energy to surround the healing center.

Morganite

MORGANITE is the palest of the colored beryls, an icy pink that is often difficult to see. The depth of this gemstone comes from its vibration for the frequency is high as it reaches towards the soul level heart. Morganite is the pivotal stone of this family, it epitomizes the love held in our soul. The pink of morganite does not have the warmth of heliodore or the dynamics of emerald, there is an aloofness about it and a sense of detachment. The love the soul holds for its physical projection is not the love of passion, it is the love of devotion, not unlike the love the Creator has for Creation. Unconditional love is the love of acceptance and honor. Love is why we are present on this planet, to re-connect with that love is the message of morganite. The spark of creation that makes life possible is LOVE.

Just as the devoted mother raises her child only to release it to the world, the soul releases the physical expression to this world to learn and grow and eventually grow up! Just as a child is always connected to his mother, as physical beings we are always connected to our soul and oversoul, even though it may not always seem that way. Morganite as a scenario stone indicates the client needs to connect with that part of their soul and awareness where the seeds of love are planted. They may have forgotten that it was love that sent them here and continually supports them. In a layout, placing the morganite on the heart center and surrounding it with crystals that connect, such as tabular quartz, will create a spark of love between the physical heart and the heart of the soul.

Calcite Family

CALCITE is a wonderful family of stones, making a tremendous impact in the healing field after being on the market only a short time. Calcite seems to be everywhere now and no longer has to struggle for recognition. The clear, beautiful colors in these stones are irresistible to client and healer alike. The calcite family has the most to do with initiation and spiritual rebirth. It nurtures new beliefs and ideas that have found their way to the physical consciousness from all areas of the light system. When calcite first began to appear, the time must have been right for us to realize that, as incarnating souls, we are in a constant state of initiation. These rites of passage are both collective and individual as the entire earth consciousness is expanding outward and upward. Calcite seems to be the wise counsel in all of us, the Jungian wise man who enters our dreams to make us aware of new gifts and potentials which have found their way into our lives from uncharted and, as yet, unexplored areas of self.

Calcite brings new light and a fresh perspective to any scenario or layout. It adds a next-step dimension to the interpretation and provides us with the incentive to move forward. We are always on the threshold of change, as individuals and as a planetary consciousness. Calcite comes along just in time to help us initiate change into our lives. We are not cast in stone, at any level of consciousness. We are always evolving, often in spite of ourselves. We maintain the status quo by staying with what is familiar and rejecting anything that feels new and strange. Calcite inspires us to move forward and welcome the unknown, just like a support group would encourage us to expand and grow.

Amber (Gold) Calcite

AMBER CALCITE, which is a clear, deep gold, puts you in touch with the innate wisdom of your soul. Specimens that are noncrystalline and somewhat more dense are reddish brown in hue, the color of dark honey. In its crystalline form, this stone is a faint reflection of the gold light you see in the spiritual body at the end of a crystal session, when you have reached the last stage of your journey through the light system. This member of the calcite family is most representative of the spiritual kind of initiation that precedes the rebirthing of consciousness into its fullest light potential.

The initiations that have been described most often and most thoroughly took place in ancient Egypt and involved lying on or in a sarcophagus in a dark chamber hidden under one of the pyramids. This rite of passage took years of preparation and was supervised by the priests. Even then, it was believed that the intervention of a holy person, or another initiate, was essential to the elevation of the spirit. Amber calcite functions as that intermediary in the expansion of our consciousness. We are our own initiators. We are responsible, as individuals, for our own evolution. We can achieve our greatest goals and highest light through our own endeavors.

When a client selects amber calcite, a spiritual initiation is at hand and some preparation is probably necessary. You might want to recommend that he meditate with amber calcite on his own. It would open a two-way channel of light into the superconscious, which would put him in touch with his own wisdom at a soul level. The clarity that is so characteristic of this stone suggests that this part of the journey requires clear focus and highest intent.

In a layout, amber calcite can be used on the third eye or in a halo around the head to assist in a personal initiation, or on any of the lower three centers to bring the energy to physical consciousness. Other stones that might be helpful are amethyst, for intuitive insight into the new consciousness, clear quartz for additional clarity, and tanzanite to bring information and energy together in the new patterning that will emerge from such an initiation. Most of the spiritual body stones would apply here, even if they are not a part of the original selection. Your part in this process should be limited to assisting in the interpretation of the symbols, if and when they occur—and only if your client asks for assistance. Your client needs to realize this experience on his own, as much as he can, for this is a part of the initiation.

Blue Calcite

BLUE CALCITE is usually opaque in its presentation. It has a soft, grayish blue color, which is similar to the tones you see in celestite, but it is very dense and often accented with streaks of white. It is usually found in spheres or eggs or fashioned into wand-like instruments. In its current stage of development, the blue version of this mineral looks very much like the early specimens of orange calcite, which was very dense when it was first mined. Blue calcite is more grounded in its intent than other members of the calcite family. It seems to be saying, "Make sure these spiritual explorations and initiations bring peace to the physical mind and heart." Sometimes in my work or meditations, a new thought appears that seems to pull ideas and perceptions from obscure parts of my consciousness and, like a revelation, causes a piece of the great puzzle to fall into place. I call moments like these spiritual ahas! Following this experience, there is, for a short time, a sense of overall well-being and a peace of mind and soul.

Blue calcite comes to mind when I recall the strange sense of peace that comes over me at such times. This may be another kind of initiation—one that sets a new belief into motion. There is movement in blue calcite, energy that pushes you gently toward the new plateaus that are eventually realized.

A client who selects blue calcite is telling you that not only is a new soul potential being realized, but also that this is a peaceful expansion. There is no resistance to growth, nothing standing in the way of change. You might mention that peaceful surroundings would greatly assist in this transition of thought and light. If other calcites are selected, then a spiritual initiation is at hand and both you and your client need to be ready for what you might call a soul shift in consciousness.

In a layout, blue calcite should be placed around the head area, to increase receptivity in the third eye and crown, and to keep the energy calm so that the expansion can continue in a peaceful manner. Blue calcite has a calming effect on the body and offers the composite being a peaceful transition to the awareness of spirit.

Green Calcite

WHEN I HELD my first piece of green calcite, I was told that it was green fluorite. I found this quite confusing. Fluorite hits me right between the eyes and, to me, this energy did not feel like fluorite. I sensed a different kind of healing coming from this stone—higher in frequency, somehow, yet softer and more gentle in its touch on the light system. The specimen in my hand was sending out a different message about the healing talent of this particular green. It took me several years to figure it out, but once I knew that this stone was not green fluorite, everything fell into place. Calcite, of course! But how did it fit into the energies of initiation and soul activation that were the central family theme? What part did healing play in these rites of passage? Sometimes the ego gets in the way of transition. The mind rises up in protest and the body rebels. The gentle vibration of green calcite balances the mind, the emotions, and the physical body. It enables the soul to send its message of light directly into the physical awareness to clear the old patterning and make way for the new. With the aid of green calcite, the entire light body system is open to change and able to accept and integrate it on all levels simultaneously.

Green calcite in a scenario indicates that the energy shifts in the light system will be dramatic. It should be incorporated into the layout wherever possible to facilitate the transition to a new level of awareness. Green calcite seems to be saying to your client, "Be mindful of change. Allow this shift in consciousness to heal you, body and soul." Green calcite, along with other members of the calcite family, is making an invaluable contribution to soul level healing.

Optical Calcite

OPTICAL CALCITE accesses other dimensions of self. These dimensions are other soul expressions or other lives. They can represent past, present or future lifetimes that are influencing the present life experience. A parallel pattern is being lived, either because it was left unresolved in the other life or because it is so powerful that it dominates all the other expressions. And I do mean powerful. A pattern like this one can make your entire life feel predestined somehow, out of your control. And if you are locked into another life pattern, it will eventually surface in your present experience as some kind of deep-seated frustration or confusion.

One of my clients came to me because he had been afflicted with severe insomnia for many years. I was a last resort, I suspect. He was desperate enough to do just about anything to uncover the cause of his sleep deprivation. He selected only a few stones, but among them were two large, clear, optical calcites. Here was my clue, but how was I going to explain parallel lives to this rather obvious skeptic? I figured I had better jump right in and make the best of it. He was looking at me doubtfully, but he had asked for my help and, after all, he was here. He would probably never come back. So I explained my work and we discussed optical calcite—much to his confusion and dismay. I decided to go right into the layout. We discovered a large thoughtform in the spiritual body that encapsulated a fascinating dramatic scene. He saw himself as a leader giving an oration of great import to his people, none of whom seemed to be listening. He was frustrated because he was trying to save their lives. It is interesting to note that, in his current life, he was using his long hours of sleeplessness to write a book of equal importance, one that was sure to make a noise in the world and awaken the spirit of many people. And he needed to see that in this past experience, his words eventually reached his people, but that they had to hear them in their own time and in their own way. Because he did not realize that his message had been received, he was left with the impression that he had failed. He was sensing the "inevitable" failure of this current project the whole time he was writing his new material, which was supposed to effect a real change in today's world. "They won't get it" was the seed of the thoughtform that had completely inundated his present life. He left the session slightly stunned, with a look of disbelief on his face. Months later he called to say he was sleeping regularly but had not wanted to tell me too soon because he was afraid of breaking the spell.

Not all your optical calcite experiences may be as dramatic as this one, but you can count on a transformative event to be happening somewhere in the light system. There are two other optical calcites—pink and peach—that are relatively new to the healing field. Pink optical calcite in a scenario seems to indicate an emotional bonding to a parallel or past life relationship. This person may be a participant in your present dramas or far removed from you in time, but it is the former relationship that is influencing your life now. If there has been a powerful event in one of your other lives, the people involved may still be linked to you emotionally and you may find yourself reliving patterns that you have already resolved. Some of my clients have recalled past events in which the other major players remain tied to the drama even after the client has released it. Some unusual past life material is coming to consciousness these days.

Peach optical calcite remains an enigma to me. It has not been selected often enough in classes or sessions for me to form a definite opinion about it. The few times it was singled out, it seemed to indicate a link to a kind of wisdom or creative talent that was developed in one of these other lives or dimensions of self and is accessible to the present life expression. The energy of peach calcite is subtle and highly refined, and because it has found its way into our lives and is utilized in healing, we must assume that there is a correspondence, an interaction, a relationship. It is far more clear than orange calcite and it very well may be an evolution of that creative energy.

Orange Calcite

YEARS AGO, a crystal class of mine gifted me with a large orange calcite sphere. We took turns holding it and marveled at the energy as we felt it penetrate our light systems. As I have mentioned before, our repertoire of stones was severely limited in the early days and we had no idea what orange calcite meant or how it worked. The ensuing years taught me that any client with a creative bent would head straight for it. The deep, orange color, in the clearer specimens now available or in the denser variety with the white inclusions, has a direct impact on the flow of creative energy. Until recently, this beautiful orange color was not available anywhere in the mineral kingdom. We are digging deeper, literally as well as figuratively, and the new mines are bringing us this wonderful, clear energy with which to work.

Orange calcite activates inspiration at the soul level to stimulate new areas of creative expression in the physical life. When it appears in a scenario, it indicates that your client has a strong creative flow that desires expression and that he is drawing his inspiration from a very spiritual part of himself. Orange calcite says that there are no limits to the ways we can creatively express ourselves, no limits to the colors on a palette or the notes on a scale. Creative soul expression—through art, music, drama and other art or communication mediums—is our divine privilege. It separates humankind from the other kingdoms in nature.

The stones surrounding orange calcite in the scenario will

be able to give you more specific information about the medium your client should use in expressing himself. Jasper, for example, would be telling your client that he would work most effectively with earth tools—wood, clay, natural fibers. Amazonite would suggest writing or speaking as a creative outlet. In a layout, orange calcite seems to belong primarily to the second center, to the birthing of new ideas, sound concepts and creative visual imaging. Orange calcite is so beautiful in its own right that it almost makes you want to rush out and buy paints, write music, or dance in the streets!

Pink Calcite

PINK CALCITE takes love to the higher realms of soul perspective. It uplifts the physical consciousness to the spirit, and uplifts the spirit to an awareness of those energies we know as God. This calcite family member is the palest of all pinks—it reminds me of those small clouds you see drifting across the sky at sunset. Meditating with this stone, you can sense the love of the Creator for creation—gentle, accepting, flowing, nurturing. Pink calcite seems to be giving us permission to overlook the dramas in our lives to reach a higher understanding of love. Sometimes all it takes to settle an issue or resolve a conflict is to see how unimportant it is—a lesson, perhaps, but with no reality beyond the four walls of this classroom.

Pink calcite stands ready to teach us more about loving, if we can just pull ourselves out of the emotional turmoil of daily living long enough to learn. This stone, along with the entire calcite family, is evolving into a more dynamic role in the healing of our composite selves and our planetary consciousness.

Red Calcite

RED CALCITE is chunky and rectangular, sometimes resembling the optical form of calcite in shape, and, of course, red. This red energy activates your spiritual adrenaline. When you are able to touch into your spiritual awareness while still remaining alert and grounded into the physical consciousness—

and this is not all that easy to do, by the way—you feel a rejuvenating surge of energy. Rather like a spiritual energy pill that settles into your light body system, red calcite raises the vibration of the emotional body and is easily assimilated by the physical body. The end result is revitalization.

In a scenario, red calcite is a good indication that your client needs to recognize that physical energy is a part of his spiritual evolution. In other words, you cannot ascend unless you take your physical body with you. The physical body is not separate from the rest of the light body system. Clear out to the soul blueprint, we are fully integrated—composite, perhaps, but nevertheless integrated into one unified consciousness. Sometimes people who are drawn to red calcite are very uncomfortable being physical. This incompatibility sometimes causes the physical body and the light body to become polarized. Red calcite seems to be able to pull that energy into oneness.

In a layout, red calcite plays first center very effectively. How we feel about being here is directly related to how much spirit we allow into our lives. When we finally realize that we are spirit on earth, that the light we represent has a purpose here, then we can activate it in our everyday lives—possibly the most meaningful initiation of all.

Violet Calcite

VIOLET CALCITE is the last of the family to be discovered and brought from the earth. Also known as cobaltocalcite, this brightly colored, fuchsia/violet specimen has an energy that is very different from the others. Refraction of light from the tiny crystals and the intensity of the color vibration make it seem powerful, moving, potent. When I first held violet calcite in my hand, I was electrified by the energy—it made me feel euphoric. I noticed that it had the physical charge of red calcite but with a connection to spirit that was, in itself, an acknowledgment of the absolute, the infinite, the eternal. Violet calcite seems to represent the ultimate initiation, Creator and creation experienced as one. All the religions say that with great effort and much hard work, we can find our way back to God. Violet calcite says we are already there! The real initiation is the realization of that perfection, the recognition of that oneness.

In a scenario, violet calcite is the wake up call that lets your client know it is time to expand the limits of his consciousness—or rather, to realize that there are no limits, that he is the light of creation, spirit incarnate. If other spiritual body stones are present, particular attention should be paid to which high vibration is being represented. Either of the apophyllites would bring into the configuration an added dimension of soul perspective or healing. One of my clients selected violet calcite along with dioptase, which told me that—with the healing of the soul wound—the spiritual blueprint would come to life.

It has always fascinated me that the whole calcite family is so connected to flow and expression of creative energy, but the violet form of this mineral is unique in its impact on the creative spirit. Many of my artist clients and students do not seem to be able to live without it. Perhaps it is the cobalt that exalts the vibration of this member of the family. Cobalt lends itself to the manufacture of a vital, periwinkle blue pigment which is used to tint glass. Yet, in combination with calcite, it presents us with this incredible shade of violet. However it came to be, violet calcite adds a dimension of transcendence to the calcite family, waiting to be acknowledged by us all and expressed through the medium of our lives.

Combination Family

NATURE HAS PRESENTED us with a special gift from the mineral kingdom. Combos are minerals that bond together in formation to create an unusual combination of energy frequencies that are worthy of our attention. Each member of the combination is enhanced by the other and sometimes an energy that is altogether different emerges from the conjoining of two different vibrations. Minerals that are fragile or brittle when they occur alone are strengthened when they bond with malachite. Malachite pushes its way into the mine pockets of a number of other stones and lends its resilience and movement capabilities to any mineral that wishes to form a friendship or, you might say, a working partnership. Whatever the combination, a new energy is created that stimulates each partner into action.

Gem Silica/Chrysocolla

THIS COMBINATION activates feminine empowerment at a much greater depth than either of these minerals is capable of reaching on its own. Here we are working with the archetypal feminine energy as well as the statement which is being made by the evolving female consciousness. Gem silica is an evolved form of chrysocolla. During this evolutionary process, there was a time when gem silica was only available in this particular combination. Now it seems to have gone its own way and can be found alone or bonded with malachite and/or azurite. You could say that chrysocolla is the parent mineral and gem silica has left home! And yet their association still exists in combination. It is interesting to note that when gem silica was first discovered, the Women's Movement was just beginning to form. Today it has established an identity of its own and women are on their way to a new independence.

When a female client selects this stone, she is probably headed towards a new self image. She is letting you know that new horizons are opening up in her life and she is feeling more confident in her identity as a woman. The other stones in the scenario would indicate where these changes are affecting her the most. Fluorite, for instance, would be saying that the changes begin in the mental body with a new way of thinking. Emotional body stones would place a greater emphasis on how she feels about them which is more than likely affecting her relationships with other people. I have never had a man select this particular combination. Mr. Macho, who swills beer down at the pub, tends to stay away from the smaller, pastel colored stones. But on the off chance that you have a client who is drawn to it, then I would have to say either that he is being forced to deal with feminine issues in a current relationship, or the ending of that relationship, or he is willing to explore the feminine aspect of himself. He has some inkling that it might be all right to be sensitive or intuitive, or there are other feminine qualities in his persona that need to be expressed. Most male clients who recognize the need to blend male and female characteristics will go for the boulder chrysocolla which is much more manly as a statement and dense enough to be safe.

In a layout, this combination does its best work at the assimilation center, where any new pattern of thought or action can be taken into the body directly. If there is a predominance of physical and emotional body stones, then any of the first three centers, or all three, would be appropriate—depending on the question that has been asked. This combination will rarely represent the primary focus of your client. It usually supplements the original thoughtform as a secondary issue or serves as an adjunct to the other stones in a layout. Gem silica/chrysocolla is the quietest of the combos. The gentleness of the feminine spirit shines through whenever your client needs to activate a new pattern of thought or action.

Malachite/Azurite

THIS COMBINATION is the transition healer. It has received more press than any of the other combos because it has been an active worker in the field of crystal healing since its inception. Those of us who were just beginning to become familiar with the energies of these stones many years ago were on the edge of a transition, to be sure. Channeling information was one thing—channeling energy was quite another. Using the stones to act directly on the patterning of the energy bodies was like inventing a science which had hundreds of variables but no facts. It took us years to figure out how it worked. The mere possibility that crystals and minerals could be an important factor in healing was pretty far out at the time.

The azurite in this combination clears away any limiting beliefs that are standing in the way of change. The malachite moves through the azurite energy to catalyze pattern shifts in the light system and transmit awareness of these changes to the physical consciousness. Anytime you break through a limitation, you are altering the configuration of all the energy bodies and the physical awareness of these pattern shifts usually lags considerably behind the others. Malachite, however, is the most powerful mover of energy on a physical level and when it enters the picture as the second half of this dynamic combination, acknowledgment of these changes is almost immediate.

When a client selects malachite/azurite, you can be sure that some kind of transition is taking place or will be very soon. It is rarely selected otherwise and the key to any successful transition seems to be your client's recognition that it is, indeed, happening and his willingness to allow these changes to implement themselves. Nothing is more difficult than trying to resist a change consciously that has already been accepted by the light system. If fear is holding your client back, look for black tourmaline in the scenario. Chrysoprase would not indicate fear, necessarily, but its presence here would emphasize your client's need to understand that he already has the courage which will see him through his changes. Fluorite would be telling you that there are thoughtforms or distortions in the mental body patterning that must be resolved before this transition can be actualized.

In a layout, malachite/azurite can be placed near any center that shows depletion or on the assimilation center, specifically, which will flow that energy directly to all parts of the light system.

Malachite/Azurite/Cuprite

THIS HIGH POWERED combination appeared only recently and has had a tremendous impact on my collection and in my work. The addition of cuprite to the dynamic malachite/azurite duo described above has so intensified the ability to shift patterns and integrate changes that its action on the light system has come to represent, to me, "mainline" changes in consciousness.

Whenever this combination appears in a scenario, I say to my client, "You no longer have time to drift aimlessly through life, second guessing your choices. This stone is telling you to get into gear. NOW!" Cuprite is a crystallized form of copper and copper conducts energy—big time. Just stand back and let her rip! When I am drawn to using this stone in a grid of my own, I know that I have reached a time in my life when movement is imperative and the only possible direction is forward. The message of this combination seems to be, "Move ahead quickly and don't look back." It is like a wake up call that is meant to shock us into the realization that change is essential if we are to meet the schedule which has been set by the terms of our own evolutionary process—a wake up call that says, "You are already awake. Get going!"

When this combo appears in a scenario, your client is telling you that he is getting ready for a big shift in consciousness and that his own energy is supporting, even compelling, these changes. You might point out to him that there is no significant resistance to this transition and that the presence of this stone in his scenario should be viewed as an opportunity for the permission that will allow these changes to happen consciously. The other stones in the scenario will show you how to locate these changes in the light system and identify areas of the physical life that will be most affected. This combination is a pivotal stone that says, "All systems are go!"

In layout, malachite/azurite/cuprite can be used just like the malachite/azurite combo described above.

Fluorite Family

FLUORITES, as a family, epitomize the energy of the mental body in activity and appearance. The tiny squares and rectangles you see on the faces of a fluorite cluster are almost a three-dimensional representation of its geometrics. Accessing the inner knowing, the instinctive wisdom, of the mental body is what fluorites do best. The mind functions like a computer data storage, and fluorite is like the floppy disk that accesses information from stored memory—which holds all our present and past life experiences as well as the information about who we truly are which filters down from the soul. This is our innate wisdom. All the information we need to sustain ourselves on this planet is somewhere in the light system—we need only retrieve that which we already know.

Of all the crystals and minerals in my collection, fluorite has had the most impact on my life. I tell people that fluorite gave me permission to be myself. When the flower children came along in the 60's, their message had to do with the open heart—peace and love. I am fairly reserved and do not enjoy being hugged or even touched at the best of times. I did not feel that I was an especially loving person and so I had a great deal of difficulty with this "free love" movement. When my spiritual life took hold, I was still confused. The type of meditation in vogue at the time was based on Eastern techniques of emptying the mind, which I was never able to do successfully. I saw the mind as a hindrance to my expansion into higher consciousness. Then I discovered fluorite. I worked with it for years before I fully understood its relationship to the mental body and the role played by the mental body in the light system.

In the book, *The Kybalion*, it says that the mind is all and everything—the reference here is to universal mind—but it also establishes that the mental aspect of our beingness is a very exalted part of ourselves and that the human mind is pivotal to existence. I began to see that some of my clients, who were primarily mental in their orientation to the world, were as confused as I had been. They were continually being told that they were not loving and demonstrative enough, that they thought too much and mentalized everything. These characteristics are typical of someone who interacts with the world and develops spiritually through the mind. At that point I realized that there are two different ways of perceiving the world—through the mind and through the heart. There is nothing wrong with that unless it is the heart that has been shut away and not allowed expression. The mind and the heart need to be balanced.

Fluorite comes in several colors and is easily obtainable as tumbled and polished pieces as well as in clusters and the double pyramids which are called octahedrons. It is the fluorite cluster that I have been able to use so successfully in meditation. I focus my mind on the stone while I am holding it in my hands or sitting in the middle of a fluorite grid. There are times when I have been able to visually walk into a specimen and I have found myself in a maze of orderly corridors, each one leading to a different facet of my own light system. Fluorite is magic to me and has been a stimulus in my life and work for many years.

A client who selects several pieces of fluorite for the scenario is making a statement about himself—"I am a mental being. This is how I learn and grow and interact with life." A mental person will always think before he feels, whereas a heart person will feel and react emotionally before he has thought the situation through. A mental person may seem cold and aloof to a heart person who needs the emotions in order to interact. This is not to say that we are not both, but one usually predominates. When your clients select a lot of fluorite, wait expectantly for a rush of ideas. These are the knowers, to be sure.

Blue Fluorite

BLUE FLUORITE is mostly found in octahedrons, often streaked with violet. When you touch into your inner knowing, there is an element of peace that goes along with it. With all the confusion in our lives, discovering a new thought or solving a problem that has perplexed you can elicit a kind of peace that breathes throughout the physical body. Lately I have had many clients select this stone as if to say that it is peace of mind they are seeking in this healing session. Depending on the other stones present in a scenario, blue fluorite can indicate that peace of mind is the goal of a spiritual pursuit. It can also indicate that your client is worried about something to the extent that a thoughtform blocking the flow of energy through the light body. Whenever you worry about something, you are not trusting in your own direction and this creates fear. Fears can develop from seeds planted in the mental body by events that have long been forgotten. Blue fluorite may be able to assist you in isolating these unsettling thoughts and bringing the full pattern to light for your review.

In a layout, blue fluorite can be placed near any center which has been affected by the issue and, being a mental body stone, will very likely end up in the throat or third eye areas. However, if your client's distress is preventing the assimilation of a thought or belief or even nutrients, the solar plexus would be a better choice. I find that having my clients meditate with blue fluorite is very effective in restoring peace of mind. "Ask and you shall be given" is the old saying, but we must remember to ask or the answers will stay hidden.

Green Fluorite

THE GREEN FLUORITE that is being discovered in the new mining areas has just a hint of violet that seems to say, "Use a spiritual focus to seek your inner knowing and explore the wisdom that will bring healing into your own life and the lives of others." Depending on the question that has been asked, it plays an important role in the interpretation of the scenario. If your client is looking for direction, green fluorite suggests the possibility of becoming a mental healer. Psychologists or people who use therapeutic techniques that involve the use of reason are mental healers. Alternative healers who incorporate counseling and methods of introspection into their holistic programs are likewise placing emphasis on the healing power of the mind. Visualization and affirmation, as well as certain types of meditation, are mind techniques.

In a layout, green fluorite is most effective at the energy center which holds the issue at hand. At the solar plexus, the healing green can be radiated throughout the light system and assimilated by the physical body. At the third eye, you will have a more direct access to the mental body. As more and more people are consciously releasing the issues which inhibit spiritual growth, green fluorite will play an increasingly important role. Keep one handy in your collection. You *will* be needing it.

Violet Fluorite

VIOLET FLUORITE is selected more often than any of the other fluorite family members and this is not too surprising when you consider that this is a time when many of us are rapidly expanding our conscious awareness into the dimension of the spiritual energy body. Violet fluorite is often confused with amethyst. They are very similar in color but not in shape or texture unless the pieces have been tumbled and/or polished.

Amethyst occurs in points or clusters of points, while fluorite occurs as octahedrons or in clusters that are so covered with tiny squares and rectangles that they look like computer chips. Amethyst and fluorite are very dissimilar in vibration. For those who are seeking a new spiritual direction and are receptive to new thought, violet fluorite works with the mental body patterning to enable the assimilation of new ideas. As amethyst stimulates the intuition and opens the door, so to speak, to a new dimension of consciousness, violet fluorite activates the inner wisdom that exists at the end of that amethyst corridor.

Violet fluorite takes you directly to the threshold of the spiritual body—that boundary between the mental body and the soul blueprint—where you can draw on the soul's wisdom and utilize it in your daily living. For some people, this is the only option they have available. As we develop spiritually, we come to a place in the journey where we have to make a commitment. Past that point, we do not seem to have as many choices. For those who choose to continue, a spiritual life is the only option they have left because they have become so far removed from their former lifestyles that they no longer feel comfortable relating to the world in a materialistic or pragmatic way. When violet fluorite appears as part of a scenario, it is telling you that your client is a seeker who can best access the spiritual dimension of himself through the mind, and that he needs to decide, at this point, whether or not to make this connection a permanent addition to his physical consciousness.

In a layout, often I place violet fluorite in a halo around the clients head, sometimes beginning at the shoulders. It keeps the violet light around the intuition center as well as the crown and connected to the 8th Ray. Violet fluorite is more than a mind stone, it radiates its violet ray energy throughout the light body system.

When a client seems to take on responsibility for other people and use their spirituality as a means to envelop those around them, I use this fluorite on the shoulders, which is the area of carrying too much responsibility for others. Many years ago, when I first opened spiritually, just beginning to channel information for myself and close friends and family, I am embarrassed to say I thought I was pretty special. I went around retrieving soul information for people whether they asked for it or not! I could have used violet fluorite then, and even now there is plenty of it around to remind me that spirituality is very personal gift. People around us will get their light and information in their own way and time! You can also use small violet fluorite octahedrons around the intuition center with other stones that enhance inner vision, such as amethyst, or clear quartz tumbled pieces.

Yellow (Gold) Fluorite

I DO NOT HAVE many pieces of gold fluorite in my collection. Usually the gold is bonded to violet and this is how it appears in the majority of my specimens. However, I do have a small octahedron or two which are rarely ever selected because my large violet and gold bonded specimens are so much more spectacular. Gold fluorite has the ability to put you in touch with the practical wisdom you need to survive in today's world. When it appears as part of a scenario, it is letting you know that your client is bright and inquisitive and learns something from everyone he comes into contact with and any situation he finds himself in the middle of.

When it is bonded to violet, it is an indication that your client has been able to successfully straddle two worlds and is as comfortable with the spiritual dimension of himself as he is with the practical side of everyday living. People who have been able to make a living from the practice of their spiritual pursuits, who have become writers and teachers, for instance—proponents of the truth that played a major part in their own processes of growth and expansion—would be very drawn to violet and gold fluorite.

In a layout, gold fluorite goes well with the integration center, where all energy, emotional, mental and spiritual is processed into the body and consciousness. The information gold fluorite has retrieved from the mental body needs to be assimilated energetically commensurate with the vibration of the client. Touching into ones innate wisdom is one thing, understanding it and processing it is another. I would like to see gold fluorite used more often, so many metaphysical teachings are rhetoric and not a way of life. Wisdom is as wisdom does.

Jade Family

Black, Green and White Jade

THE JADE FAMILY seems to stimulate those areas of the unconscious that reveal themselves in heavily symbolic dreams. There are hundreds of books on dream interpretation, but my feeling is that dreams are far more personal than universal and that the symbology of our personal life script is known only to us. We must learn to bring our dreams into waking consciousness and interpret them ourselves. I have only three pieces of jade in my collection—black, green, and white—and only the black has ever been selected more than once.

One of my students likes to use all three varieties on the third eye because it seems to bring through information during the layout that, without any "insulation" around it, would create a certain amount of conscious resistance on behalf of the client and, in some cases, even deliver a shock to the system. In other words, its function here is very similar to that of lepidolite but, instead of peeling back layers of emotional pain, it works with the mental body patterning to bring forth deeply buried memories. Not by "erupting" them as obsidian would do—but by bringing them smoothly, painlessly, to light.

Western culture is oriented to action rather than contemplation and, while I have received some invaluable information through dreams, I have never been drawn to use dream work as an adjunct to my own growth process, nor do I have much experience in working with jade. I can tell you that black jade uses the dream state to process activities and events that are part of daily living and can give you a great deal of insight into your experience of the mundane world. Green jade seems to provide an outlet for information of a healing nature that can be pertinent to your own life situation or specific to the problems of friends or family members. White jade is a highly spiritual vibration that can be used to stimulate the precognitive faculty which is sometimes very active in the dream state or to enhance a talent for lucid dreaming. There is a delicate lavender version of this stone that helps us to merge with the energy of group consciousness and is the vibration of what some of us have come to recognize as "dream school," the level at which we are able to connect with our masters and teachers and other members of our spiritual family.

I have never worked with either red or gold jade. My information these stones is sketchy at best, they need to be explored further Remember, however, that in order to utilize the jade energy effectively, you must keep a dream journal and be willing to commit a certain amount of time each day to reviewing the material, and this is what I tell my clients whenever jade appears in the scenario. Dream work is a solitary activity that involves discipline.

Quartz Family

IN THE EARLY DAYS of my counseling, quartz crystal was the full extent of my stone repertoire and I have used it as an amplifier from the very beginning, when I put these crystals with their colored gels on light boxes my son had made and used them as aids to visualization. The first thing that happened is that I was able to expand my use of color as a therapeutic technique and new horizons in healing opened up for me. The second thing that happened is that I learned how to work with the geometrics of the light body. Fluorite was the real catalyst there, but without quartz there would have been no foundation on which to build. Quartz fascinates me even today. In my meditations I have seen the center of this planet as a gold core of liquid quartz crystal. What the implications are, I cannot begin to tell you, but we are, indeed, the crystal planet.

There has been much speculation on the role played by quartz crystal in Atlantean times and a great deal of material has been channeled on this subject. Some of us are beginning to remember our connections to Atlantis as we use meditative techniques to go further and further back through planetary history in search of our roots. When Katrina and I were gathering material for *Crystal Enlightenment*, we stumbled on some very interesting information regarding large man-made crystal points that were used for everything from physical energy enhancement to soul transition. Much of our information came from a large Dow crystal that showed us ancient transition ceremonies and initiation rites and left the door open for further exploration.

Some of the crystals I saw were infused with color—red, blue or gold—and enclosed in large cylindrical rooms which were open at the top. These were stellar communications devices. These large quartz points, often higher than a two-story building, are lying on the floor of the Atlantic Ocean, still emitting a type of "radar." So, if, in fact, quartz crystal is at the core of our earth and played such a major role in our history, then it probably still has a great deal of untapped knowledge that we can utilize today and we need to learn as much about it as we can.

Quartz crystals are not often selected as scenario stones except for Dow crystals. Most of my clients will overlook them in favor of other, brightly-colored minerals or faceted specimens, but I always add them to the layout as amplifiers, clarifiers or mandala stones, or I use them to set up a powerful grid around the physical body. If a client does select clear quartz, it means they are looking for clarification on some issue, so look for stones placed around it for further insight. When you review the quartz family, greater detail about each formation of quartz will add to your information. The family of quartz crystal is the foundation of all crystal healing and will always be an important part of this work.

Cluster

Clusters

A QUARTZ CRYSTAL cluster is beautiful to behold. Light pours in, out and through a multitude of points that have formed and grown together. Clusters can be used to pull light in from one or more directions or to project light out in a broader spectrum of wavelength or frequency. They can also be used to clear negativity from other stones or to heal fractures. I purchased a small, bi-colored tourmaline one day and, when I got home, I noticed a small crack deep inside the stone. I placed it on a quartz cluster and forgot about it. Over a year later, I rediscovered it and, to my astonishment, the fracture had completely disappeared. I wish I could explain how this happened, but the lesson in it for me was that quartz, with its powerful light and clear vibration, can heal a fracture in the light system of an individual or a physical fracture in another stone. You may want to tune into your collection of quartz cluster to see if one would be appropriate for such healing and a hint would be to look for the one that likes to be separate from all the others!

If a cluster is chosen during the selection process, your client is someone who is open to new ideas, ready to broaden the horizons of his experience and express in a number of different ways. It could mean also that your client needs to become aware of new dimensions of light within himself and not be too narrow in his views or too focused in his pursuits. The other stones in the scenario will help you to decipher the message that is being sent. In a layout, a small cluster at the solar plexus will expand light throughout the system. Other minerals can be placed within it and those vibrations will be expanded also. Clusters can be filled, say, with tourmaline to ensure the opening of a center.

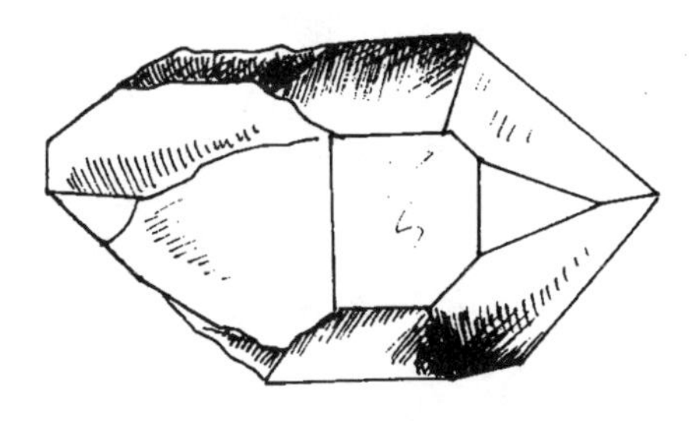

Double terminated quartz

Double Terminated Quartz

THESE CRYSTAL POINTS have terminations at either end and I have always considered them to be channeling crystals to create a two-way channel of communication linking physical consciousness to the rest of the light system, or to an entity from another dimension. In crystal healing, doubles move energy in and out of an energy center or a light field and are often used to create a bridge between one center and another. In a scenario, double terminated crystals can tell you a great deal about the ability of your clients to open to new dimensions of light in themselves, or it can point to an area in need of light. If azurite is a part of that same scenario, there are self-imposed limits to the ability to open their consciousness. If moonstone is there, then psychic opening is more than a possibility. In a layout, doubles can be placed between energy centers to connect them or below the feet to enhance the earth connection or above the head to connect to the higher self. If, when you test the energy centers for a light body reading, there is a sluggish center or two, place double terminated quartz among the layout to assist in their flow.

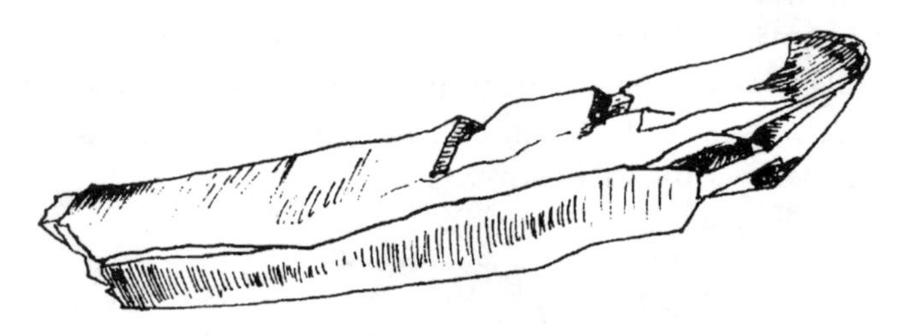

Laser crystal

Laser Crystal

THE APPEARANCE of a laser quartz crystal is highly distinctive. Lasers are always flattened like a tabular and there is a kind of wave-like movement to the sides and to the energy as it flows from one end to the other. Laser wands were originally used as a psychic surgery tool to excise thoughtforms from the energy bodies. I am not in favor of using lasers or any other stone for the purposes of cutting energy out of the light system. If a client is not able to release the thoughtform on his own, it should stay where it is. Otherwise, the pattern will simply reform. I use laser crystals to reach inaccessible areas of consciousness in people who have so much density around an issue in the light body that the awareness, as well as the energy, is totally blocked. To surgically remove such a thoughtform would deny your client the opportunity to own it and decide for himself whether or not he is ready to release it. The powerful beam of a laser, however, when it is present as part of the layout, can cut through the layers of density surrounding a seed thought to make it accessible to the physical consciousness—at which point it can be reviewed, reinterpreted and released, or retained in its resolved form.

In a scenario, a laser can indicate the presence of a heavily layered thoughtform in the light system or it can be describing the intense focus and clarity of your client's energy and vision. The stones around it will allow you to be more specific. Rose quartz, for example, would be telling you that the inability to feel love or respect for self has impacted a whole series of lifetimes and given rise to negative situations or relationships in the present life. In a layout, lasers can be used alongside the body or placed on any of the energy centers—or anywhere on the body, for that matter. Malachite/azurite or sugilite pieces on the flat surface of a laser crystal can help break up areas of density in the light system and the vibration of any stone that is likewise projected with the laser energy can be powerfully enhanced.

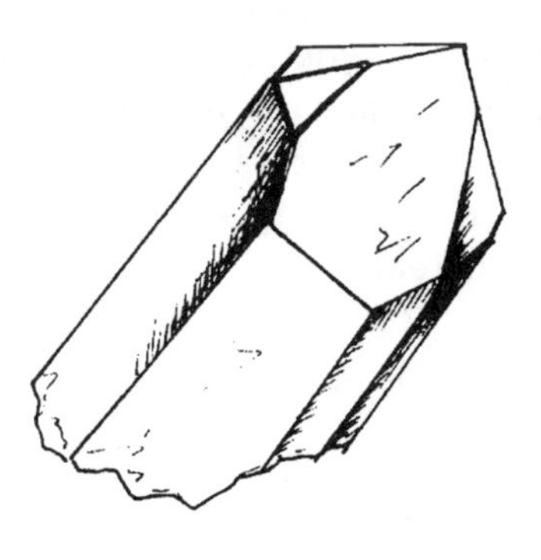

Quartz points

Quartz Points

QUARTZ POINTS always signify a focusing of the attention or a narrowing of perspective. Focus has always been an important issue in my own life—I am one of those people who simply cannot walk and chew gum at the same time. I need those crystal points! So I work with them as much as I can. Focus is the key to clarity and balance. There is so much distraction in the world today, to say nothing of crisis. We seem to be inundated with extracurricular activities and world class emergencies. If you watch the morning news, you can be overwhelmed before you finish your first cup of morning coffee.

Most of my clients will select the large generators over the small crystal points. Generators are larger than hand sized quartz points and used in layouts around the body to create an energy flow. However, the size of the quartz specimen is not really important and points can be substituted for generators in any layout to emphasize the energy of a center. I like to use them in mandalas or in forming a grid around the physical body of the client. They can be placed wherever your client seems to need an infusion of clarity or light. I often hold a crystal point in my hand during the breathing segment of a session. It helps me to stay focused and clear. If your client is agitated or confused, put a clear quartz point in each hand and ask him to breathe that energy throughout the body—an exercise which will relax your client and focus the attention. Using crystal points to make a grid within the room might also be helpful. The more you work with these small quartz points, the better you will understand the true function of quartz in our light system.

Rutilated quartz

Rutilated Quartz

AS YOU WANDER through rock shops and gem shows, you will probably see tumbled or faceted pieces of quartz crystal that are filled with tiny gold thread. These are called rutiles, and they step up the quartz vibration so that it is even more powerful as an amplifier. Rutilated quartz has an electric charge and energizes any layout or scenario in which it appears. I have one piece of heavily rutilated, polished quartz that surrounds a piece of hematite. It gets a lot of attention from my clients during the selection process and projects the hematite as well as the quartz vibration in such a way that it colors the whole energetic configuration, regardless of what the other stones are. There is little doubt as to the charged energy of a situation when rutilated quartz is present in the scenario.

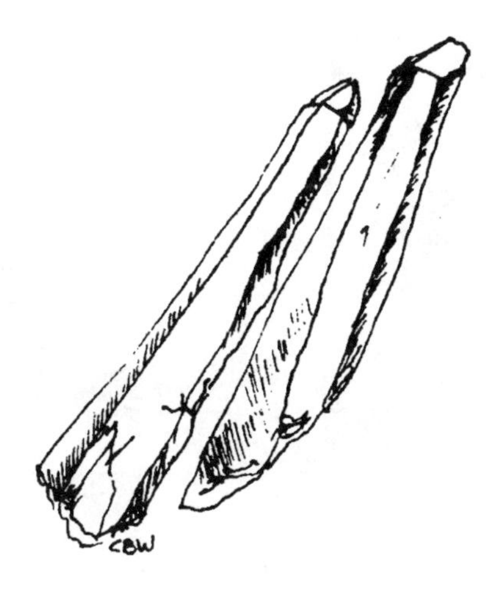

Seed crystals

Seed Crystals

I BELIEVE it was Frank Alper who first brought seed crystals to our attention some years ago. These crystals are believed to be the original seeds of thought and energy that brought consciousness to this planet. When the earth was formed, they were planted deep beneath the surface and supposedly came to fruition when we were advanced enough to use their power intelligently. That says a lot for these tiny quartz specimens that differ in formation only slightly from the quartz points.

Seed crystals are broader at the base and flow gently to a point at the apex. Their lines are not as clear and straight as quartz points, which tend to be more uniform in diameter. I use them almost exclusively in mandalas as support for energy centers that have been blocked or seem to need building up. They are rarely ever selected by clients. If this were to happen, however, I would interpret these seed crystals as seed thoughts very close to the surface of physical consciousness and ready for review. Seed crystals may hold the key to all the inner secrets of our earth if they carry memory enough and energy enough to penetrate the shadow that surrounds them.

Tabular crystal

Tabular Crystals

TABULAR QUARTZ crystals are wonderful reminders of the importance of connection and communication in our lives. Tabulars form when the crystals approach each other during the formation process. The molecular structure changes and they flatten, while still retaining their six-sided quartz features. For me, tabulars are bridging crystals—connecting one energy center with another, one light field with another, the soul awareness with the physical consciousness.

Years ago, a friend called to say that her daughter was very late in coming home and she was afraid that something had happened to her. I was not sure that I could help, but I walked over to my crystal case and said, "Who wants to find the lost child?" My eye went to a tabular quartz piece, slightly larger than my hand could hold. I created a grid of quartz points and lay down inside, holding the tabular to my forehead. I asked for a connection to the child and saw her almost immediately, in a car on a mountain road. She was quite lost and confused. Telepathically I stayed with her for a while, sending a calm blue light. By the time I was able to reach the mother on the phone, the daughter had arrived safely. This was when I fully realized the importance of tabular quartz, which has the ability to establish a link between any two light centers or light fields.

In a scenario, tabular quartz crystal indicates the need to connect with some aspect of the light system that will be further explained by the surrounding stones. If fluorite is also present, information in the mental body needs to be accessed. Emotional stones would focus awareness on the reactive emotional body. We have suppressed our feelings about an issue that is obviously more important than we think it is. In layouts, I often place tabular quartz between energy centers or above the head to enhance an eighth center or holographic awareness.

Tourmalinated Quartz

THIS TONGUE-TWISTER of a name identifies those pieces of clear quartz crystal which are filled with tiny needles of black tourmaline. The specimens are usually quite small but their presence in a scenario can be pivotal to its interpretation. The ability of black tourmaline to neutralize negativity is amplified by the clarity in the quartz, so as an indicator, tourmalinated quartz puts your client on notice that there are areas of confusion or anger or fear in his life that need to be scrutinized very carefully, cleared and released. These extraordinary little quartz pieces act as exclamation points in a scenario with emphasis on timing—"the time is now" to resolve these conflicts or tie up those loose ends. They can penetrate any shadow or any area of density in the light system and, when placed in a grid, they can do sort of an abbreviated crystal healing all by themselves, if you have enough of them.

Topaz Family

TOPAZ INITIATES the path of the heart, as opposed to the path of the mind, and shows us how to access the light body through feeling. People who are drawn to topaz normally make very good empathic healers. An empathic healer does not need scenario stones or energy measurements to locate imbalances in the light system. An empathic healer is one who intuitively feels any problem or affliction of a client or anyone around them. This capacity is present in all of us to some extent, but when the empathic abilities are present and activated, but not fully understood, these individuals may not realize that they are picking up physical and emotional pain from other people. A fully developed empathic healer has set up an internal flow of communication between the heart center and the third eye, integrating the energies of heart and mind. The sensitivity is still there, but any physical pain or emotional turmoil present in the environment is acknowledged mentally and not experienced as being quite so personal. I feel very strongly that in order to be an effective healer, you must remain objective. Identifying with the trauma that is being experienced by a client is one way of sensing the area of conflict, but it could create problems for you if your issues in that area are unresolved. It is not helpful to your client, either.

The film *Resurrection* portrayed a woman who was able to heal physical trauma and disease in other people by taking it on and healing it in herself. There are a number of healers today who continue to use this method and some of us take these things on without being consciously aware of it. This pattern seems to be an almost reflexive response that goes along with the wish to do something about a painful situation. Subconsciously, we volunteer. We do something about it.

One of my clients, another healer, came to me because she was experiencing severe kidney problems. They had started shortly after she opened her counseling practice and, though she was not on dialysis, she was progressing rapidly towards shutdown. She selected topaz, tourmaline—almost all emotional body stones. As it turned out, her method of healing the emotional problems of her clients was to take them on herself. She was unable to release them from her light system, however, and so they were congesting the energy bodies and piling up in the physical body, until it was so full of toxins that her kidneys had almost stopped working altogether. We worked together on dissolving some of these thoughtforms and had a very long talk.

When we take on the imbalance or disharmony of another, we are not allowing that person to be responsible for his own illness. We are denying him the opportunity to understand how he created it and to make the decision about whether or not he has learned enough from the experience to be able to let it go. Unless your client is able to recognize and release the thoughtform on his own, it could reoccur. And what will you have accomplished then? If topaz teaches us anything, it is that to be the empath does not mean to be the sponge. You should be able to sense another's pain without experiencing it as your own. That is the first pitfall. The second has to do with responsibility. To take responsibility for your own life decisions is an act of freedom, and we do not have the right to make these decisions for anyone else.

Blue Topaz

NATURAL BLUE TOPAZ is not easy to find. It is normally a very pale aqua that is often dyed or irradiated to intensify the color before the stones are cut, faceted and set into jewelry. As with most blue stones, the energy has a peaceful and calming effect that is, in this case, focused almost exclusively on the emotional body though it can be sensed physically as well. When it appears in a scenario, empathic abilities are present and activated, and there is a need to establish personal boundaries.

Perhaps your client is just now becoming aware that the emotions can be a conduit for perception. He may be confused about what he is feeling and might even be picking up on physical pain. When this kind of sensitivity is present in children, they may be taking on physical traumas or chronic illnesses for the parents. This situation requires delicate handling and you need to be very cautious in explaining "empathy" to your client. It goes beyond the dictionary definition of "identification with and understanding of another's feelings, situation or motives."

In a layout, I usually place blue topaz just above the heart, near the throat. This placement seems to be effective in identifying the boundaries of personal consciousness, enabling your client to discriminate between those energies that are the expression of his own persona, and those which represent the expression of someone else.

Gold Topaz

OF ALL THE topaz family, the gold is my favorite. These specimens are especially beautiful and powerful to me. I find it interesting that the rich, gold tones of imperial topaz are often tinged with pink, as if to say that the heart is able to add a whole new dimension to the inner wisdom which is ours by divine right. It is this wisdom that makes us realize that we need to define our personal boundaries and limit our emotional involvement with others so we can be effective healers.

Gold topaz represents that flow of communication between mind and heart that allows for the perspective of pure objectivity. When the empathic healer uses this perspective to merge with another personality, perception becomes a "full light-body" response. There is an immediate acknowledgment of the areas in the light system which contain shadows or distortions, an awareness of what these thoughtforms contain, fleeting impressions of feeling, a sense of the physical body.

With this perspective, it is an easy matter to disengage. There is no confusion, no holding onto another's pain, no drama.

When gold topaz is selected for the scenario, I know that my client is a sensitive who is fully aware of the need for personal boundaries but has not yet been able to attain that perspective of pure objectivity which is so essential to the healer. The emotions are not fully under control and it may still be something of a struggle to keep the equilibrium always in balance. When gold topaz dominates the selection, it is a good indication that the person sitting in front of you is a natural healer who might enjoy exploring different ways of utilizing this ability. Some of these individuals play a very supportive role in their families and use their sensitivity to become "caretakers" rather than going public with crystals or massage therapy or iridology, whatever. If gold topaz is serving as an adjunct to the energy of other stones, it is telling you that your client is too emotionally involved in the situation at hand and needs to view it more objectively from a distance.

In a layout, I generally place gold topaz on the heart, the throat or the third eye, but it can be used wherever that wisdom which is soul's gift to the heart might be considered healing for the body.

Silver (Clear) Topaz

THIS STONE is representative of the empathic healer who has been able to attain control of the emotions which so often "short circuit" the perception, but those individuals who live with this kind of clarity on a daily basis may feel ambivalent about having it. People drawn to silver topaz have well-defined personal boundaries and are very controlled where their own emotions are concerned—the emotional body is very clear. But they are so acutely sensitive that spending any length of time in even a small crowd of people can be physically traumatic because they get overwhelmed by the sheer quantity of input.

It can be helpful for people to understand and acknowledge this quality in themselves so that they can begin to work with their sensitivities, and when silver topaz appears in the scenario, this is what I tell my clients to do. They make very good healers and learning to work with energy—using crystals or some other medium—also teaches them how to keep themselves clear.

The one time I used silver topaz in a layout, my client was looking for a specific answer to a question she had. I do not remember what the question was but I do remember that after placing this stone on her third eye she went far out of her body for her answer. I believe that silver topaz can put you in touch with dimensions that are far beyond the perspective of eighth chakra, or holographic center, experience. It should probably be used with stones like variscite or red calcite that would enable your client to maintain enough contact with the physical body to be able to communicate clearly.

Tourmaline Family

TOURMALINES ARE the true givers of the mineral kingdom. They work by emitting or beaming energy outward rather than by drawing it into and through themselves. They also tend to be somewhat kinetic, approximating the ability of quartz crystal to catalyze events or make things happen. There is always a lot of movement taking place in the light system when tourmalines are around. The first time I put a necklace of them around my neck I thought my head would explode and, though they do not have that effect on me today, they are not subtle workers and their energy can be perceived easily even by people who do not have a lot of sensitivity to the stones. Tourmalines are the one family that has every energy center represented in the color spectrum, ranging from the deepest black to the most delicate lavender. Green tourmaline was one of my first healing stones. Pink and green tourmaline, and malachite, were all I had to work with in the very early days of crystal healing.

In a scenario, the presence of tourmaline is letting you

know that your client has a care giver type of personality—he feels the need to give something of himself to the people around him. Because there is so much "give" in the energy of tourmalines, they help to open centers that are energetically blocked and can accelerate the flow of energy in a center which seems to be moving sluggishly. Tourmalines are not quiet stones. They are assertive by nature—pushing open closed doors and demanding to be heard!

Black Tourmaline

BLACK TOURMALINE is a wonder stone. It has the ability to neutralize negative energy due to excessive emotionalism—anger, fear, resentment—in the light body or the physical environment. If a client selects black tourmaline for the scenario, you might suggest that someone or something in the immediate environment does not have his best interests at heart and could be the source of the emotional stress that he is experiencing in a difficult work situation or a family conflict. You do not want to frighten your client so you may want to soft-pedal this kind of information, especially at the beginning. The surrounding stones should be able to identify the problem for you. A predominance of emotional body stones will confirm that there is a relationship with someone who is creating a lot of confusion and difficulty in the immediate environment. If sulfur is close at hand the situation, whatever it is, is interfering with the ability to digest food or assimilate nutrients. Fluorite would indicate that something in the belief system is a source of confusion and/or stress. I have found that black tourmaline works best of all in the solar plexus area, regardless of the nature of the problem. I often create medicine wheels or mandalas at that center with citrine and quartz points and any other stones that may be pertinent to the issue.

I had a client whose work situation was becoming intolerable. He was a supervisor, responsible for a number of people who were difficult to work with because they were so angry and confused. And they had reason. The problem was not correctable, however, and so the work environment was tense and unhappy. He took three black tourmalines to his office one day and placed them strategically around the room. Soon his office was filling up with disgruntled workers who came in to complain but, inexplicably, felt much better when they left. There are limits to what these stones can do and some of the changes are very subtle, but there are times when even a small change can make all the difference. Black tourmaline has also been very successful in calming hyperactive children. I met one mother who kept several of them around her house. Whatever works!

Blue Tourmaline

BLUE TOURMALINE, known as indicolite, is the rarest member of this family and the most difficult to obtain, but well worth the extra effort and expense. Working with this stone will help you to feel at peace with who you are. We are rarely ever completely happy with ourselves, and so this beautiful energy, which is vibrant and peaceful at the same time, would be a useful adjunct to any program of affirmation or meditation with self improvement as its goal. In a scenario, indicolite usually indicates shyness or a lack of self confidence, and my experience has been that it often turns up in the selections of people who are overachievers. They are not workaholics, necessarily, and they tend to be very loving and forgiving people, but they have very high standards for themselves. You could almost call them saintly. The message of blue tourmaline seems to be "live in the present moment"—this is the key to serenity—and "be gentle with yourself."

In a layout, blue tourmaline belongs at the throat—almost exclusively—and works especially well in combination with turquoise and lapis to create a tangible, physical experience of contentment.

Green, Pink and Watermelon Tourmaline

AS I HAVE SAID BEFORE, green tourmaline was one of my first healing stones. So many of my critically ill children were drawn to green tourmaline and able to benefit from its energy, that I have come to wonder if tourmaline, in general, is the stone that best exemplifies the cancer-prone personality and holds out the most hope for its cure. People who have cancer tend to be "care giver personalities" and I include myself among them. When I had cancer some years ago and came out of surgery, my first thought was not "did they get it all and am I going to be all right" but "are my children all right—my husband, my mother, etc."

My young friend Billy told me once that he became ill because his parents either fought all the time or did not speak at all. He felt he had to do something to bring them together and bring peace to the family. His remarks stunned me when he said , "don't you see it had to be serious - and it worked!"

Billy was very drawn to green and pink tourmaline. When he was undergoing a particularly harsh chemotherapy that made it impossible for him to eat, I would put the tourmalines into a glass of water and give it to him to drink. Surprisingly enough, it was able to sustain him energetically through those really difficult treatment periods. He was still unable to eat—that did not change—but he had energy and he did not feel weak, which was unusual. The conclusion I eventually came to was that the tourmaline was a loving, healing energy he was replacing from his loving giving spirit. The heart has two chambers—blood is pumped into one and out the other. And so the energy circulating through the heart center was assigned two functions—one, which later became identified with pink tourmaline, focuses love and appreciation inward, to the self, and the other, the green tourmaline, sends loving, healing energy out into the world.

Watermelon tourmaline, the pink and green combined in a single specimen, has come to represent, for me, the balance of these two different kinds of heart energy. It seems to me that this is the stone that could be used most effectively with cancer patients who care so deeply for others that there is nothing left over to give to themselves. It is not that caring for others is wrong, but you need to be able to give to yourself, to love yourself, so that you can continue to give to other people. The issue here is a lack of balance.

Green tourmaline in a scenario or layout is considered to be the activating heart energy and pink is the energy of the loving heart that needs to acknowledge the love which is already present in self and others. The presence of watermelon tourmaline lets you know that the heart is balanced, so any issues present are coming from another part of the light system. Any of these stones can be used to open the heart center if the energy is blocked.

Orange, gold and lavender tourmalines are quite rare and detailed descriptions and explanations have not been included here.

Scenario Stones

STONES THAT ARE relatively inert energy-wise but able to trigger memories or energetic associations through bonding are called scenario stones, because they are always so pivotal in the interpretation of the scenario. Sometimes they acquire symbolic value through my agreements with them—like my crystal pyramids, which represent past-life initiations, or my I-Ching coins I keep in a small woven basket, which may indicate a very earth-based, materialistic type of consciousness. And these stones may not feel inert to everyone. There are some people, for example, who get a real energy hit from moldavite, but that was not my experience with this stone. I am writing about my own knowledge and agreements with the scenario stones.

My experience has been that these stones say more than they do. Scenario stones should always be incorporated into the layout because, even though some of them will not be able to heal the patterning or change the energy of a configuration, their inherent symbolism may help to focus the energy of the other stones. Others can easily stand alone or among a layout pattern and contribute to the energy shift or healing.

Angelite

ANGELITE is relatively new to the healing field. My specimen is fist-sized, pale blue in color with flecks of white, very dense—it is very similar in appearance to blue calcite, for which it is sometimes mistaken. From the very beginning, angelite has had Lemurian associations for me. Lemuria was psychic Edgar Cayce's name for the lost continent of Mu, which was where many of us had our first experience of earth. Life there was so similar to what I remember from my planet of origin that there was almost no difference in vibration and no sense of separation.

The imprinting was relatively painless and there was no trauma associated with this first experience of earth existence. Lemurians were, for the most part, very gentle spirits and not as polarized in the mental body as were the Atlanteans who came later. I remember a synthesis of color and sound—the air filling with tones and shades of blue. The civilization of Lemuria used healing techniques based on differing combinations of color, water and tone. Large reflecting pools surrounded open columned courtyards, where people who served in a healing capacity stood in certain positions and emitted sounds in the appropriate healing frequencies. This kind of treatment was available to everyone.

Lemurian civilization was highly advanced in its healing techniques, so it is not really so surprising that I chose to experience a lifetime there. In all of my expressions, I have been either a teacher or a healer who has specialized in soul transition—the movement of consciousness from light to form and back to light again—and this is the thread that runs through the tapestry of all my lifetimes. Many of my clients who select angelite for the scenario have this same background or specialization—not in transition, necessarily, but there is almost always an interest in healing that does not seem to want to travel the conventional route of medical school, internship, residency, practice. Angelite is always an indication of Lemurian influence and heritage, whether or not

Lemuria was the first earth experience. People who are drawn to this stone tend to be very gentle souls who are interested in alternative lifestyles and do not seem to have much ambition. Once they see themselves from a Lemurian perspective, however, they have a better understanding of what motivates them to be the silent iconoclasts. They are not rebels by any stretch of the imagination—they simply have a different vision of community.

In a layout, I place angelite on the heart center or in one of the hands—usually at my client's request. People seem to enjoy holding it. Perhaps it reminds them of a distant home. Perhaps it is just the deep stirring of a familiar association that is becoming activated in the present life.

Labradorite

LABRADORITE IS ALSO known as spectrolite— some say the name depends on the location of the mining of the stone. First discovered in Labrador, this deep, penetrating stone acts like a mirror to an inner light within us all. Rotating a cabochon of labradorite in the light elicits colors of blue, green, white and gold, colors so moving and beautiful against the dark black background, you can almost see your own soul reflected there. For many years of my healing, I ignored this mineral, it never felt like much, seemed too dark and brooding to be of much help! As I have often said: when the student is ready, the teacher appears. Labradorite patiently waited for me to discover a part of my soul history that could be enhanced by its vibration.

During a visual journey through my last days in Atlantis, labradorite suddenly appeared in tall obelisk columns where I was pacing about like a mad scientist, frustrated and angry that the civilization I was so devoted to was not paying attention to its purpose. Destiny for Atlantis changed when the majority of the ruling class chose to implode the entire civilization. The separation of classes was too great, there was an abuse of power and intellect that was out of control.

At first I thought labradorite was a stone that indicated Atlantis lives, but it turned out to be far more than that. Labradorite in those times was the mirror to the soul and symbolized the roots of the soul to be from the star system Sirius. It was the Sirius connection that brought most of the healers and teachers to Atlantis, and this Dog Star still influences this planet today. Labradorite was seeded here from those early settlers as a healing tool to be used as a soul mirror, to see, I suppose, the very same patterning we see now in crystal healing.

Labradorite in a scenario selection opens a door for discussion of Sirius as the root of the soul of the client. Awakening that early memory of soul is important at this time. Sirius is the pass through for souls who come to this planet to be teachers. In American Indian traditions, the Dog Star is associated with the Wolf, the teacher, and some tribes consider themselves as direct decedents of the star Sirius. If the client needs to recognize themselves as having something to offer this planet, then labradorite will share its message of teaching. Something from their soul level is being awakened from their distant past to their present. The presence of labradorite in the scenario may also mean that the client may have strong leanings towards mental or spiritual healing, such as one of the many psychologies around now, or may be attracted to the soul level healing crystal work offers. If the Sirius soul roots have been established through the scenario, then their role here may be to bring the teaching from Sirius in a healing way.

Labradorite is a scenario stone, it tells its story and stirs long dormant memories. It does not heal any distortion of these memories, it is a mirror that is held before the client for them to see a greater dimension of themselves. You will find that once a Sirius Soul reconnects with a mineral like labradorite from their home planet or star system, there will be an immediate attraction.

It may be that labradorite for your client may come to mean a powerful Atlantis connection, they may be one of the root race from there and need to get in touch with that past. It is up to you to decide how labradorite plays out in the scenario and what prominence the client gives to the stone. Is it one of the first stones selected, or is it placed in a dominate position to the other stones? Does the mention of Atlantis and a possible connection to that civilization trigger memories or strong feelings? As for a pure Atlantis indicator, I use a crystal point that has a pocket of gold imbedded in it. For some reason, that is more of an Atlantis totem than labradorite, because the Sirius Star teachers can be a part of any root race or early civilization.

In a layout, I would place labradorite at the feet between large generator quartz specimens or over the top of the head with crystals pointing towards the body. Labradorite is a symbol, yet when placed with clear crystal points, the message and the mirror is intensified and can shed new light not only on the root of the soul projection, but its connection to present time living. If the client wants to experience their Sirius Star visually, then place a small piece at the third eye or intuition center with herkimer diamonds or small quartz points on either side. Labradorite likes to be around quartz crystals, perhaps the clear vibration of the quartz penetrates deeper into the depths of the dark light of the labradorite.

Moldavite

MOLDAVITE is a glassy green tektite mineral that came here via a meteorite to Czechoslovakia. When I first heard of moldavite everyone was excited about its mysterious origin and extolling its virtues as a miraculous healing stone. Some people who wore it in jewelry said they had a difficult time staying in their body, others felt they were being balanced by its presence, still others felt they could communicate with our sister planets and star systems, and I got a terrible headache! Well, there you go. This is exactly what makes crystal healing such a challenge, six different folks will give six different interpretations to the same stone. This is one of the reasons I stress that you find out for yourself how your crystals will work best with you.

Moldavite, upon further contemplation, seemed be a

Pleiadian activation. Experimenting with clients and classes, I found that those who were drawn to moldavite and were enamored by it, all felt a strong connection to the Pleiades star system. Ah-ha! I was on to something here. Not only does moldavite activate the connection, it will create a psychic link between those Pleiadian souls who are healers here and those interdimensional beings from that star system who continually serve this planet. So, those people who were blown away by moldavite were being activated, those who sensed a communication connection were right and my headache must have manifested because I have no Pleiadian roots in my soul. Well, I felt better knowing that! I discovered through my studies that all Pleiadian beings, there and here, have a deep love and reverence for Earth and are a vital part of its evolution. Many of our emotional healers and counselors are initially from there and the presence of moldavite seems to intensify that connection. Our mental and spiritual healers seem to have prominent Sirius soul roots and together, maybe this earthplane can indeed be healed. And, no, I do not get headaches from moldavite anymore.

In a scenario selection, moldavite states its message clearly. The client has strong Pleiadian connections and if he is not already in the healing arts, perhaps he should be. Having moldavite in the scenario already activates the Pleiades patterns in the client's light body and it would be helpful to know which one is the key. If there are emotional stones nearby, then some kind of emotional healing and counseling would be a start. Physical stones indicate a physical therapy, such a massage or acupressure. For the layout, moldavite would be best either at the integration or heart centers, where the devotion and energy of the Pleiadian roots would most likely be held. Surrounding it with the stones found near it in the scenario may give an additional boost to the connection. Moldavite is quite an interesting mineral, worthy of your attention and exploration.

Tigers

WITHIN THE classification of quartz is what I call the Tigers. The only member of this family that remotely resembles quartz is the quartz cat's eye, part of the chrysoberyls, that looks something like a cross between moonstones and opals. This is the only member of the Tiger family that is not included in my repertoire of stones, but it bears mentioning just in case you stumble into them. With all the 'eyes' family they appear to look like the eyes of animals that change in depth of color and pattern as the light moves before them. I have placed this family in the scenario stones because it is my opinion that they tell more than they do! Even though there is movement in these stones, I see that more as a reflective quality than the ability to shift patterns, thought or feeling in the light body. These are pensive stones that draw you into their energy flow to give some clues about living on this planet.

Bull's Eye (Red)

BULL'S EYE QUARTZ is the least known of this family, not as easy to find unless you hang around rock shops. Despite the movement as light falls on a polished specimen, it is rather inert. The message of bull's eye is adaptability. When it appears in a scenario, the client needs to be informed of the importance of remaining flexible, to learn to gently flow with the tides of life. The red of this stone adds energy to the message that in order to be more adaptable it often requires great strength and agility. As a facilitator you might suggest he explore nutrients or vitamins that may enhance his vitality.

In a layout, bull's eye will likely play best at a lower, more physical energy center, one that particularly shows a need for energy and adaptability. I have never used this stone alone, always with others like carnelian to learn more creative ways of being flexible or garnet to boost the red energy.

Hawk's Eye (Blue)

ANOTHER LITTLE KNOWN eye family member, but one of my favorites. Hawk's Eye reminds me of the American Indian Hawk medicine, the messenger. The message of this deep blue stone is alertness. It indicates a need for keener observance of your physical surroundings. Whenever it appears in a scenario, I tell the client that he must be the hawk, ever alert to what is going on around him, he is missing something very important. Messages from spirit come from all around us, from situations, from friends, from turmoil and from beauty. Hawk's eye says to be watchful not only of the reality we are creating but that of those that we surround ourselves with. There can a lesson in everything we do and say, in everything we hear and receive. Spirit says to stay alert, most especially when you or your client are expanding awareness by following a spiritual path.

In a layout, hawk's eye would be good at the third eye of the intuition, where the mind sees, where the vision can be sharpened. Placing stones of clarity around it would be helpful, clear quartz points or amethyst.

Tiger's Eye (Gold)

TIGER'S EYES carry the most light, have the most movement and reflect the most light. These golden/brown stones offer us greater insight into our life path by drawing us deep into a meditative state to find our place between the mind and the heart. Tiger's eye is the message of resolution, creating a balance between what we know and what we feel and reminds us of the scope and breadth of our soul. Tiger's eye can lead us on a journey into self to discover how best to manifest our light on this planet. This stone does not alter the energy field in any way, it is a meditative journey. When a client selects tiger's eye, he is telling you he is an old soul, been around the planet a few times, and is likely in need of some direction. He needs to go deeper into his patterning to find what may have become obscure over many life expressions. Rather like a person who spins around looking for himself but gets lost in the confusion. Tiger's eye says to stand in the eye of the storm of confusion for a better perspective of ones destiny. This stone along with the tempest stone would be a sure indication that turmoil is a major distraction with the client.

In a layout, the best place for tiger's eye is the integration center where manifestation of light and life is focused. Placing stones such as gold calcite around it for greater soul wisdom connected with the message of tiger's eye or larimar to calm down any resistance to the resolution. There is something endearing about these stones, they seem to symbolize spirit watching all of us through the eyes of the tiger.

Vanadanite

A PIECE of vanadanite was given to me by a friend who found it at a flea market. We had a difficult time finding out what it was, a reddish rock, with flashes of light coming from its many facets. If a client chose it from my case, I would smile and say that vanadanite was my 'hippy' stone, bright lights amidst the density of the red rock. I always think of the hippy generation as initiators of free expression and alternative thought, earthy folks who gained our attention by simply living in their own light. As an indicator, vanadanite tells the client that maybe his true destiny lies with him just being who he is, to live spontaneously, true to his beliefs. Just to be in their light, in the moment! That is a lot to ask of most people, simple as it sounds. The hippy generation opened our eyes to love, loving the planet, freedom of expression, honoring the moment. Although vanadanite is inert energetically, there is a quality of inner light about it that may stir a client into greater self realization.

Volcanic Glass

IF YOU ARE fortunate enough to find volcanic glass, ashes from an active volcano fired with heat to create a green class, you will have a vital addition to your healing stones. Following the eruption of Mt. St.. Helen in Washington state, someone experimented with the ashes and came up with an incredible teal green color, yet to be represented in the mineral kingdom. People were fascinated with my one small cylinder piece and as I worked with it as an indicator, there appeared a correlation between the eruptive qualities of a volcano and the disruptions we can create in our lives.

Obsidian brings up the hidden issues from the depths of our consciousness. Volcanic glass warns that a major eruption is about to take place, emotionally, mentally or spiritually, depending on the surrounding stones in the scenario.

The presence of volcanic glass puts the client on notice to prepare for this shift and welcome it as an opportunity for change and growth. Only through change do we grow, otherwise we stay stuck in a belief or behavior that can dictate lifetimes! There is no passivity with volcanic glass around, it tells us to face up to our challenges.

Organics

ORGANICS ARE stones and minerals that come from living organisms, some even considered to be gem stones. All of the organics, with the exception of amber, are used as indicators. There is a hint of living energy in all of them, a sense that a transmuted energy exists inside that is unlike other crystals. The question of their ability to move energy from their inert form arises when organics are introduced as healing stones. I found they were most valuable as indicators, stones that told their story or could lead a session into a specific direction rather than actually moving energy about in the light or physical bodies.

Amber

AMBER is the only organic that has the ability to shift energy. Its specific job is to ground scattered ethereal energies found in the light system, especially near the physical body. Whenever I feel like energy is flying around my body, disorganized and jumpy, I head for my amber necklace! Amber is really sap from trees in Russia and Santo Domingo, that lends itself to be polished into beads, carved into amulets or set into jewelry. Sometimes the amber has hardened so quickly as it runs down a tree trunk that small insects are trapped in its path. To many, the soul of the bug intensifies the amber energy making it more valuable. Amber varies from a buttery yellow to deep brown with all the golden tones in between. There is a mellowness about amber, a warmth that calms the spirit. However, it is not a powerful healer and cannot be counted on to combat severe psychological imbalances.

When selected in a scenario, amber tells you that the client is etherically scattered and in need of some focus before the session begins. Placing amber pieces around an overly active center in the layout will bring it into balance with the others.

Coral

CORAL IS REALLY crystalized calcite with color ranges the same as their calcite source. Coral is considered a strong emotional stone and I suppose that is because they come from the water. They seem to be bundles of emotional energy not sure of where they are going! It was pink coral that led me to the discovery of the association of coral to the latest therapeutic interest in the 'inner child.' These are the only stones that could energetically activate the childlike quality of innocence so important to the search for the 'inner child.' In a scenario coral indicates the need for the client to bring key issues from the unconscious to a conscious state of awareness, and a crystal journey is a good place to start. Pink coral is the only specimen ever chosen by clients and I have never used the other colors in my work.

Ivory

STRENGTH AND TENACITY are the key messages of ivory. The source of ivory is whales and elephants. Their ability to survive on this planet as a species and the strength they symbolize is powerful. There is so little ivory available now, but in case you have some around, beads or small amulets, they can be a good indicator stone for your scenario readings.

When a client selects ivory it is usually to be reminded that they have the inner strength, the will and ability to reach their goals.

Pearl

PEARLS, whose very existence begins as an irritation, speak to us as physical stresses and agitation in our lives as lessons. The story pearls tell us from the seeding of a piece of sand that evolves through agitation, ending up as a beautiful gemstone is certainly unique and worthy of our attention. Clients who draw pearls can be the kinds of people who live a constantly stressful life. There are some folks who think that if things come too easy they are not learning anything! That is the old 'no pain, no gain' theory, which has never held much fascination for me! This does not mean the clients who choose pearls are not as beautiful as the pearls they select or wear. I learned about pearls from my mother who lived much of her life in a pretty highly charged state. She was a small volatile woman with the strength of ten, and a high strung personality. She loved life. She loved pearls. I used to look at her in utter amazement. I loved my mother, but I never cared much for pearls.

Petrified Wood

THERE ARE SOME who say that petrified wood does not belong among healing stones, but I have gained insight and respect for this stilted rock formation. It has come to represent rigidity of thought or belief or behavior that can lead to diseases like arthritis.

People who get so locked into a physical perspective, unbending, unmoving, can lock up their entire light system and endanger their health and well being. I consider arthritis to be the major disease of our future and when clients select my one piece of petrified wood, the scenario reading leads directly to the possibility that a controlling personality is present with very strong beliefs about what is right for themselves and others. When we cannot solve global issues or impact a time of great change, we turn to our immediate surroundings, control within our grasp. Devastating eating disorders and serious arthritis tendencies can result from the need to limit our lives and control everything around us. Rigid beliefs and thinking severely effect our entire light system and physical body.

Petrified wood does not heal a belief or change a living pattern in any way. It acts as a powerful indicator that it is time for greater flow in the clients' life and to put their energies in a more proper perspective and proportion to those around them.

Adjunct Stones

I CALL THESE stones the A Team. A for adjunct. A for accent. A for activate. At one time each of these stones was assigned to a specific energy center like all the other healing crystals. Then I discovered that all other crystals and minerals work best when accompanied by adjuncts, particularly in layouts and grids. Adjuncts work well with all the other stones on any center or by themselves as powerful healers. There was a television program several years ago called the *A Team*, a group of detectives that worked together in solving crimes. They had a special gift for combining their energies for a common goal, each member participating on behalf of the whole. When I put my special A Team together, each one of the stones had a special energy to offer all the other stones and all energy centers as well. The adjunct stones presented here are all favorites of mine and are used quite often in my sessions.

Apatite

WHEN YOU first see apatite, it looks like a very yellow form of citrine. Apatite, however, has a slight green or chartreuse cast to it that gives it a totally different energy. Apatite works best in association with the integration center that we call solar plexus, because it heals the disharmony that is created when energy is not properly assimilated. When a client selects apatite in the scenario, you are assured that there is some conflict of energy in the integration center. If the source of that energy is not apparent, then ask the client to select more stones for clarification or more detailed information. Apatite can appear in the scenario when there is no conscious problem, but this quiet unobtrusive mineral can be of great assistance in indicating and healing a disharmony in the center that takes in energy from all the other centers.

In a layout, apatite works best in the assimilation or third center, but is not limited to that one area. Any energy center that is having difficulty taking in the energy flow from the light system can benefit from apatite. In your measurements of these centers, one that is depleted is usually unable to flow energy outward from the body as well as taking energy in. Apatite strongly effects the flow inward, telling us it is important to receive as well as to give! When the energy flow is out of balance or very one sided, consider apatite as an adjunct to the other stones around the integration center and when you re-measure the energy flow, see if there is a difference.

Kunzite/Hiddenite

BOTH KUNZITE AND HIDDENITE are gem varieties of the spodumene group of minerals. They look a bit like tourmalines with similar striations of lines, but are dependant on a perpendicular axis to hold their light. Kunzite particularly, if seen from the side looks pale and uninviting. As soon as you view one from its top, the color intensifies and the light pours through. Its colors range from pink to light violet.

I first found kunzite in a gem show, sitting atop a wooden stand on display at one of the sales counters. I could not take my eyes or hands off of it for the longest time. The salesman, out of desperation, asked if I were buying it or not! He even included the stand when I finally purchased it! It took a long while to understand kunzite. Again, in the early days of crystal healing, all pink stones had something to do with love. So there it went, lumped in with the rest of the love stones as an activator of the heart chakra. The more I worked with kunzite, the more I intuited its energy of balance. I noticed clients placing it very consciously among the scenario stones, usually between two other stones or pointing directly to another stone. Invariably, when the reading of the scenario unfolded, kunzite had pointed to a specific issue in need of attention. It was as if this pink stone acted like the needle of a gauge, giving a reading of the situation, that almost always was out of balance.

My advanced crystal class did experiments with kunzite and found that its message had most to do with an imbalance between the physical and emotional bodies. Something was out of sync between action and feeling and kunzite not only indicated that, it bridged the gap by enhancing the other crystals and stones around it. Far more influential in a layout, as an adjunct stone kunzite works well when placed between the integration center of action and the feeling center of the heart.

The stones that surrounded kunzite in the scenario should be placed in the same pattern on the body. If there has been no direction indicated by the kunzite, watch carefully how you intuit the placement of this stone on the body. Where is it pointing to? What stones are being connected by the striations of the kunzite? Is an area of the physical body in need of attention outside of the linear energy body system?

Follow the direction of the striations in the kunzite and it will enhance your layouts energetically and symbolically.

Hiddenite is a close relative of kunzite and newer on the healing scene. It is a pale green, sometimes yellow/green, spodumene whose perpendicular axis also deepens its color. The striations are not as visible as kunzite, the vibration seems calmer, more subtle. Hiddenite is the mental/spiritual partner of kunzite, to create a bridge from thought to spirit, wisdom connected to the blueprint of the soul. And quite a bridge this is, especially when surrounded by other stones in the scenario that will pull the puzzle together. As an adjunct stone, hiddentite lends its direction and healing clarity to the surrounding centers and stones.

Watch for the direction of its placement in the scenario as well as the layout on the body. Hiddenite may give valuable clues to any disharmony that may exist between soul and mind, particularly if there is a strong present life belief that may contradict a message from the spiritual patterning. Look for the gem quality of azurite to indicate a real limitation in the mental body, or apophyllites that ask for a focus on the spiritual patterning that may be in need of clarification and balance with a current or past belief. Hiddenite, although it is a relatively new healing stone, shows great promise as an adjunct for balance between the mental and spiritual bodies.

Kyanite

KYANITE is a blue striated mineral that most crystal healers have in a very dense form. Looking like an elongated blue mica rock with streaks of white, kyanite has only recently made its impact in crystal healing. The layered appearance of kyanite reminded me of mica lepidolite. This was my biggest clue into the value and energy of kyanite, to access the patterning of the soul blueprint that held information from other lifetimes. Kyanite is the best tool for past life regression, it peels away the layers of time to reveal an insight into another expression that may hold a key to this one. In my opinion, past life regression is only important if this 'past' information has an impact on the present. Nonetheless, as an adjunct stone, kyanite catalyses the exploration into the spiritual body patterning.

When a client selects kyanite they are telling you that whatever the problem is, the roots lie in another lifetime. If dioptase is also part of the scenario, along with kyanite you are assured that this is the direction to take in the layout. If there is any resistance to this journey, indicated by azurite showing limitation or black tourmaline showing negativity surrounding the pattern, kyanite will forge its way through the energy of the other stones to make the past life drama available.

Kyanite always indicates the need to look into another expression of the soul, and sets the energy in motion to get there.

In a layout kyanite can be placed on the body at the integration center to assure connection of this consciousness with the journey. Often I place kyanite above the head bridging the physical light system with the 8th Ray center, or holographic center where the information you seek may really be. If it is not a part of this lifetime patterning, you may have to accesses the 8th Ray center for the data of another lifetime.

Skeletal Quartz

I REMOVED skeletal quartz from the quartz family because of its unique and special qualities as an adjunct stone. Katrina calls this quartz "elestial" for its etheral light vibration, but its original name is skeletal. You can see where it got this name, this quartz is dark like a smoky, with many inclusions of light that make it look like a skeleton. And although it has six sides like all quartz, it is often shaped like a tabular quartz or a group of them fused together. When I first held a skeletal I was drawn right into a deep soul patterning that showed me that common to all life expressions, there is one theme, one oversoul expression that is played out in life after life. In my personal lives, the theme has been healing by helping souls through life/death transitions. Flashed before my eyes was a series of lifetimes in which I saw myself in some counseling capacity.

Initially I wondered if we kept coming back until we got it right, but soon I discovered that each lifetime is a refinement of the initial theme. How did this skelatal quartz impact soul level healing? It was my clients that showed me the way. The more skeletals were selected the more I could experiment with my theory of life theme and sure enough, it turned out to be right on.

When a client selects a skeletal for the scenario, they are looking for their theme either to give direction to their present life, or connect with their oversoul pattern. Once a client or anyone has a better idea of what their cycles of lives is really about, there is a greater continuity and purpose to their living. Stones around the skeletal will give vital clues to the theme: green apophyllite indicates a soul level healer, mental stones for a teacher theme or emotional stones like sodalite show a theme of personal expression. Often a client who is trying to find himself or is lost on this life path, will select skeletal in hopes of finding better or new direction to take. Skeletal quartz definitely enhances this exploration with its smoky quartz qualities to bring the process into consciousness.

In layouts, grids and wheels, skeletals really do their thing! I usually use this quartz at the first center of seeding of consciousness where the root of our being exists. Being able to connect that root to the overall soul patterning can certainly impact that energy center. Wherever the patterning lies in the light body, seeded in the soul or manifest in the mind or emotions, skeletal will seek out the information, especially along with other appropriate stones.

If your skeletal specimen is large, place it at the feet of the client and surround it with large generator quartz to amplify the energy, or black onyx to really ground the ethereal energies of the skeletal into the body. I sometimes think that our oversoul must look like a skeletal quartz, perfectly formed yet filled with our light of awareness and shadows of thought-forms. Perhaps that is why skeletals are so thought-provoking.

Sugilite

SUGILITE has become such a personal favorite of so many people, as a healing stone and in jewelry, it made its way rapidly into our hearts. This deep violet mineral was discovered in Africa less than twenty years ago, only one huge rock of it. Also called Royal Lazelle and Luvulite, Sugilite, because of its hardness and consistent coloring, has lent itself to stone carvings, cabochons, amulets and, of course, due to the violet color is considered a spiritual stone. When sugilite first entered crystal healing it was thought to be a stone to heal cancer, which was on the rise at the same time of its discovery. Synchronicity we all thought, and looked for the correlation between our spirituality and the physical manifestation of cancer. The vibration of sugilite reminded me of malachite, there was movement and there was a slight variations in color tone, but the frequency of the sugilite was above the physical body.

I started out with two carved diamond shaped pieces that wanted to be placed on the lymphatic locations of the body, particularly around the neck and groin areas. There was some relief there when clients complained of congestion or swelling of lymph nodes. When I looked into their light system, I saw much greater movement than was visible on a physical level and this led me to the true meaning of sugilite. I discovered that we have an etheric lymphatic system in our light bodies, a energy that continually flows throughout the aura. When this flow of energy is slowed or blocked completely by thoughtforms or congestion in the light body from excessive emotions or mental confusion, the entire light system is effected.

Sugilite is able to move the energy along, increase the flow of light and ease the congestion of thoughtforms. As an adjunct stone, sugilite works along the healers of the thoughtforms to keep the energy moving. There are many who think that cancer is an emotional or mental disease and if this is true, it begins in the sluggish light system that eventually moves its way into the physical body, carrying the message of congestion that seriously effects the lymphatic and immune systems. So, in a round about way, sugilite can still be thought of as a stone that addresses cancer, but healing it is another matter. Stones and crystals do not heal cancer, but if you want to find out where it truly came from, thought or emotion, or even spiritual patterning, then crystal healing can certainly help. I think cancer can be healed, I have seen it happen, but only through a great deal of self-evaluation and processing, dedication to diet and medical assistance.

If a client selects sugilite, chances are there is light body work to be done, clearing out congested areas and working along with the surrounding scenario stones to find precisely where in the light body the thoughtforms are and how to address them. As an adjunct stone, sugilite can greatly assist the exploration and movement of ethereal energies. In a layout, sugilite should be placed at any center that measures lower than the rest that may be indicating where the congested light body energy is slowly entering the physical body. If the outer vision needs to be enhanced, then place sugilite at the intuition center along with amethyst for greater intuitive ability, or lapis to penetrate any illusion surrounding the thoughtform. Sugilite is a powerful adjunct to any crystal healing, especially when the entire light body energy flow is in question.

Wulfenite

WULFENITE is another rather obscure healing stone, often overlooked as valuable for healing, but it has the unique ability to pull creative energy into focus and bring order and construct to the light body. It is a bright orange crystalline mineral, usually found imbedded in a rock matrix. Tetragonal in shape and very brittle, wulfenite lends its special energy to crystal healing. Its gem quality has a light like fire agate, but is more difficult to find.

I have placed it among the adjunct stones because its light and keen vibration seems to enhance just about every stone it is around, as if to pull a creative spark of light and order from each of its neighbors. Wulfenite is a kind of stone that grows on you, sort of creeps into your consciousness and quietly puts light patterning in order. I imagine this process to be like putting your aura on Rolodex cards! It does not heal or alter the pattering in any way, but just moves it around for a greater clarity. It is the creative energy about wulfenite that is so interesting, you cannot miss the influence of the brilliant orange color. That must be what effects the stones around it so much. As an adjunct, this crystalline mineral pushes other stones into action.

In a scenario, wulfenite tells the client that there is some confusion and disorganization in his light body that needs to be put into order. That, in turn, will facilitate better communication between the light patterning and physical awareness, most likely to bring about greater creativity. There is little doubt that this stone can move energy about! In a layout, wulfenite would belong at the second center, the place of birthing new ideas. This is the seat of our creativity and if you surround wulfenite with other creative stones such as orange calcite or carnelian, you will get a lot of information about the client's creative abilities.

Facet V

High Gear Crystals Dow and Trigonic

In Search of the Dow Within

THE SHAMAN DOW, on the cover of this book, has really taught me the most about the crystal journey. We have within our spiritual patterning an exact imprint of who we are that is reflected outward through our living expression. Crystal healing is one of the ways to reach that imprint, taking the journey through the emotional and mental light bodies, creating a corridor of light to see our way. And when we arrive at the spiritual light body, there is the original template for our evolving consciousness. All of the lessons that are to be learned, all of the experiences that are to be lived, all of the potentials of this lifetime are coded into the master plan. And the most surprising thing to realize is that we are living our lives perfectly and have been all along. If there is a thoughtform that casts a shadow in the spiritual body, then it is waiting to be resolved from lifetimes past. This does not mean there is anything wrong or negative in our lives, it is merely a pattern that is a part of our total soul package. We have come back again either to re-live the experience in order to gain another point of view or to dissolve it all together with a new awareness and discipline. The Shaman Dow with its white phantom, is that perfect reflection, the clear shaman mirror that shows us that light and perfection is present in us all.

By perfection, I do not mean saintliness or living a flawless life according to the dogmatic principles set forth in some religious creed. The Dow crystal has something to say about our potential, about living by the guidelines set forth in the spiritual blueprint of each individual soul, as balanced and as harmoniously as possible. I believe that the end result of our evolutionary process is our perfection as imprinted on the original template for our evolving consciousness. Many Master Teachers have walked this earth as exemplars of this template to offer us precepts to live by and valuable insights into our personal spiritual master plan. Now we have the magic of crystal healing to reveal our template as well as the vibrational energy to sustain our balance.

When you look at a Dow crystal from the top of the apex, you will see the geometric pattern that so captivated my interest years ago. There are three perfect triangles separated by seven-sided facets that create a mandala of harmony. This pattern, of all the quartz crystal patterns I have explored, is the most perfectly balanced. Even without the phantom inside, the Dow reflects the perfection we have innately within us. The first time I held a Dow, my crystal journey began, not only into crystal healing but into my own spiritual light body.

In all the healing modalities, alternative or otherwise, there is growth that coincides with the expansion of the consciousness of the times. When we first began exploring crystal energy, over a dozen years ago, we knew that we were working with a new form of healing. We did not have the knowledge we do now of the light body system and how it works, or did we have the ability to sense or comprehend the subtleties of crystal energy. It was like being on one side of a portal that was very slowly opening. Some healers peered through it cautiously and saw great potential for change in the healing paradigm, but did not feel confident enough to carry the vision any further. Some of us stepped boldly onto this new threshold and found ourselves immersed in a light filled with crystals and minerals of every color and dimension. We felt an incredible surge of energy and knew that crystal healing was our next step.

It was then that the Dow crystals came into my life. First, there were two large specimens from Gary Fleck, who was mining in Arkansas at the time. It was not long before many more Dows began to fill my crystal cabinet. Every time I worked with them an aura of balance came over the session. One day a woman came to see me and picked up a Dow right away. Within minutes her body began to vibrate, almost uncontrollably. During the session it became apparent that her spiritual light body patterning matched the Dow vibration exactly. She was, in fact, a living Dow crystal, balanced and living her life pattern perfectly. Regardless of what she felt about her life, any traumas or disappointments, she was in perfect harmony with her soul patterning. Here was my greatest Dow teaching, that we have the potential within our lifetime to attain the highest vibration of our soul possible and live our lives accordingly. Balance is the key. The geometric pattern of the Dow denotes balance, the three triangles represent the body, mind and spirit balance so necessary for us to reach our individual perfection.

A Toltec Shaman of my acquaintance, Miguel, is the only other individual I have known whose life is entirely in line with his soul patterning. He is a living example of the totally blissful being and fully understands the role love plays in our lives as energy and as the essence of who and what we are. Whenever he talks about love, you can see that it is not emotion which gives fullness to his words or beauty to his smile. It is the essence of his being that is shining and speaking through him. Miguel is in near perfect attunement with this soul template. Miguel is also a living Dow!

There is an acupuncturist in Santa Fe, Tom Duckworth, who teaches Inochi Oriental Medicine and Kototama sounds. The theory behind this medicine is the essential balance of body, mind and spirit. It is a natural law that says the excess of any one means there is a depletion in another. If a person is overly mental, analyses and intellectualizes everything, then some aspect of his physical body or his spirituality is diminished. If he is excessively physical, obsessed with exercise and fitness, there will be an imbalance somewhere in his mental capacity or spirit. Religious zealots, even metaphysical fanatics, can be severely out of balance physically and mentally if there is no life outside of their beliefs. The use of sounding the three Kototama vowels for the body, mind and spirit is how greater balanced is achieved in this medicine. It is certainly an interesting concept and method of aligning energy. Now take me, for instance, my mind never stops, my spirit soars, but my body is not in very great shape! I hum Kototama sounds a lot!

Crystal healing is another means of attaining greater balance and the Dow crystal epitomizes that balance. Its function is a healing session is to set the template of perfection, as well as the potential of balance to be realized, into each of the energy centers. For those few moments of the healing session, each center will energetically perceive the soul blueprint in complete clarity. The conscious feeling of this perception is one of ecstasy or bliss, and deep sense of what it feels like to be balanced. This is why I always include Dow crystals somewhere in the layout, either placed between two vital centers pertinent to the scenario, or around the body at the head or feet of the client.

The Dow constantly emits an energy of balance and regardless of where it is in the layout, the vibration of balance fills the light system. I had a client who came for the 'cosmic experience' of crystal healing with no real issues in mind. In her layout, I intuited that several Dows wanted to be pointing down over her left shoulder along with a blue fluorite octahedron. During the breathing part of the session, the energy around this area became agitated and obviously there was an thoughtform resting there that was resisting the balanced vibration of the Dows. Sure enough, when she explored the thoughtform, it was a very old issue of conflict in her belief system that she thought had been resolved years before.

If a Dow crystal is selected for the scenario, your client is telling you that there may be an imbalance between the original spiritual template and his behavior. Or, that he seeks a greater understanding of this template and how it relates to his living. In either case, the Dow, and the surrounding stones will indicate which of the light bodies is carrying the spiritual/physical imbalance and needs to be the focus of the healing session. Whenever the Dow is part of a scenario and there are spiritual body stones such as celestite, herkimer diamond or phenakite, your client is ready for a conscious alignment with his template. Get out all your Dow crystals and create a spiritual grid with the other spiritual body stones around the client, or over his head, and proceed with the layout.

It is important to remember that Dow crystals do not heal energy patterns or alter them in any way. They are vibrationally similar to adjunct stones that work along side other crystals and minerals by effectively sharing the template of balance and perfection that comes from the highest vibration the soul. The more active healing stones will carry the responsibility of moving energy or clearing thoughtforms. Accessing the blueprint can be accomplished through several spiritual body stones along with the Dow, clear apophyllite, selenite, tanzanite.

The purpose of the Dow here is to emphasize the perfection innate in all of our patterning, rather than actualizing it. How it feels to be balanced is essential to any crystal healing. Once a thoughtform is resolved the light patterning must adjust to the absence of the shadow. That shift of pattern in any of the light bodies needs to expand to the other bands of light and energy so that the entire aura receives the message that a thoughtform, once dictating a behavior, is now gone. And it is imperative that this energy shift be brought back to the physical body, visually and with the breath as the client concludes their crystal journey. In this way, the client is able to actually feel the difference the light body shift makes in their body, gain a new reference point for balance and breathe a new sense of well being right into their physical body. Telling a client to be balanced is meaningless if he does not feel it for himself. Placing a Dow crystal at the center of breath, or near the entrance of the thoughtform into consciousness, helps to align the center with the new light body pattern, a new perfection reached, a new balance achieved.

Our unfolding consciousness will eventually lead us to the Dow within us all, living the perfect reflection of our spiritual template. Working with the Dow will not hasten that process, but it will put us in touch with our potential for perfection. It may even give us guidelines to that process by observing the stones that surround the Dow to see where any imbalances may reside that impede our spiritual progress. If the Dow crystal does any healing at all with its vibrational frequency, it creates balance. Other healing stones can heal the imbalance while the Dow provides the template for the healing energy.

The Dow can have a specific function in each of the energy centers in a layout beginning with the first center, the seeding of consciousness. Many people feel separate from their spiritual blueprint, if indeed they even know they have one, which can impact this center severely. Placing the Dow here will focus part of the session on how the client feels about being physical and put him in touch with the soul patterning of his life expression. In the second center of creativity, the Dow can help, along with other creative stones such as orange calcite or carnelian, to bring greater clarity to what may be out of balance creatively speaking, what ideas are unable to manifest. The third center is assimilation/integration, the most active of all the centers. The Dow here would insure the client's integration of the soul patterning into his living by breathing through this center from the spiritual body to the physical body.

The fourth center is the loving heart, the center of feeling and emotion. Perfection in this center is the realization that there needs to be harmony between receiving love with the same intensity as we give love. A Dow at this center also aligns the heart with the intention of the soul to experience love in its many forms. The throat and intuitive centers have to do with the mind, the mind that expresses and the mind that intuits to gather information. Balance here is an essential

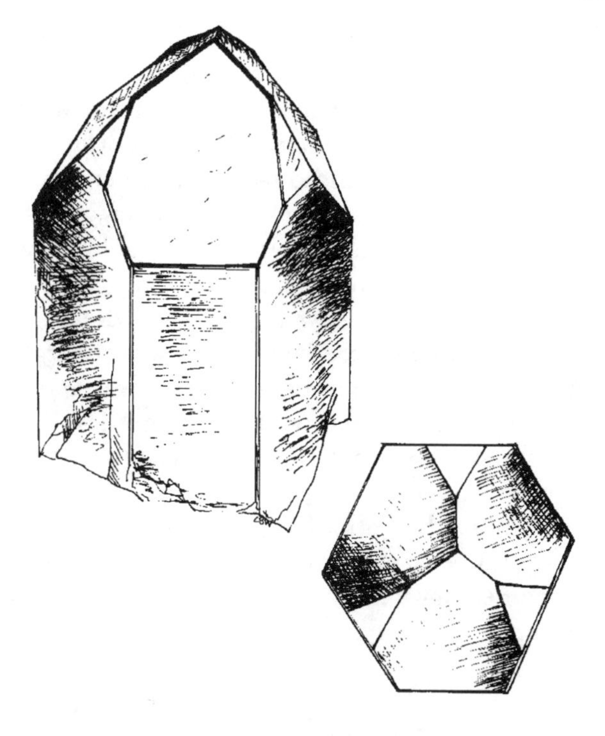

Dow crystal

part of the triangle of body, mind and spirit, the Dow template insures that balance.

Spirit resides in the crown energy center. The Dow crystal at this center does not create a physical reaction or stimulation at all. Instead it subtly balances your spiritual nature. This center is never blocked or limited. It flows in accordance with the spiritual dimension of each individual. If crystals are placed here at all, they should be spiritual body stones along with the Dow. Here they do more to indicate a potency of our light than altering it in any way. This center is the true portal of light through which the soul enters and leaves the body. All channeled information and vision enter here and must be in strict accordance with the frequency of our vibration. A Dow crystal here will not create a spiritual opening, it will enhance the opening as it unfolds by setting the template of spiritual balance into place. The Shaman Dow and ordinary Dow crystals have come to play a significant role in crystal healing. Just by having them among other healing stones seems to cast an aura of harmony over my entire collection. Seeing their perfectly balanced faces stirs an energy deep inside that gives me a sense of well being. They certainly were responsible for pushing me further into crystal healing by captivating my interest with their symmetrical geometric patterns. I used to give my Dows away, or sell them to clients, but not any more! I am experimenting now with large grids of Dow crystals for meditation on self awareness and balance. And, because of my fascination with geometrics, Dows have led me to the patterns that all quartz crystals make in their terminating facets.

I invite you to the Path of Dow, to explore their patterns and energy and perhaps you too will be just as intrigued as I am with their energy will want to take a crystal journey to the Dow within.

Trigonic Connection

ABOUT AN HOUR north of Santa Fe is the small community of Taos, nestled in the mountains and inhabited mostly by the post-hippy generation. Just as the highway enters town, there is a small crystal shop that is the best I have seen called Taos Gem and Mineral. Not only is it stylishly filled with stones and gems from all over the world, it is filled with the nicest people in the crystal business who call me periodically when something special comes into the shop. On one of my many journeys there, a new shipment of crystals arrived from Brazil and among them were crystals they called 'Trigonics.' I noticed an abundance of small triangles naturally etched in the quartz points and when I held one in my hand, there was an energy shift in my body. It was not an altering vibration of change, but more like one that sets a pattern into place. It was as if the Trigonic had a quality of a silent initiation about it.

When I looked more closely at this mysterious quartz, the triangles on the faces of the terminations were going in both directions, towards the apex and towards the body of the crystal. This is quite unusual, for most triangle formations on a quartz align with the direction of the apex as if to reflect the faces themselves. The Trigonic looked and felt differently than any other quartz I had ever seen! On the body and faces of this crystal there were etched lines of triangles, each one penetrating the next, creating a wavelike pattern. Under a microscope, the pattern of triangles looked just like the free flowing triangular shapes I see in the spiritual light body, only they formed a chain that was far more condensed. True to the friendly nature of the crystal shop, the owner Pam lent me their finest Trigonic to work with a while.

My obsession with triangles began when I was a child when I drew them incessantly much like others doodle with flowers or lines. It was not so surprising many years later when I discovered their importance in my intuitive counseling especially with terminally ill clients. Not really sure how I knew, I was able to sense when someone was about to die. Not only was there a diminishing in their light body, there was something I saw that I could not define or describe. It was years before I would fully understand what I was really seeing.

I met a woman who was very ill with cancer and was asked by a local hospice program to sit with her several hours a week between the nurses on duty. Every time I went to see her she fell deeply asleep. 'Well, this is great' I thought, wanting to share my understandings and insights about death and the transition of the soul, but never had the opportunity. I resorted to sitting nearby and sending her 'light for right action' which allows the soul to use light and intent for its own purposes. During one of my visits, while in meditative contemplation, I saw her light body and there were triangles pointing towards her physical body that were in a state of disarray, shifting positions and beginning to point outward from her body. The transformation of pattern from one direction to the other was actually quite orderly and precise. I intuitively knew what this meant, she was dying. The imaging was the opposite of the geometric picture I saw while attending a home birthing. There, the small soul was filled with many triangles as she entered the light body of the mother, all pointing towards the earth. It looked like an angelic chorus-line! It was as beautiful and moving an experience as seeing the dying woman transitioning her light body to leave the earthplane.

Holding the Trigonic rekindled my interest in the life/death triangles. The intricate tailings of triangles etched into these crystals seemed similar to the triangular pattern in the spiritual light body, yet they were more organized and deliberate in their direction. I had seen the wafting tailings of triangles outside the light body that seemed to connect consciousness with the oversoul. Outside the auric light system, the triangles flow in both directions. Inside the light body the direction is only towards the body. How was this all connected to the Trigonic crystal? It seems that these rare and unusual quartz points take our consciousness on a journey, out from our limited light body and create a psychic link to our oversoul. When I first experienced this phenomenon, I saw the triangles like a ladder, each rung a step to our overseeing light. The deeply etched chain of triangles in the Trigonic represent the connecting link between physical consciousness and our superconsciousness, or oversoul expression. The vibration of the Trigonic within our light body system pulls the consciousness to its outer edge and places us on the threshold of the true shamanic journey, out through the tunnel of light through which the consciousness travels at the time of physical death.

While the Shaman Dow Phantom pulls you into the holographic memory of wholeness, the Trigonic takes you out beyond the soul's patterning to the super-conscious Self. That is the initiation energy you feel when first holding a Trigonic crystal. The light body patterning sets the journey in motion, not by changing the energy pattern, but by pushing your consciousness to the shamanic threshold. The Trigonic vibration does not heal or alter patterns or destinies. Those deeply imbedded tailings of triangles in the Trigonic epitomize the true journey of the soul—soul into life living, soul return to oversoul.

We are just beginning to glimpse into the many possibilities of the shamanic journey and the Trigonic is a journeying crystal that leads us back to our source of Light. Etched into each crevice of a Trigonic is the message that we need to understand ourselves and all of creation from a new point of view, the Soul. When we die, physical life flashes before us like a snap of a finger, a brief moment in the foreverness of time. All of our learning, our experiences and expression, merge into triangles of coded information that trails out from the body at the time of death, the great egress of triangles. We could even consider the Trigonic as the crystal of life and death cycles.

Giving one to a dying person to hold, so he could feel the ultimate cycle and connect with the triangles reforming beyond the light system, would greatly enhance the passage of the soul from life to the next dimension, the next beginning. In my own death experience years ago, I had the revelation of freedom, being beyond life and body, completely unencumbered by the limitations of this planet. I felt like a kite flowing free yet held to earth by a thin thread of light. Had I been more observant, I would have seen that thread filled with the same etched triangles so evident in the Trigonic crystals. Small wonder I was struck by the vibrations and images of this unique quartz crystal.

The Trigonic would also be a good crystal to place in the hands of a birthing mother so she could feel, or possible see, the triangles surround the small light entering the earthplane through her body. This would give her a greater sense of birthing a new light for the planet. Seeded within those triangles, which will become the geometric patterning of the spiritual body, is all the soul information the small light being, the new child, will need.

The Trigonic is clearly the crystal of soul level realization, not only of soul level healing. It takes you on a journey to your superconscious self, the place of true neutrality where there is no judgement, only the wisdom encoded into the triangles which has been amassed by your physical experience. These triangles in the outer light body flow in both directions and are filled with

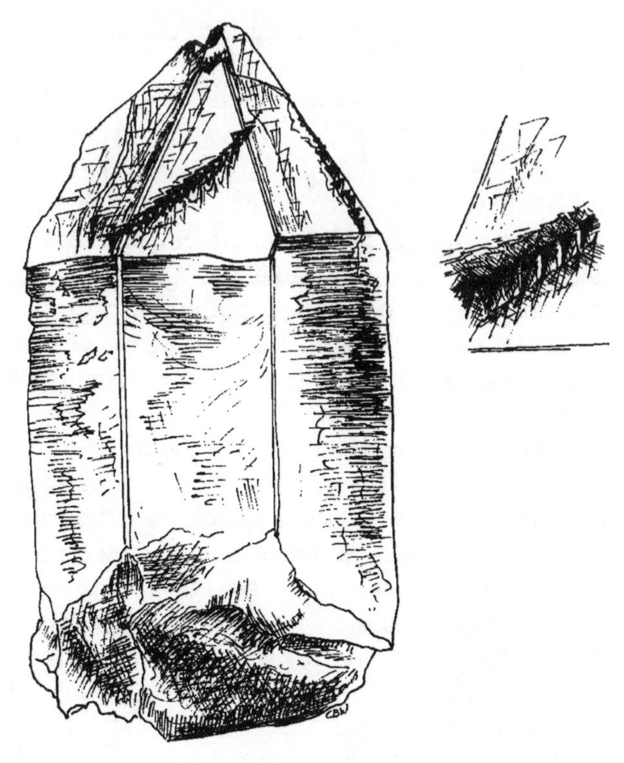

Trigonic crystal

light and information. Those traveling outward take the physical experience to the oversoul, those coming in bring us the light and wisdom of the universe, to feed our minds and sustain our souls. This is the key to the Trigonic crystal, putting us in contact with our own coding and opening the doorway to our superconscious self. All of this occurs only when we are prepared to take in the high vibrational energy and information required to take us to the next step of our unfoldment. This is why the Trigonic is not placed among my other healing stones or even within sight of them. Only when a client has experienced a major shift of consciousness does the session call for the kind of ceremony the Trigonic vibration initiates. Then I will take out the Trigonic and have the client hold it for as long as it takes to set their journey into motion. As the corridor of light opens to new awareness and energetic frequency, the new patterns of consciousness is set.

True to the nature of the Trigonic, there are three uses for this crystal: creating the shamanic journey of the soul to set new patterns of consciousness, assisting in the transition of a soul at the time of death, and welcoming a new soul to the planet. There are very few Trigonics available at this time. For those of you who are fortunate enough to find one, you have been chosen to act as a guardian of their sacred energy. Trigonics should be set apart from other healing stones so that they are not selected as a scenario stone. It is your intuition and agreement with your Trigonic that will determine whether the client is ready for the high vibrational energy and rites of passage the Trigonic creates. Trigonics like to be wrapped in a natural cloth and seem to prefer red! The only assumption I can make about this is that red is the color of the seeding of consciousness energy center in our physical body. This is the center most effected by the Trigonic vibrations. The coding of information in the many triangle formations has been silent since earth-time began. Now, with the presence of Trigonic crystals, we must be ready for the emergence of the crystal journey to our Soul.

FACET VI

Creative Side Trips

Grids and Wheels

IN ADDITION to the scenario and layout sequences discussed in the previous chapters, the stones can be used to create grids and what I call "wheels" of light and energy for absent or long-distance healing. Any pattern of stones that has been deliberately placed to create a channel for this energy is a grid. A grid is similar to a layout in that both configurations transmit a healing vibration, but the focus of your healing need not be physically present for a grid to work. Wheels are just elaborate grids based on a central theme, and they have the added advantage of allowing an entire group of people to participate in their creation. Because the group energy carries a tremendous impact, wheels are normally used for the treatment of global or planetary situations with repercussions that affect large numbers of people. Wheels can also be marvelous, creative teaching tools for a class or even a study group, should several of you decide to get together and learn how to work with the stones on your own.

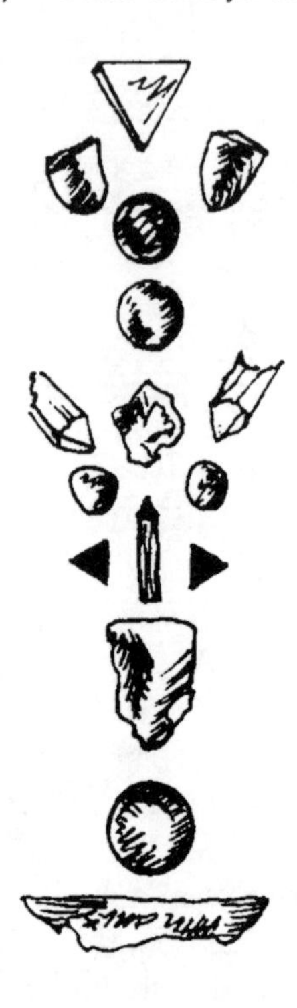

Example of a grid

Grids

EVERY NOW AND THEN you will have a client who cannot attend a session in person. You can conduct a session for him by, first of all, sitting quietly and focusing your attention on the situation at hand. Touch into his personal vibration by sensing his presence all around you. You should feel almost as if you have become this other individual. You might experience fleeting thoughts or feelings that you recognize as not being your own, or you might just get a very strong feeling that he is in the room with you. Holding onto this awareness, select some stones from your collection and place them in a pattern on the floor. In this particular instance, you are trying to create an energy dynamic with the stones so it is important to place them in patterned grids that will interact with one another and generate energy. This part of the process does require a great deal of sensitivity, but do not allow yourself to become discouraged if you do not feel much at first. I can assure you that this kind of awareness develops very quickly with practice.

Interpret the stones as you would if your client were sitting in front of you. If you have questions or the issue is not clear, select a few more stones for each area that is in need of definition. This will give you some idea of what you are dealing with. At this point, the stones in front of you are functioning like any other scenario and you should be able to locate the source of the problem in the light system. When you have finished your interpretation, sit quietly for a few minutes and focus on the energy of the grid. How does it feel? Is it strong enough? Is the energy rough or smooth? Does it feel complete to you? In a manner of speaking, you are now in the layout portion of the session. If you feel that you need additional stones you can add them now, or you may just need to rearrange the stones you already have to get the energy flowing. When the grid feels complete to you and you can sense that the vibration is strong enough, release your hold on the energy. It will be transmitted directly to your client. Leave the room and put the session out of your mind. You may want to write down your insights if you intend to include this information in a letter or talk with your client on the phone later on, but once this has been done, try to forget about it. Otherwise your release of the energy will not be complete and your client will not be able to utilize it as effectively.

I had an occasion to really see grids in action a few years ago when a friend called to say that her husband, who had a bad accident, was not improving his condition as rapidly as he should. What began as a rather routine case of a few broken ribs had catapulted into a serious infection with life threatening side effects. Just as soon as he began to feel better, another problem would arise, and the situation seemed out of control. Was there anything I could do to help, my friend asked desperately. I told her about my grid work and that I would do one immediately. What came up was a small grid pattern of six stones surrounding a large orange calcite sphere and a strong indication that her husband was at a major cross roads in his life. If he did not change his direction to include a more creative flow from his spiritual patterning to his physical expression, he was fully prepared to leave the planet!

There were no emotional or mental stones present in the grid, it was strictly a matter of spirit to earth, a message from his life script to his physical consciousness. When I reported the grid findings they were astounded at the similarity between my grid information and what a psychic had told them the week before. They were both listening now. The husband committed to a deep conscious effort to explore his life purpose and was able to get in touch with a light within himself that showed his true potential. He had real tools to work with now to confront his illness and heal himself.

A very important issue that needs to be addressed in any discussion of absent healing is permission. No healing, absent or otherwise, should be administered without the permission of the client himself or a close friend or relative. Perhaps not the least of your considerations should be that it is a waste of time and effort. When you send healing to someone who is not ready for it, it either lingers in the aura without being assimilated by the light system or, depending on the strength of the rejection, comes flying back to you. If the client does not desire healing and wishes the situation to continue as it is, then that choice should be honored and respected.

Years ago before I really understood all of this, a woman came to visit me who had a nasty cold. I told her that I would try to help her feel better. The energy I sent her came back on me so hard, it nearly knocked me over. She really wanted that cold! She needed it, and there was no way she was going to let me take it away from her. I eventually discovered that the most appropriate way to do long-distance or any other kind of healing is to send light for right action. This allows the recipient to decide how to use the energy—whether to heal himself, complete a transition or to enhance soul development. If you find that you have a certain amount of facility with these grids, discretion will ensure your success. Never send light or energy without permission. Honor the soul's choice. And be unattached to the results—give what you are given and let it go.

A few years ago a friend called to extol talents of a new psychic healer in California who could enter the light body of a client long distance and clear out thoughtforms. Further into the conversation I was told that this healer had done work in my light body the night before and was told: "oh, she found a few problems, but they're gone now!" I was astonished and dismayed and felt psychically violated. Then I began to wonder about what she found and why these thoughtforms needed to be removed, especially without my knowledge or permission. This incident confirmed my adamant feelings about asking permission before any light, healing or grid is sent to anyone!

You can also use grids to gain insight into some of your own dilemmas. Issues can be clarified and problems in living viewed with a new perspective. With your focus in mind, put yourself in neutral and allow your intuition to guide you in selecting the stones and placing them in a grid. You will be surprised at some of the answers that come out of the selection process alone. Often when I am puzzled over something or seeking an answer to a personal problem, I will use a grid to bring to light additional factors I may not have seen clearly or overlooked completely. If it is just information you are after, you may want to stop here, but if you are trying to effect some kind of change in the situation, work with energy of the stones just as if you were doing an absent healing. When the energetic configuration is powerful and complete, release your hold on it and go on with your life.

Grids do not have to be restricted to therapeutic issues of personal healing. They can help you to understand what is going on in a relationship or resolve a work-related or business problem. You can practice with them to learn how the energies of the stones interact with one another or to experience their effect on your own light system. Grids can give you information on more universal problems, such as natural disasters or political unrest, and also can be used to send light and energy to people who are suffering all over the world. You can select stones on just about anything to get some idea of what is going on "behind the scenes" and actually do something about resolving the conflict or healing a pattern Every little bit helps, though for global issues you might prefer to use a wheel configuration which will carry a more powerful impact with the group energy. This type of energy work is very similar to meditation or prayer but, in my opinion, carries a little more punch. I usually leave my grids intact for three days as that seems to be my magic number for effecting a change.

Just prior to the Gulf War, a friend and I did a grid for Saddam Hussein. There was a threat of war in the air and we were curious to find out what was going on and what kind of person Saddam really was. We were not trying to heal anything, just get more information. The end result was a physical outline of the human figure that had two distinctly different sides that were connected by a network of quartz crystals. This scenario indicated to me that balance between war and peace was a very delicate one that could go either way, depending on which public persona he decided to draw from energetically. He had the potential to either exert a tremendous influence for good in the world or create destruction. The war happened, but our work with the stones gave me a more complete understanding of the man and the world event that followed.

As you become sensitive to the stones and more familiar with their energies, you will be able to employ what I call "quick fixes." These are simple healing grids of no more than three stones that will, over a period of time, alleviate certain kinds of physical or emotional disharmony or meet other specific needs. You can use these mini-grids for absent healing or suggest them to those clients who feel comfortable enough with the stones to be able to work with them at home. Following are some suggestions. If you can see how each grouping of three stones applies to the situation at hand, you are ready to start creating your own.

Abuse (physical or emotional)
Larimar, Malachite/Azurite, Rock ruby
Addiction
Malachite/Azurite, Red calcite, Red jasper
Anger
Blue lace agate, Fluorite, Sodalite
Anxiety
Amber, Onyx, Turquoise
Apathy
Azurite, Malachite, Pyrite
Arthritis
Lepidolite, Obsidian, Opal
Assertiveness
Chrysoprase, Fire opal, Lapis
Birthing
Lingam, Malachite, Water opal
Blood disorders
Bloodstone, Garnet, Malachite
Colds
Malachite, Kunzite or Citrine, Hiddenite
Confusion
Charoite, Fluorite, Howlite
Communication
Amazonite, Cuprite, Lapis
Creative blocks
Azurite, Carnelian, Orange calcite
Depression
Endogenous (physiological)
Azurite, Malachite, Sugilite
Exogenous (situational)
Azurite, Laser quartz, Sugilite
Dysmenorrhea (painful menstruation)
Gem silica, Malachite, Water opal
Fear
Dow crystal, Fluorite, Obsidian
Focus
Emotional
Blue aventurine, Citrine, Kunzite

Mental
Amethyst, Gold fluorite, Quartz point
Spiritual
Dow crystal, Herkimer, Lapis
Grief
Black tourmaline, Chrysoprase, Sunstone
Grounding
Onyx, Smoky quartz, Variscite
Guilt
Lapis, Rose quartz, Malachite
Joy
Scolecite, Sugilite, Topaz
Next Step
Chrysoprase, Dow crystal, Tabular quartz
Past-life regression
Kyanite, Skeletal quartz, Smoky amethyst
Physical wound or injury
Larimar, Malachite, Peridot
PMS
Lepidolite, Kunzite, Smithsonite
Prosperity
Galena, Quartz point, Variscite
Self-esteem
Chrysoprase, Rose quartz, White apophyllite
Shock
Bloodstone, Larimar, Sunstone
Spiritual void
Chalcanthite, Moonstone, Smoky quartz
Trauma
Emotional
Citrine, Green aventurine, Larimar
Physical
Larimar, Orange aventurine, Red calcite

Wheels

CRYSTAL/MINERAL wheels create corridors of light around the stone which functions as the central focus at the hub. I started using them as a teaching tool when I formed my advanced crystal class two years ago. Many of these students were practicing alternative healers who wanted to use crystals as an adjunct to the work they were already doing with clients. They wanted to become familiar with subtle nuances in the energy of each stone. Most of them had never used crystals as a diagnostic or interpretive tool, so they needed practice in reading the scenarios. Rather than spend class time demonstrating scenarios and layouts on one or two students, I devised a way for everyone to participate in each class session. With one stone representing an issue that the entire group wished to explore, each student selected stones which were then laid out around the center like spokes on a wheel and interpreted individually. The students read their own stones and commented on the other layouts. Not only were they able to become familiar with the stones and get lots of practice in reading scenarios, but they gained some valuable insights into themselves and each other.

Some very interesting topics for class discussion emerged from these sessions. As an exercise for the class, I had invited a writer who was having trouble understanding motivations behind some of the characters in a play she was writing. She drew stones for all of her characters. The class was able to do a study of each one, clear up any questions she had regarding motivation, and add a whole new dimension to the plot outline. Current events provided us with plenty of material for study. We looked at personal issues and global disasters. With angelite at the center of the wheel, we explored our Lemurian past lives. With labradorite, we were able to explore our connection to Sirius and with Moldavite, our connection to the Pleiades. There was no restriction as to theme.

Example of a wheel

Should you decide to use these wheels as a teaching tool or incorporate them into your study group, just be sure that everyone agrees on the central theme or focus of your meeting. This is just as important as setting the intent of a crystal session. Otherwise people will get off track when they are selecting stones, the information that comes out of the layout will not be as clear, and there will be a tendency to confuse the issues during the discussion. Talk about whether the issue you will be exploring together is personal and individual, or whether it is part of a collective pattern.

In crystal healing a collective pattern is a universal issue or problem that many souls incarnate in order to heal. A lot of women's issues are collective: abuse, abandonment, sexuality, identity, and the like. Sometimes a very sensitive person can tune into the collective and begin to identify with the pattern. I have had clients who were told there was abuse in their childhood and we could fine nothing. Suggesting the idea of the collective and selecting stones around that almost always indicated it was a collective they were experiencing, primarily through their emotions, not a personal experience. At that time, the client can make a choice as to whether to continue the pattern in their living or not.

Do a short meditation and breathe in the group focus, then have people select their stones one at a time. It is important that all members of the group remain silent as the selection process is going on. It is very easy to get distracted when people are talking among themselves, even when they are making an effort to talk quietly. If someone wishes to use a stone that has already been selected, the stone can be "loaned out" and moved around the circle as the interpretation is going on. The energy remains as part of the original configuration even when the stone is not physically present.

Begin the analysis with anyone who feels like sharing, and if people are shy about speaking out, just make a beginning somewhere and continue on from that point. People should feel free to comment on their own spokes and on each other's. When this part of the process is complete, you may want to do a longer group meditation which will reinforce the group energy and enhance the focus of the wheel, or you may prefer have each person sit quietly for a minute in front of his own spoke to absorb the energy into his light system. If the focus of your wheel has been a world problem or planetary issue, you may want to touch into the energy of the wheel as a group and individually to see if there are areas that need additional stones. When the energy feels complete and you sense that it is flowing and strong, have the group release it.

Here are some sample wheel themes.

Amber

Are you scattered? Do you need to focus yourself mentally, emotionally or spiritually?

Clear Apophyllite

Is there any information in your soul blueprint that you need in order to grow spiritually?

Dioptase

Do I have a soul wound that is affecting you in present time? Is there a pattern you need to get in touch with that is causing you to suffer?

Fluorite

Are there thoughtforms in the mental body that you need to get in touch with?

Obsidian

Are there memories or experiences you have suppressed that now need to brought forward and be processed?

Orange Calcite

How does your spirit wish to create?

Shaman Dow Crystal

What is your next step on the shaman journey? Where in your light system is the shamanic part of your being? Are you an earth shaman? A mental wizard? A space being? How should you be utilizing your abilities?

Skeletal Quartz

What are your life themes? How are they played out in this life?

Sugilite

Where in your light system is energy not flowing? Why?

Tabular Quartz

What are the connections that your conscious mind needs to make with your light body system? What are the implications?

APEX
Journey's End

AS I WAS WRITING THIS BOOK, many thoughts about healers and healing came to mind, as well as memories of classes and clients that inspired me. By including some last thoughts about crystal healing and the shaman journey, I complete my own crystal journey.

The journey of a crystal ends at the apex or terminating point of the quartz. When a crystal ends its journey, it is totally clear and focused, it is pure light. I have always thought of our life journeys in the same way. When all of our physical expressions are completed, we become totally clear and pure light. When you walk into a crystal shop or a gem show and see tables filled with quartz crystals, each one is different, each one has its own light, each one has been on its own journey. Inclusions of light and water inside the crystals remind me of the experiences that teach us the lessons we need to learn. And no matter how many bumps and chips are along the body of the quartz, almost all of them end in a clear point. Even the totally clear crystals seem like people whose lives are relatively uneventful, not much to learn, but perhaps much to teach about clarity, flow and balance.

Each one of my stones has taught me something about energy, light and healing. Just when it looks like another crystal could not possibly fit into my cabinet, along will come a spectacular or unusual specimen I cannot live without! As you add to your collection, be on the alert for interesting combinations, like my newest citrine tabular quartz filled with spikes of black and green tourmalines. Now there is a statement for a quartz to make! Negativity penetrating the emotional body that needs to be healed. Tourmalines like to hang around with quartz, you may find a clear quartz with a large pink or green tourmaline inside that tells you greater clarity is needed regarding the client's ability to give from the heart. Whatever stones come your way with a feeling of fondness, they will become an important part of your scenario and healing crystals and minerals.

The most important aspect of the crystal journey is to enjoy your stones and your work. Because no two clients are ever alike, no two scenario selections are ever alike. You will be challenged with each new client. Crystal healing is the most colorful and artistic counseling tool to come along since color therapy. It adds the dimension of vibration and energy to the color each stone brings along. When you have completed the session and your client has reached an important thoughtform and has breathed resolution throughout his light and physical body, you will feel exhilarated. If your sessions deplete your energy, then you are doing something wrong. The only way this happens is if you are taking too much responsibility for your client. Your true responsibility begins and ends with how you conduct your healing steps and the integrity with which you present yourself. Your responsibility does not include taking on the imbalance of your client, nor does it include being answerable to the outcome of the session. You must understand that some people are very attached to their issues and problems which may be a much needed vehicle for the expression of their life. It is not up to you to whisk away every shadow in their light system. If you are too attached to the outcome of the session and want in the worse way for everyone to feel better, then you will be exhausted when your client leaves. This may be your biggest clue that your role may just be that of helper, not healer.

It is difficult to understand that not everyone wants to be healed, even those who come to you for crystal healing. What they may really want is information, more clarity in their situation, more reason to justify their plight. In such cases, I urge you to put your thoughts of healing aside and offer the knowledge that helps the client to resolve issues on their own. A woman came to be with a debilitating muscular disease and the crystal scenario revealed the answers to her questions about what it meant and where it really came from, but the layout was never intended to change any of her light patterning. It was not my role to heal her, she had claimed the illness and did not want the pattern altered in any way. You are going to have clients that will not take responsibility for themselves and may even argue your basic metaphysical beliefs at every turn. All you can do is offer what you know and hopefully plant a seed or two in their consciousness that may later grow into a revelation.

A very wise, old discarnate soul once said to me, 'Do not look back to see what blooms from the light seeds of consciousness you sow, it will only impede your journey.' When your client leaves the session, he takes his drama with him, it belongs to him, not to you. If you find yourself mulling over the client's problems, reviewing the session, reevaluating your efforts, you will find yourself in a lot of anguish and possibly become discouraged and disheartened. If you become overly attached to your clients, and worry about them and wonder if they really got the point of the healing, then you will most certainly impede your journey. And here is where the ego can become unduly inflated. If you take full responsibility for the well being of your clients, then most probably you will be unbearable to live with very soon! You will be doing harm to yourself and to the clients by denying them the right to heal themselves. Crystal healing and all healing is a cooperative effort and the ultimate responsibility of creating change rests with the clients.

At a crystal healing you may be approached to handle some very serious and delicate situations. A client may come to you in the last stages of a devastating disease and expect you to make a difference. The greatest affect you can have on such a person is to help him discover what the imbalance is really all about and most importantly, what the true intended lessons are. A most delightful woman came to see me who was very ill, nearly blind and asked for a healing. In utter amazement I saw that her aura was strong and vibrant, yet her body was barely functioning. Through the stones she selected, not by sight, but by feel, she portrayed a determined woman whose life was ending. I put her in touch with her own patterning to inwardly see and feel that according to her blueprint, she was right on schedule, her destiny was fulfilled. We had a marvelous discussion about choices, about her lessons and the journey that was ahead for her. A remarkable woman, a true gift to the planet.

There are a few things to say about cancer, the major disease of our times. Undoubtedly, along with your crystal journey, you will have clients with cancer. There are many theories that cancer is an emotional or mental disease, brought about by too much or too little emotion, or bad thoughts. There is a profile of the cancer personality or the cancer behavior and there is a great deal of guilt because of these theories. The one drawback to holistic healing is the way some facilitators can make a client feel guilty for creating a terrible disease. 'Creating your own reality', a basic metaphysical premise, needs to be handled very delicately when you are approaching a client who faces a life threatening problem. As a crystal healer it is your role to find out where in the light body patterning the seed thought or emotion for cancer lies, and explore the thoughtform for all the information it holds regarding the need to manifest the disease.

I had a few sessions with a friend who had breast cancer that taught me more about the disease than my own personal cancer experience. A writer and actress, she was emotional and dramatic about her situation and who could blame her! Through the stones she selected and the scenario discussion she revealed that a difficult family relationship had left her extremely angry for many years. Now, we all know what inordinate anger can do to a body, mind and spirit, but rather than blurt out that her anger caused her cancer, the stones told about another aspect to the same theory. When there is a powerful emotion, like anger, hatred, fear and even grief, compounded over many years of anguish along with an intense focus, a pocket of disharmony is created in the emotional or mental light body. This pocket acts as a receptacle for the emotion. When these pockets cannot hold any more anger or other emotions, they explode. The energy, once contained in a thoughtform, finds its way to the physical body and manifests as a tumor or disease. This strong emotion once held in the light body, pours onto the physical receptacle which contains the anger until it too bursts open and floods the body with cancer.

My friend with breast cancer was treated successfully with surgery and months of chemotherapies and counseling, but has yet to completely resolve the painful anger or heal the old conflict. The role of the crystal healer in such cases to open the client's consciousness to the pockets of disharmony, and find the seed thought or event that created the thoughtform. The client needs to gain a clearer and better understanding of the initial issue before any healing on any level can take place.

We all have pockets of disharmony in our light body where we store unresolved issues, old beliefs, powerful emotions like anger and feelings long forgotten. Some of us choose to intensify these disharmonies to the point of creating disease and others never empower them enough to manifest a problem. We carry around a whole lot of emotional and mental baggage collected for a lifetime. One of the gifts of crystal healing is the ability of this work to scope out this baggage and help lighten the load.

There will be many joyful moments in your crystal healing: when you see a client's face light up from a new self awareness, when you see a light body suddenly take on new light, when you feel a deep sense of commitment and satisfaction in your work. Your enthusiasm for crystal will increase many times over! Then, of course, you will want to teach about healing and crystals. This book is designed as a teaching tool

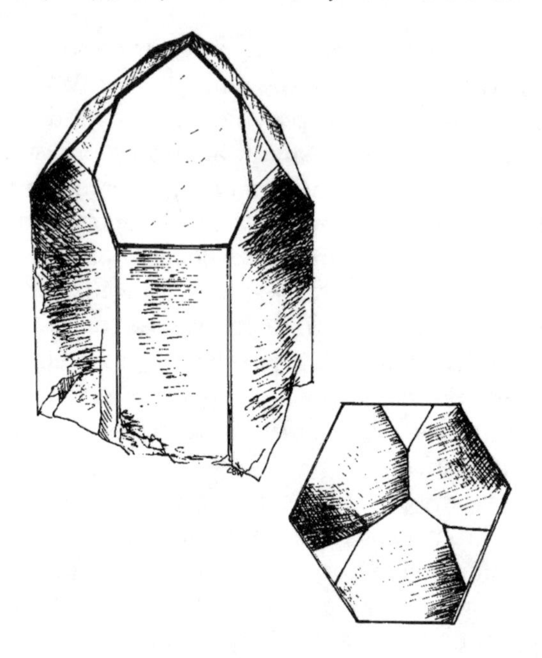

The Shaman Dow

for anyone who wishes to set up classes and I encourage you to do so. The more experience you have with your stones and the Six Steps to Healing, the more you will learn. Students and clients will raise questions and issues that will greatly assist your work. You will gain a great deal from the practice. There is an old saying that a teacher teaches what they most need to learn! Please, take what you want from this book, create your own relationship with your stones and crystals and do your own work.

Crystals are the final gift from Mother Earth, offering us her last healing tool. Herbs, flower essences, minerals, clay, trees and color have all come from Nature to help us help ourselves. Now, her most brilliant and colorful healing vibrations rise again from the earth, bright enough to gain our attention and powerful enough to create the necessary changes in our life and light patterning.

Crystal Journey is filled with nearly all I have come to

know about crystals, gems and minerals, and some of what they offer this planet in energy, vibration, light and healing. There will always be new information from those who experiment with crystals and discover more about the mineral kingdom. As your consciousness reaches ever higher and gains greater clarity, the stones will reveal even more of themselves. The crystal journey never really ends!

Crystal Chart

Keys to Chart

P = Physical body	E = Emotional body
M = Mental body	S = Spiritual body
F = Family	O = Organic
A = Adjunct	SS = Scenario

ANGELITE (SS) .... Indicates Lemurian soul roots
AMAZONITE (P) .... Self expression, activates ego
AMBER (O) .... Calms scattered etheric energy
AMETHYST (M) .... Develops intuition, aids meditation
APATITE (A) .... Heals inner disharmony, 3rd center
APOPHYLLITE (S) .... Accesses soul level patterning/ healing
AVENTURINE (E) .... Neutralizes emotional stress
AZURITE (M) .... Breaks up patterns of limitation

BERYL (F) .... Soul level heart
Aquamarine .... Memory of early angelic life
Bixbite .... Releases emotional trauma
Emerald .... Soul level transitional changes
Goshenite .... Heals birth/death trauma
Heliodore .... Heals loneliness for home planet
Morganite .... Holds love soul has for life here

BLOODSTONE (P) .... Stimulates life force flow
BLUE LACE AGATE (P) .... Alleviates physical tension
BOJI STONE (P) .... Balance life destiny with earth life

CALCITE (F) .... Initiation and spiritual rebirth
Amber .... Spiritual initiation
Blue .... New soul potential
Green .... Dramatic energy shifts
Optical .... Living parallel life pattern
Orange .... Activates inspiration at soul level
Pink .... Love from soul perspective
Red .... Spiritual evolution/physical energy
Violet .... Expand limits of consciousness
CARNELIAN (P) .... Removes blocks to creativity
CELESTITE (S) .... Transforms spiritual warrior to knower
CHALCANTHITE (E) .... Alleviates fear of change
CHARIOTE (E) .... Ready to confront issues
CHRYSOCOLLA (P) .... Activates feminine persona
CHRYSOPRASE (M) .... Courage
Rock form .... Courage to stay on the planet
Gemstone .... Courage to be spiritual self
CITRINE ((E) .... Integrates emotional trauma
COMBINATIONS (F) .... Minerals bonded together
Gem Silica/Chrysocolla .... Activates feminine empowerment
Malachite/Azurite .... Moves energy to clear way for change
Mal/Azur/Cuprite .... Mainline changes in consciousness
CORAL (O) .... Aids in discovery of inner child
CROCOITE (P) .... Sexual expression, activate kundalini

DIOPTASE (S) .... Soul level wound, heart-ache
DOW CRYSTAL .... Reflects innate perfection

FLUORITE (F) .... Information stored in memory
Blue .... Peace from inner knowing

Green .... Mental/psychological healer
Violet .... Spiritual seeker
Yellow .... Integrates wisdom into expression
GARNET (P) .... Stimulates energy flow in body
GEM SILICA (E) .... Honoring the feminine

HALITE (M) .... Sets new energy shifts in light body
HEMATITE (M) .... Associates with other dimensions
HERKIMER (S) .... New Age light and awareness
HIDDENITE (A) .... Imbalance between mental/spirit
HOWLITE (P) .... Information to cellular level

IVORY (O) .... Strength, tenacity, boldness

JADE (F) .... Dream activation, symbology
Green .... Dreams of prosperity, success
Black .... Dreams revealing hidden issues
Lavender .... Dreams of spirituality
White .... Dreams revealing clarity
JASPER (P) .... Creativity from nature

KUNZITE (A) .... Imbalance between physical/emotions
KYANITE (A) .... Tool for past life regression

LABRADORITE (SS) .... Root of soul in Sirius star system
LAPIS (M) .... Clears mental/thought debris
LARIMAR (E) .... Calms emotional storm or trauma
LEPIDOLITE (E) .... Numbs emotional pain
LINGAM (P) .... Nurtures 2nd energy center

MALACHITE (P) .... Moves energy in body for healing
MOLDAVITE (SS) .... Activation of Pleiadian soul roots
MOONSTONE (M) .... Activates psychic ability

OBSIDIAN (P) .... Surfaces hidden issues

OPAL (M)	Energy flow between feminine/ masculine
Water opal	Emotional release
Fire opal	Catalyses assertiveness/leadership
White opal	Activates Universal mother archetype
ONYX (P)	Grounded on planet
PEARL (O)	Growth from struggle
PERIDOT (P)	Heals physical pain
PHENAKITE (S)	Softens light body boundaries
PETRIFIED WOOD (O)	Rigidity of thought, belief, behavior
QUARTZ (F)	Clarity
Double terminated	Channeling
Cluster	Broadens horizons and perspective
Laser	Accesses seed thoughts
Points	Focus, clarity
Rutilated	Steps up quartz vibration
Seed	Original seeds of thought and energy
Tabular	Connection/communication
Tourmalinated	Clears areas of confusion
RHODOCHROSITE (S)	Heralds coming age of enlightenment
RHODONITE (P)	Awakens compassion for service
ROCK RUBY (E)	Breathes through emotional pain
ROSE QUARTZ (E)	Enhances self esteem, self love
SCOLECITE (S)	Activates joy for being spirit on earth
SELENITE (M)	Scans entire light body system
SKELETAL QUARTZ (A)	Commonality of all life expressions
SODALITE (E)	Speaking from the heart

SMITHSONITE (M) .... Gender identification
SMOKY QUARTZ (P) .... Physical level focus/clarity
SULFUR (P) .... Issues affect digestive system
SUGILITE (A) .... Moves light body energy flow
SUNSTONE (P) .... Activates integration center

TANZANITE (S) .... Merges cosmic fabric of lifetimes
TEMPEST STONE (E) .... Chaos in transitional period
TIGER'S EYE (SS) .... Balance knowing and feeling
TOPAZ (F) .... Initiates path of the heart
  Blue .... Need for personal boundaries
  Gold .... Communication between mind/heart
  Silver .... Control emotions, sensitivity
TOURMALINE (F) .... Emits energy, catalyzes events
  Black .... Neutralizes negativity
  Blue .... At peace with who you are, being
  Green .... Activates the healing heart/loving
  Pink .... Activates the loving heart/feeling
TURQUOISE (P) .... Peace of heart/mind/soul
TRIGONIC QUARTZ .... Physical/oversoul energy connection

VANADINITE (SS) .... Light of self realization
VARISCITE (P).................... Rekindles love for planet
VOLCANIC GLASS (SS) .. Major change/shift ahead

WULFENITE (A) .... Brings order to light body confusion

About the Author

JANEANN DOW began her journey into the New Age Healing Arts nearly thirty years ago in California, where she was born on New Year's Eve, 1936. It was a near-death experience that sent her into the world of Holistic Health seeking answers to what had happened to her and why.

Within alternative healing practices there are many avenues to explore and over a dozen years ago, at the age of 44, JaneAnn returned to college for a doctoral degree in Thanatology, the psychology of death and dying. Among her field of study was Color Therapy, a valuable tool for counseling the terminally ill children she worked with in the KITE foundation she founded as the doctoral project. KITE, Kids in Transitional Experiences, offered many innovative and creative ways to counsel critically ill children and their families. It was the color therapies that led to the discovery of the high vibrational energy achieved when colored theatrical gels were placed under light boxes of quartz crystals. Soon, JaneAnn and her friend Katrina Raphaell expanded their interests in exploring new healing methods into the vast array of color and energy of the minerals kingdom. They spent nearly a year tuning into each colored stone specimen, carefully recording their intuitive findings and formulating a viable healing practice. Out of their collaboration came Katrina's first book: *Crystal Enlightenment*. Katrina continued on with crystal healing while JaneAnn turned more to counseling and spiritual healing. In the mid-1980s the Edenic Light Center was founded in Newport Beach, California, based on JaneAnn's work and interest in spiritual teaching, channeling, counseling, and crystal healing. Classes formed, clients appeared and when she moved to Santa Fe, New Mexico in 1988, it was apparent that crystal healing was to be her focus, again.

Combining so many years of study, clients, students and life experience has culminated in this book: *Crystal Journey–Travel Guide for the New Shaman*. Now, JaneAnn concentrates on writing and teaching, occasionally seeing clients at her ranch outside of Santa Fe. Rough roads and river crossings keep her fairly isolated at Red Cloud Ranch, where she lives with her husband Scott, two horses, an assortment of pets and a studio filled with crystals and rocks! Scott is a CPA, their two adult children live on the West Coast where SJ is an aero-space engineer and Kate is a Ph.D. psychologist. A diversified family indeed!